A Whimsy about the Author

Fantasy:
Petra Ceason was born on Friday 21 June 1972, on the right side of the tracks in a small town in Somerset, South-west of Bath. She was the first member of her family for several generations to fail to get into an Academically Biased institution, which left a severe, but deeply hidden open wound, until she was emergency blind dated with an older man. Although the wound took years to heal, Easteruprising O'Grady packed it with salve and sewed the edges back tightly together, on their first date.

She embarked on a passionate, friendly, Sexual Education Affair with Pi until Mr Right came knocking barely two months later. They were married when he graduated, and she joined him in the frozen North, where they now live, with their two children, on the Estate he manages.

Pi, now retired, and with no children of his own that he is aware of, is a God Parent of each of the youngsters, and a regular, and eagerly awaited, welcome visitor to the house.

Reality:
These Short Stories were written while learning the craft, so they are pretty rough. They have been extensively edited but not by a professional English Academic, so most of the typos have been corrected, but the English Grammar may still be wild. In particular, the comma and myself have a love/hate relationship on about a 5/95 ratio. Consequently, some stories are rougher than others.

Petra Ceason.

Also by Petra Ceason

West Novochester Chronicles Group
Karen, The Girl Who Would Be A Plumber.
Delia, Chef In A Wheelchair.
Rita -- Who?
Janie, Mechanic On A Motorbike.

Nearly Ready
Rosalind And Timothy, An Essay In Deflated Self Worth.

Work in Progress
Anna, CEO In Short Socks.
Ash And Cindy.
Fred And Louise, Reluctant Athletes
Jennifer And Sylvie, Flouting Convention, But Politely.
Jill.
Jo.
Kerry, Musician On A Mission.
Pealle, Sporty Sparks.
Samantha, Under Age Working Girl.
Shelley And William, Autistic Artist.
Shirley And John, Monta's Secret Weapon.
Stewart And Jean.

Autobiography {Whimsy}
Writes En Passion

Petra Ceason

Collected Short Stories and Pomes
{And No, It's Not A Typo.}
Most of these were Homeworks set by
our Creative Writing Tutor Mr E. E. Coleman-Hughes.
According to him we can't write poetry,
so we've resorted to the Geordie Vernacular,
and just called them pomes!

**Collected Short Stories And Pomes
And No It's Not A Typo**

A catalogue record for this book is available from the British Library.
ISBN 978-0-9930419-6-9

Published by Double Sausage
For more copies of this book,
please contact Lulu: www.lulu.com

Designed and Set by Petra Ceason
www.petraceason.co.uk
Printed in Great Britain.
Set in Georgia 12 point and other fonts.

If the Ancestor had ever owned a boat, he would have called it The Double Sausage.
The publication of this First Commercial Edition funded by Double-Sausage.

This book is Fiction. Consequently although every precaution has been taken in the preparation of this book, the publisher and author assume no responsibility for errors or omissions. Neither is any liability assumed for damages resulting from the use of this information contained herein.
The Laws of Man and maybe even of Physics occasionally may have been ignored.

Author's Comment

Underneath some titles I have written a note referring to the brief given for the work, and occasionally more background.

Most of the Characters are fictitious.

However, although in most cases the characters are fictitious, some of these stories are true, or based on fact. Apart from a few cases, I leave you, Dear True Reader, to decide which are one, which the other, and which are neither.

Also, at least one is screaming to be expanded into a novel, watch this space.

My Characters' wild-child character traits, free thinking, and non-mainstream exploits are, however, very largely their own. Consequently, views expressed by characters in this book are are always theirs, but, occasionally, mine too.

Petra Ceason

July 2014

This Collection
For
My Creative Writing Tutor,
E. E. Coleman-Hughes,
who banged his head against the wall at me regularly,
for my innovative interpretation of the rules
of when and where to use a comma,
but gave me the confidence to keep trying.
With thanks.
However, any erroneous possessive,
or character missing apostrophes,
any incorrect its, your or who's are typos,
not grammatical mistakes,
and down to me.
In this one book
I probably kept herself in check sufficiently
to allow you to show most of it to your Maiden Aunt.
But for all the others, as always:
Don't blame me,
blame Petra.
She did it,
all I did was hit the keys,

Mervyn Waine.

Contents

Collected Short Stories and Pomes
{And No, It's Not A Typo}

Take Your Pick
(With Michael Miles)

{The prequel to Technology is wonderful,
when it works.}

"I won't be long. I telephoned the order in earlier."
Cindy sat patiently in the car watching her date walk along past the Dry-cleaners and into the Chinese takeaway next door. The row of shops was a catholic selection, Greengrocer; Chippy; Replacement Windows; further along, she could see others. Ash was already returning, laden down.

That was quick! He hadn't asked her what she liked, but then she liked most Chinese.

His home was a double fronted downstairs flat in a quiet cul-de-sac. He carried her wheelchair in first, then came back for her.

"It's the door on the left."

The dining table was already laid for two, the candles new, just waiting to be lit; she rolled to a halt next to it. Ash closed up the house, pulled up a chair beside her and presented her with a list,

"If Milady would choose --"

"Barbecued spare ribs please."

"And --"

"Sweet and sour Pork."

"And --"

"What are the House Specials?"

"Mixed meats, that one's mainly with vegetables, that one, bean sprouts and that one, noodles."

"Have you got all of these?"

"I bought everything that I really like, and some that I will eat, what we don't eat tonight goes in the freezer, and comes out after a hard day at the chalk face. Keep choosing!"

Cindy obediently chose without inhibition, and Ash went off into the kitchen.

She took the opportunity to look around her. *Their first dinner date,*

Our first date, she corrected herself, was in his living room. It was a male room, quite bare and simply furnished, with a few quality pieces, but no frills or chintz. She guessed correctly that there hadn't been a wife, or London-style live-in girlfriend for a while, if ever. Ash reappeared pushing a heated trolley,

"Wow!"

"Yes, and it tastes as nice as it looks, but it does mean I am ruined, I buy ready-to-eat in other parts of the country, and I end up wishing I hadn't."

After that appraisal, despite her attempts to smother it, Cindy's expectation of the food was seriously high.

She was not disappointed. The produce of the Cedar Garden was even better than she had hoped and served on a Wedgwood 'Mayfield' dinner service, the deep wine-red version, worthy of the food it bore.

Such a shame that the gravy boat doesn't match the rest of the set.

Apparently reading her thoughts, he explained,

"The gravy boat has a hairline crack; I prefer not to use it in case I affect the hairline bit."

"You read minds too?" She was regretting the quip as she said it.

He shrugged deprecatingly.

"I really like this pattern," she continued pointedly changing the subject away from shoal water. "It's much nicer than the grey one.”

“I didn’t know there was a grey version.”

“You probably didn’t notice it next to this one when you bought it; it’s classy but dull.”

Ash got up, went to the sideboard and took an envelope out from beside the rest of the service. He returned and gave it to her.

“I didn’t buy this one, I won it; Michael Miles bought it.” Inside the envelope was a buff card with a red typed legend congratulating the winner of a heated trolley and 32 piece Wedgwood Dinner Service, on the television quiz show, ‘Take Your Pick’.

“Is this for real?”

“Mmm!” Ash couldn’t help it. “Sorry for grinning like an imbecile, but it’s my one claim to Media Fame, and I loved every second of the experience.”

“Were you on the television?”

“Mmm.”

“When?”

“Years ago, a decade ago. Dad had been given a couple of tickets to the local Ford Dealership’s new premises warming, which was an extra un-transmitted edition of the show; it had Michael Miles, Bob Danvers-Walker, the whole shebang, box 13 the lot, but he hadn’t got on as a contestant. He was disappointed and when Michael Miles came to do one from the local commercial station, a scheduled one this time, he applied for tickets and got a couple. Mum didn’t want to go a second time, and offered the other one to me.”

Cindy could see the joy in Ash’s eyes that the memories were giving him,

“Tell me about it,” she said obligingly, but she did want to know too.

“On our way down to the show, I belatedly asked Dad how the contestants were chosen. You had to do a forfeit, he could only remember a couple, and anyway, they were from weeks before, there was no guarantee it would be the same format. I actually had to press him to tell me. One was that you were a barrow boy selling faulty stockings, they had the seam down the front, another was a Sergeant Major dressing down troops. Dad had remembered that one because he had been a Staff Sergeant during the Second World War, that was the one he was going to do, but Michael Miles filled his quota before he got to it. Dad also told me that if someone got up and just burbled on, he used their time to look in the audience for people with interesting faces to invite to have a go. So if you got the chance, you had to grab it."

"One take only, real life."

"Yeah. We went in and found our seats; they were absolutely the business, smack in the middle of the raised area at the back, about halfway up and next to an aisle. They were just a couple of rows back from the natural place anyone would look from the stage. On my seat was a list of forfeits, the first one, the very first, was the barrow boy selling the faulty stockings, and I had thought of a theme, in the car. I spent the next three-quarters of an hour rehearsing it in my mind. The show was supposed to start at seven, but Michael Miles was nowhere to be seen. Everyone assumed he was in the Pyramid, the station's local, next door." Ash readjusted himself in his seat and smiled at his young guest. "There was no hurry anyway because one of the cameras was faulty, technicians were swarming all over it. They finally decided it was beyond resurrection dead, and took it off its bogey and replaced it with another one. Michael Miles appeared and after apologising, agreed that they had better get the show on the road and just called out to the audience, 'Who would like to do Forfeit Number One?'"

"The one you'd been rehearsing. You'd got your cue." She laid her palm on his flaming cheek; it was really hot: "And even now, telling me, you're blushing."

"I know. I know what people see when they look at me, but it's all an act. I'm really quite shy, most of the time. But I had been girding up for this moment for two whole weeks and rehearsing my spiel for nearly an hour. I jumped up into the aisle pointed in his general direction and shouted 'I will!'

He glanced at me and waved me on, 'OK you have a go.'"

Ash gazed deeply into her eyes, shaking his head,

"But he hadn't really seen me. He wasn't looking at me. He was apologising again to Bob Danvers-Walker. Half the audience were watching the camera being changed. The rest were squabbling over sweets, or seating, or the price of fish. Not a soul was paying a blind bit of attention to me; it was exactly like taking an assembly."

He grinned,

"I had to grab them by the throat. So I took a deep breath and bellowed at the miscreants hiding at the back, 'Ladies! Tonight we're going to talk about attracting men!'"

Ash paused and opened her hand, and looked down at it for a moment, and caressed it,

"Cindy, I had them in the palm of my hand, Michael Miles pointing back at me protesting that I couldn't do that here, sweets poised halfway to mouths, camera cables waving about aimlessly in the hands of technicians suffering short-term memory loss, and everybody looking straight at me! The silence was tangible; you could have scooped it up, squashed it into balls and thrown it. After that it was easy, I was on, I just didn't have to blow it."

"What was the spiel?"

"Oh something about, one way of getting your legs noticed is to kink the seam of your stockings, the kink is seen, then the gorgeous leg it's caressing, but all the wolf whistles come from behind, with these-'

"The whistles come from in front, where you can size up the talent, neat, very neat, well done."

"Well, it was good enough to get me on."

"How long did you last in the 'Yes No interlude'?"

"About ten seconds, until he asked me if I went to School on my bike."

"What were the questions?"

"What is the atomic weight of uranium? 'Who was Jack the Ripper? 'In what sport is there a pitcher and a catcher?"

"I would have failed!"

"No, you wouldn't. He only asked me that one because he knew that I was temporarily teaching Science, and I was lucky, he picked one I knew, if he'd said Lead, or Silicon, I'd have been dead. And it wasn't a question on his sheet; he'd already told me that he had no Science questions,

'I've got no Science questionswhat's the atomic weight of Uranium?' and he really did say questionswhat's as one word."

"What did you answer?"

"There are two, 238 and 235; the stuff that explodes is 235. He asked the audience if that could be the first question and of course they all shouted 'Yes!" and clapped and stamped their feet, but he checked with me carefully on the quiet that it was the right answer. I think it was that; that got me on the box, there are always seven contestants, one for each of the good prizes, but only about four are transmitted. It was Jack the Ripper that had me going; because I was sure that he was never caught, so I just said 'Murderer', and that was all that was wanted."

There was something else. Ash had another memory of that night; he was glowing with pride.

"What's the other thing, the thing you're more proud of than winning a prize on a quiz show?"

"My Dad, also a teacher, a gifted, genius teacher, my unattainable target to emulate, was also impressed with the Barrow Boy Performance enough to say, and repeat variations of, 'Well done, that was very good.' It was the best bit of the night."

That was the moment; when the curtain drew back for a second and allowed her to glimpse the man behind the face, that she fell in love with him.

Enforcing the Deal

{Write a story suggested by a picture of a middle-aged couple sitting in a comfortable living room, either side of an unlit fire. There was a dog in the scene, as well as a hint of polite tension. Bovin already existed in Birthday Present/Birthday Future; this story explains how Vera made her mistake.}

Paraphrase of the note to our tutor:-

Dear True Reader,

Writing for Himself is like a disease, he sits down, and he writes. Then suddenly he writes something, nonsensical, or impossible. The choice is between erase, or pick it up and run with it. Before 1999 he would have erased and written something staid, but now I take over, pick it up and run, because the wilder the words, to me the more interesting the story.

Because I frequently take over in the middle of an idea, I often wonder how the protagonists reached the beginning, Paragraph One. Sometimes I go back to research them. I did so in our novel Delia, where it took well over fifty pages to find out, and Karen, where it took over twice as many.

One of our less enchanting expendables, Bovin B. Bovin, appeared in one of our homeworks in January of 2006, pp 112. Since then he and his story have been fleshed out a bit. He may yet have a role to play in our novel 'Pealle'.

'Enforcing the Deal' was a recent homework, but while writing it, I went back in time and discovered how come a lovely girl like Vera, ended up marrying such a gargoyle as Bovin in the first place.

I also found out why he was as he was, and that Vera had even less reason to mourn his departure than I thought

.

Petra.

Enforcing the Deal

{Prequel to Birthday Present/Birthday Future}

"No," said James. "I've got my book from the library; I'm settled. I'm not."

"It's your turn," Mavis insisted.

"It's Monday."

The supercilious tone and mild patronising manner infuriated her. What made matters worse was that he knew it.

"It's still your turn, we agreed. This week, you'd do Monday."

Again he spoke like a disinterested schoolmaster addressing a petulant child,

"It was a package deal. You did not fulfil your part."

"Yes, I did. I cooked Sunday lunch for your Mother, and she was as obnoxious as usual, and I smiled and said nothing."

"You agreed to cook Sunday lunch for Mother regularly; that was part of the deal."

"I agreed to cook Sunday lunch for your harpy of a Mother, on two Sundays a month. It's been three this month already, and there are fifteen days not yet broken into."

James ignored her as if she hadn't replied. The silence stretched out and out, until he moistened his middle finger, reached out, and with precision turned the page with it. Presently Mavis could stand the calculated insult no longer,

"Well?"

"I've had to put a jumper on."

"We agreed."

"And you've had to put your jacket on. And it doesn't go with that skirt."

"I would have had one that went with the skirt. But a certain person, not seven leagues away from here wouldn't buy it for me."

"I offered. You refused."

"You offered to buy a jacket that no girl would have been seen dead in. There were at least ten others all suitable. Some of them were even cheaper! But of course I liked them, so you would not agree with me spending my own money on one."

"It was your choice."

The incredible level of Orwellian Double-Think needed to generate such a statement silenced Mavis. This allowed her to backtrack and realise that they had not been talking about clothes, but about,

"We agreed. We wouldn't light the fire today because it's such a lovely day."

"So you're an item short on the deal. You do it. It's Monday anyway."

The silence resumed. James read several pages more.

Despite trying to concentrate her thoughts on him, as if to attract his attention by willpower alone, Mavis found her concentration wandering. She would do it; she always did. Eventually, she always obeyed.

Something inside her snapped, causing actual physical pain. "Oh!"

James ignored the involuntary exclamation, and in doing so tempered the previously indifferent metal into the finest steel. Mavis arose, not even now convinced herself, but her steps towards the kitchen were purposeful and sure.

"Where are you going? It's that way," said James waving in the direction of the front door.

"I'm going to prepare my lunch. Do you want some?"

"Of course. I'll have a beaten up egg sandwich. With mushrooms. Done the way I like it."

"Anything else?"

"No. Yes, do the bun how I like it."

"Anything else?"

"I'll have a coke, and a cheesecake to finish off with."

"Anything else?"

"No that'll do."

Mavis went through to the kitchen and retrieved the remains of yesterday's joint. She cut herself a couple of slices and built a sandwich of meat, pickle and salad. Then she transferred all the ready to eat food from the small kitchen fridge to the larger main fridge out in the garage, the one that James hardly knew how to find, never mind open. A couple of minutes spent rearranging the larder ensured that only makings could be seen when the cupboard was opened, no ready to eat. In James's eyes, they would be the only foodstuffs there. Finally, she brewed her tea and carried her lunch through on her tray. James put his book down on the chair beside him and prepared to receive his food.

Without a word, Mavis placed the tray on her table, sat down, and began to eat.

"Where's mine?"

"Various bits are in the freezer, larder and fridge. The frying pan's in the second drawer down under the hob. Your coke is in the garage stacked up against the far wall."

"What?"

"When you stick to our agreed deal, then and only then will I cook for you. Until you do it, I look after myself and Queenie, but not you."

"We had a deal which you--."

"I am sticking to our agreement. If you don't, all bets are off. Everything's off. Food, TV -- Bed."

"Don't be silly. You're being childish."

The new, hardened Mavis didn't even pause in her feeding.

"I want my lunch."

Fastidiously Mavis continued until she had finished, studiously ignoring the stare boring into her from across the hearthrug. She sipped her tea, and presently returned to the kitchen for her second cup.

"I said; I want my lunch!"

"Oh, didn't I make myself clear? Everything's off, and that includes conversation."

"What?" James was standing in the kitchen doorway, visibly irate and annoyed for the first time since she could remember.

"Until I deem it necessary, and for other short periods if and when of course. Excuse me."

"What?" But he had stepped out of her way; it was either that or risk a hot cup of tea down his front.

Mavis sat down and once again began sipping her tea. James banged about in the kitchen for a few minutes, and she mentally traced his progress around the room from the different sounds that the doors and drawers made. When he strode through to the hallway, the new Mavis didn't even consider the possibility that he was relenting and fulfilling the agreement. More like going--

"I'm going out! To the Plough." A moment later the door banged. The dog had risen from her basket, she whined, looking puzzled and lost. James walked past down the lane, the picture of righteous indignation.

"It's alright Queenie; I'm taking you out when I've finished my tea. James's gone to have lunch at the Plough. Had he taken you, you would have known to go the other way to the Swan, wouldn't you?" She soothed their pet: "But the Plough's nearer, closed for renovations, but nearer. Well, the exercise will do him good. Ten minutes to the Plough, another forty through Highfield Woods back to the Swan, half an hour to get back, plus eating time. I reckon we've got a good hour for your walk. Come on, out the back. We'll make it a special." She leaned in closer to speak conspiratorially,

The dog's eyes were alight with expectation.

"Today we'll make it -- The Spinney!"

Queenie's tail began to wag her whole body with pleasure; she made little noises while running back and forth between Mavis and the back door.

Until the Spinney came in sight Mavis kept Queenie on her lead, but then the dog stopped, waiting. Obediently Mavis slipped the leash, and the lurcher vanished like a wraith.

Ten minutes and two rabbits later,

"Hello, Mavis," said the Squire.

She turned, slightly startled,

"Oh! Hello, John. You're nearly as quiet as Queenie; I didn't hear you."

"Sorry, didn't mean to surprise you, but I have come to see you, specifically you." His face was grave and sad.

"What's wrong?"

"Did you know that I've been elected to the Board of Governors--"

"Again? Congratulations."

"The Board of Governors of West Novochester, as well as the Village Primary School."

"Oh." The sombre manner was getting through to her. "What's happened? Is Bovin alright?"

"Your son is in the very best of health, well virility at least. But he will be summarily fired on the twelfth of next month, at the next Governors meeting."

"What's happened?"

"He's got the latest one pregnant."

Mavis froze, appreciating all the unsaid nuances immediately.

"And her parents want his hide nailed to his classroom door."

"Oh."

"Preferably with a power nailer, and preferably with him in it. They suspect that their daughter is not the first, and are attempting to verify that suspicion. You and I both know that his history in that area couldn't stand too close an examination."

"Oh John, I thought he was over all that."

"So did I, but apparently not. But -- there is a possible way out."

"He's my son."

John outlined the Governors' requirements for lenient treatment as Queenie returned with her third rabbit.

Mavis put the dog back on the lead.

"I'll go home and make a start. When must you know by?"

"Tomorrow at the latest, Vera's parents are already asking around. You and I know of three, how many more are there that we don't know about? Or even more likely, how many more know, and would be only too willing to tell?"

Back home Mavis telephoned her solicitor, who came straight around to complete her instructions immediately.

She had cleaned and prepared the rabbits and set them aside to hang in the larder by the time James returned.

He walked into the living room and haughtily sat down without greeting her. When he reached for his book, it wasn't there; Mavis was holding it.

"Give me my book."

"While you were out I talked to the Squire."

"Book!"

"Apparently, Bovin has seduced another of his pupils."

"He's just sowing his wild oats; that's what peasant girls are there for. Book!"

"Yes. If I remember rightly, that's what you said to him. Well, you are correct in one detail, this time he has successfully sown one. The latest is pregnant."

"Oldest trick in the book. She--"

"Beyond any reasonable doubt without blood tests. On that School Trip to Austria, they slept together every night. All her friends are prepared to testify, and baby or no baby, that is gross malfeasance and instant dismissal. With no prospect of ever getting another teaching job."

She'd got through; James's face showed that he had at last appreciated that his darling son might be in a bit of real bother.

"This one, thankfully, is in the Lower Sixth, she's sixteen. I am told that she's a very nice girl and that he doesn't deserve her. But if he is prepared to marry her, and change her parents from his most ardent foes into complicit allies, there is just a chance that he'll get off with merely a severe verbal reprimand, and no entry on his record. And most important of all bearing in mind the circumstances, and his new responsibilities, keep his job."

James heard her out in silence.

"His behaviour is directly attributable to the way you have brought him up, despite my best efforts to the contrary. So you are going to break the glad tidings. You are going to go to him now and tell him the news. Tell him her parents want him lynched and are assembling the lynch mob as we speak, and offer the way out."

"Now?"

"Now!"

Unsteadily James got to his feet.

"For your information, you can use it as a lever, or not, I don't care, but it is a fact. This afternoon I changed my will. The girl is called Vera Wright, I have left everything to her and her children, and I've organised a pension of twelve thousand a year for her during my lifetime. The only way Bovin will get his hands on any of my money is by marrying it."

"You can't do that; all money transactions have to be jointly agreed."

"You forgot, currently all bets are off, I just did! This afternoon. It's done. Signed, witnessed, sealed and filed with the Probate Court. Vera will be informed and given the first monthly cheque tomorrow, along with a polite request that I may be allowed to visit my common-law daughter-in-law and my grandchild regularly."

"You're serious aren't you?"

"It's done, you may tell him."

James went out to the hall.

"James."

He poked his head back around the door.

Mavis was holding up Queenie's lead. Slowly he returned and took it; Queenie was already waiting by the front door.

"All this, just because I wouldn't walk the dog this morning?"

Mavis just tipped her head non-commitally.

Stick

{Write a story in only fifty words. This was a challenge issued on 'Richard and Judy' by a published author. We found it hard!}

Maud saw Sadie stick the toffee paper on the post above the bin.

Shouting complaints, she took it and thrust it into the bin. Cursing, she returned to bin it. Gibbering, she returned a second time.

Disgusted, Winifred saw Maud stick the paper on the post, above the bin.

{The 50 count includes the title, 'Stick'. If required 'young' may be placed in front of 'Sadie'.}

Jennifer Jackson's First Journey

*{A Journey. Make it as unusual as possible. Okay,
so how about one of about thirty centimetres?
Jennifer is a major, pivotal character in
the West Novochester Chronicles Novels,
and one of the eponymous characters in our
novel, Jennifer and Sylvie, Flouting Convention,
But Politely. }*

L-L-L-L-LATE-SEPTEMBER 1970
Awareness.
Pleasure in awareness.
She is aware of me, pleasure.
Lack of pleasure is followed by pleasure.
Lack of pleasure does not hurt because pleasure follows.
Knowledge.
There are two pleasures, one constant with waves, from inside.
The other comes, deeper, far away, gives double pleasure.
Jennifer looks forward to double pleasure.
NOVEMBER
"How about Algernon?" Far away pleasure.
"Algie no way! Bernard?"
"Is Bernie any better than Algie?"

"Cuthbert, that's your grandfather's name."
"And he's had 'Dibble, Grub' added to it for years."
Jennifer!
There's Now and Was and Soon.
Now is always different.
Soon is always the same.
Was is -- is there a was?
"The seafood platter please, with celery."
"Celery Madame?"
"I'm pregnant!"
"Very good, Madame."
"Then the steak, with celery, and can you do me the cheesecake with a side serving of celery to finish with?"
"Certainly Madame."
Lots of Pleasure.
Everyone calm and happy.
"Happy Anniversary Darling."
Double pleasure.
"Here's the starter."
Foul smell!
Objection.
Protest!
Must be sick!
Must be sick NOW!
"I'm sorry! So sorry. I've filled your ice bucket, I'm afraid. It was the smell of, what are they?"
"Green-lipped mussels, flown in specially from New Zealand, this morning. There are just six to a portion because they're so expensive."
"I'll just have the celery thanks. And sorry about the bucket."
"Better in the bucket than on the floor Madame, don't worry about it."
FEBRUARY
"Margaret. The name of a Princess." Inside pleasure.
"A princess that was maligned and misunderstood, who had to put family before self, and paid for it for the rest of her life." Far away pleasure.

"Helen? The most beautiful Queen in history."

It's Jennifer!

"Who started a war. Anyway, the diminutive is Nellie, and it's only a short step from there to elephant!"

"Why don't you ask the child?" The new sound was warm and round and reassuring.

I keep telling you it's Jennifer!

"All children have to get used to a name they didn't choose; many would change if they could. I went to School with an Anne, who was a Margaret."

"There's always that I suppose, give it the choice when it's old enough."

"I meant now. But you'd know the sex too; I couldn't give you the name without revealing the sex too."

"I'm not into witchcraft and old wives tales step-moth--"

"Please call me Greta, Marjorie. I'm not stealing your Dad away, nor am I trying to be the Mum you never had."

"Mum died having me."

"Nor am I trying to give you sage advice from the lofty heights of being three years older than you. Just offering an alternative view to a girl I would like as a friend."

Deep struggles.

Calm and soothe the pain away.

Allow the new sound in to help calm and soothe.

Leave it to fill the aching void that has been there always.

Gently move objections to one side.

"What -- I mean how -- I--"

"I stand behind you, cuddle up tightly to you, put my arms around you with my hands on your bare tummy. Then I tell you what baby tells me."

Soothe and calm.

"What if it tells you it's deformed?"

I am deformed. My hair!

Soothe and calm.

"I would tell you, I've done it before, and sadly I was right, or I should say the baby was correct. I tell you what baby tells me."

Soothe and calm.

"All right Greta, you can give it a try."

"Marjorie?"

"I'm going to find out in three months anyway; I'm sick, and sick of waiting, and sick of arguing over every name either of us thinks up. Let the baby choose. Now?"

"If you wish."

"Marjorie! Pull them back up now!"

"Oh whisht, Saul. There'll be a lot more than this on lewd display in May, come on Greta, never mind him, cuddle up and grope me."

My name is Jennifer I'm deformed my hair is red--

"It's okay baby; I'm getting it all, take your time --"

I'm plain, and thick, and ugly --

"Item one; she's not deformed in any way."

Yes, I am! I told you I was!

"Quiet child, she's perfect. Her name is Jennifer--"

"Oh, we never thought of that one. Jennifer--"

"I like Jennifer."

"So do I. Jennifer. Jenny--"

Jennifer!

"Quiet! There's no need to shout at me I know. It's Jennifer, not Jenny! She's going to be tall, and very fair skinned. She will re-define the concept of grace. She is overflowing with loving care, which is something about which you two will have to be aware."

"You mean, not take her for granted?"

"Yes, Saul I do. She will cover you with love; that doesn't mean automatically that she has enough for herself too. You have to provide your fair share."

"We will have to put away the self-centred me and you, and put someone else first for a change."

"I'll start now; anyone want a cup of tea?"

Tell them!

"Shut up; I'm going to! I'm not finished, there's more."

"Why do you keep telling me to be quiet?"

"I'm not, I'm telling Jennifer to be quiet, she's bombarding me with information, I'm telling it in a different order to what she wants me to, and she's complaining."

"Oh."

"She wants me to tell you that she is academically dull. She isn't--"

I am!

"Quiet! She's a genius, but she's modest and self-effacing, to a fault. She wants me to tell you she's ugly--"

I am!

"Oh for crying out loud Jennifer, shut up! She will never be pretty, but when she grows up, she will be beautiful. Shut up, Jennifer!"

I never said anything!

"I know, that was in case you did. She will have freckles, lots of freckles, because, and this is why she's shouting away at me, she is a redhead."

"Uncle Alfie was ginger."

Red!

"Not ginger, red! As in scarlet. Red!"

"You mean pillar-box red!"

"I mean red as in Ferrari, with flame orange highlights."

"Oh no!"

"What's the matter, darling?"

"That's what the Aunts were always on about, that I should have had red hair, like my father."

"Your father's blond."

"Her Dad is blond Saul, but her father is red."

"Dad used to laugh it off--"

"He'll still laugh it off Marjorie, he told me as soon as he knew you were pregnant that the truth would come out. He married your Mum knowing she was pregnant by someone else. But you are his daughter, and he loves you."

"So who was my father?"

"An itinerant jobbing gardener, travelling around sowing seed wherever he stopped. It is believed that you have siblings scattered all over the country."

A new pleasure, marching about.

Jennifer, marching about.

"It won't be long now."

"It better hadn't be. I've seen other people, but I never imagined I'd swell up like this. Greta, can I ask you a big favour?"

"What?"

"Would you be with me? Saul's going to be with me, but I'd like you to be there to hold my other hand. I know you haven't, but I'd like someone to be there who can at least imagine what I'm going through."

"I'll gladly be there. Would you do the honours for me?"

"Of course -- What are you saying? When?"

"December, middle of December."

"Oh, Greta. Congratulations."

MAY 15 1971

Need!

Need to what?

Turn ready.

Turn ready to what?

Now!

What?

Need now!

Desperate!

Need what?

SPACE!

Being squashed!

Unpleasant!

Protest!

PROTEST!

"Listen! That's your baby crying. She's still in the birth channel, and she's yelling her little red head off."

Cold!

Objection Your Honour!

I didn't sign up for this!

But now, with a breath, I can let really rip!

"There you are Marjorie, ten fingers, ten toes, two ears, two eyes, and as you can hear there's nothing wrong with her lungs, your daughter is perfect."

-- pant -- "What do you mean?" -- pant -- "Redhead?" -- pant

-- "Let me see her!"

"She means she's got red hair Darling!"

"But she won't look so red after we've washed her--"

"Oh, yes she will." -- pant -- "The blood's masking the colour." -- pant -- "Not intensifying it." -- pant -- "That's my Father's hair." -- pant -- "You were right Greta." -- pant -- "In every detail."

"Jennifer was correct, in every detail, not me, I just relayed the message."

Anna's Ankh

{The Treasure}

Anna Dawson was waiting.

She'd try again in a minute, hopefully before he broke something irreplaceable.

She'd turned her music up loud, but she could still hear him between numbers. As the current track faded, she used menial tasks to block out the noise tearing her heart. She checked her watch against the clock on her wall that listened to Rugby and was never wrong.

Except when the batteries ran down.

Or Rugby went off the air for servicing.

Or -- impatiently she let her eyes range over her pictures, the largest Suzie Q poster, and her cartoon style drawing of a swimming aid donkey. She had coloured it in the fiercest bright yellow, with huge red blotches. Why would anyone want to keep such a childish, garish, picture on her wall?

She knew why, but always crushed the thought on the bearable side of pain. Another burst of music did the blocking out for her.

Her gaze ranged over the neatly folded School Uniform, contrasting with the day before yesterday's discarded hockey kit crouched behind the door. The tiny desk in her study corner had open books, although the work was finished. The girl that was always looking at her was sitting on her bed in that other Universe behind the mirror.

"Anything yet?" Asked the girl.

She pouted her chest and pulled the blue denim bolero aside. The yellow Tee shirt's smooth curve was broken only by the two tiny nubs she'd always had. No nothing yet, but soon.

"Hopefully, very soon," she added looking straight into Anna's eyes again.

The track was finishing.

She turned her find over and over in her hands, concentrating on it, not the last few chords. It was a good size, not too big, in a couple of years or so, she'd be tall enough to wear it as a necklace, or a brooch. She laid it on her knee and spread her jeans behind it. It looked really good against blue denim.

* * *

Earlier that day Peter Dawson had been sitting glumly on the School Bus,

Just another drawback of living in the sticks.

Anna had tried hard to lift her brother's spirits but failed. Five miles into the journey she had had to get off at the Junior School; it was another ten minutes at least before Peter reached his destination.

"A Museum visit. A bloody Museum. 8A went to the Zoo, why a Museum?"

"We went to the coast last year." Argued Amy, the stickler for fairness.

"And Rogers got us all into trouble pinching ice cream," Peter replied: "8D went to an Engine Works; I think he's punishing us."

Brassneck's inclination to punish pupils in an arbitrary and random fashion was well known; the truth of Peter's surmise wasn't challenged, not even by their teacher's blue-eyed girl who was secretly looking forward to the trip out.

* * *

The visit was even worse than had been feared, it wasn't

a museum, it was an archaeological dig, with a hut to display the thrilling and priceless trophies found. Items which in their day, were junk to throw away, and to the untrained eye had had millennia to accrue the added value of corrosion, accretion, and damage, and now looked like knobbly stones and pointy stones and muddy stones, and any combination of the three.

Tables of it; racks of it; boxes of it. Some of it had been cleaned up,

(*sic*), thought Peter,

Each exhibit had a handwritten label, and some a pencil sketch.

'A Granary Vessel.' Four pieces of broken plant pot, with beside it a drawing of an urn. Peter dug the girl he fancied in the ribs and waved at 'A Granary Vessel.'

"That's like presenting a Martian with four suckers and expecting her to draw an octopus."

Amy giggled,

"Not quite, but I know what you mean."

'An Ethnic Necklace.' Some beads. 'A Warrior's Clothing Repair kit.' Part of a ripped and filthy bum bag, with some spikes of bone and a ravel of snapped threads. And among the swine, of interest only to academics, some pearls. A tiny bronze dagger, with intricately pierced hilt and tooled scabbard,

"I'm having that." Said Rogers.

"Don't be daft; you'll get caught, get us all into trouble again."

"You shut up Dawson, and say nowt."

In other boxes were six highly polished marble spheres; a comb-like hair adornment made from polished horn; a tiny beaded drawstring bag, minus its strings and ornamental coral. In a box by itself were a selection of bangles, from a merely nice, remarkably well preserved one, in five-way plaited leather with no obvious joins, to a stunningly beautiful bronze serpent with a diamond pattern of amber and jet tooled into it.

In all, a dozen or so gems to delight the eye scattered among the dross.

"So what are you nicking?" Peter found himself hemmed in by the bullies.

"This?" A tent peg circa 100AD was thrust under his nose. "Suits your style all rusty and bent."

"Nah! This for him." The comb. More items were brandished, taunts hurled. Peter was bent over the table backwards, in desperation, he scrabbled for something, anything. His hand, palm up, grasping air.

"Outside you lot," Brassneck's voice, close by: "The bus is waiting," He felt himself twisted and pushed; he spun around, flinging his hand out to stop his fall. His fingers closed on the small item; it gave slightly in his grasp.

"Say nowt!" As they scurried outside Peter unslung his bag and thrust his hand into the top, but unable to find the drawstring in his hurry, he gave up and shouldered it again.

Brassneck directed all the boys to the lower deck, while most of the girls were allowed to go upstairs.

Having settled the brood downstairs, he went up to check on the rest of the girls.

Knowing this was the most likely time, Peter grabbed his bag firmly, but too late, it had already been torn from his grasp, across his face.

His glasses went flying one way; his bag hoisted out of the bus window another. Rogers jiggled the bag up and down, pretending to drop it. Peter was desperate for his glasses; the schoolbag could wait.

"I've got them; you get your bag." Amy flashed him a quick peek at the glasses securely in her hand.

"Lookout Brassneck!" The warning was hissed from the stairs. Thankfully Peter grabbed his now withdrawn bag and retreated towards his glasses.

"Dawson! What are you doing out of your seat?"

"I dropped my glasses; Sir, Amy saved them for me."

The sight of his favourite handing the glasses back momentarily softened Brassneck's eyes and most probably was what stopped the tirade boiling up. The teacher contented himself with merely glaring at the boy as he returned to his seat.

* * *

The reception committee back at School was a new experience for most of them.

8B were marched into the Dining Hall and stood at separate tables. While half a dozen teachers patrolled among them, watching their every move, they were ordered to empty their bags, pockets, pencil cases.

"We've had a telephone call from the Museum; some of the exhibits seem to be missing."

Despite the sometimes-ingenious efforts to hide it, the swag appeared item by item, Rogers' dagger; Prunt's bronze serpent; the marbles; and coral; and beads.

"Put your stuff here." Obediently Peter pulled his books from his bag and emptied the contents of his pockets onto the table beside them. Miss Cage fastidiously eased aside his hanky to view the locker keys, toffee papers, string and other mess, wrestling underneath it.

She picked up the bag.

He'd never felt such shame.

He was discovered, so weak, despicable, wretched.

The deal flashed through his brain,

Never again! I'll reform now. I'll never be weak, or small or spiteful again. Just don't let her find it. I'll send it back.

But too late, she tipped his contraband out.

Except that, nothing came out of the bag. She looked in it, patted inside it and searched through the books. Presently she moved on. Peter stood woodenly as Mr Cross followed her and searched through his pockets. Eventually, he too was satisfied,

"OK, Peter. Thank you, you can put your socks and shoes back on."

He'd got away.

Thank you, Guardian Angel.

He'd never felt so free, and yet, so duty bound. But where was it? He'd been given the reprieve, but now he had to deliver his half of the bargain. And he had to deliver it, obligated. The end of School bell signalled his release, as innocent of all crimes, he was free to go for the bus; others would have parents sent for, or transport home arranged.

Where is it?

While on the bus he rechecked everything, slowly, carefully, and as unobtrusively as possible.

It wasn't there.

He sat up, worried sick, Mockton was in view across the valley, home next stop but one.

He'd search again there, strip search himself.

* * *

Anna had come out of the School gate and surveyed the bus queue, but only for a moment. She cut across the hillside at a trot to the previous stop, to give herself a fighting chance of getting on the first bus. When the isolated shelter came into view around the shoulder of the hill the small knot of people waiting were grouped talking, she stopped hurrying and settled to a walk, had the bus been in sight the queue would have been formed up.

It was as she reached the road again, gathering herself to leap the ditch that she found it.

Plunged into the ditch was the drawstring bag, with the Ankh spilled out of it, buried in the ooze. She only found the Ankh because she scraped her finger upon it when she picked up the bag.

"What's that you've got?" Anna didn't want to say. Fortunately,

"Here's the bus," terminated the conversation nicely.

At home, she laid the bag on her radiator to dry and gently cleaned the Ankh with an old soft toothbrush. Being careful to remove only dirt, not patina.

The true splendour of her find slowly appeared. The yellow background metal had had silver and copper wires beaten into the surface in a swirling pattern. The blue and green enamel fillings apparently formed a picture, which shimmered and receded as you tried to home in on it. She'd never seen anything so beautiful.

She couldn't wait for Peter to come home, to show him.

And when he'd come home, he'd blanked her, shut himself in his room, and judging by the sounds, trashed it.

The jungle beat died away.

Silence.

No bangs or thumps, then a new noise.

The new track began.

She urgently turned her music down.

What she could hear now was sobbing, her big brother sobbing, her idol distraught.

Anna leaped up; the discarded Ankh fell unheeded; she hurried through to soothe and comfort. Peter was sitting on his bed. The room wasn't that bad; it was his clothes and shoes, school bag and school-books that had been thrown about. She moved straight over and hugged the naked boy.

"Don't cry; I hate it when people cry." He clung to her tightly, hurting her with the power of his need. She blocked out the pain, stroked his hair and let him get it all out.

The story emerged in phrases and concepts, disjointed, uncivilised.

The threats and intimidation. His weakness, grabbing something, instead of fighting back. Hiding it in his bag, and then it vanishing before the search, and now he couldn't return it, and he needed to return it.

"I made a deal, I've got to find it, give it back."

"And you've no idea where it is?"

"There's only one place it could be. Rogers hung my bag out the window; it'll have dropped out. Near your School it was. But that's a big only one place to go looking."

"Come with me." She drew him through into her room picked up the Ankh and gave it to him. "I found it, walking for the bus."

"It's lovely. It's very nice."

That wasn't the expected reaction,

"Isn't it what you lost?"

"No, it's a tiny bead bag, drawstring bag. It hasn't got any strings left, though." She reached the drying bag from off the radiator.

"Like this one?"

"That's it. Not like it, that's what I'm looking for."

"But the Ankh was in it, well it had fallen out, but it was right under it. They were together." He shook his head,

"No, there wasn't anything in it. Look it won't go in, it's too big." He kissed his sister, wet-faced but smiling now. "You didn't find one lost thing; you found two lost things, just lost in the same place."

* * *

"How much will the postage be?" Asked Peter
"Dunno, it's a one-ounce limit."
"This weighs three ounces."
"Put three stamps on then; that'll cover it."
Anna watched him stick the stamps on,
"How do you know where to send it?
"I got a handout; it had the address on."
"Come on; we'll just catch the last post."
The padded envelope slid into the pillar box and fell onto other mail with a swishing sound. As brother and sister set off back home, cuddled tightly together,
"I can't thank you enough for finding it for me."
Anna caressed her Ankh, fiddling with the string around her neck. She wasn't sure whether to replace it with a leather thong or a chain. She looked up at him,
"Yes, you can, three ways. At least three ways."
"Go on."
"Firstly, stand up to the bullies. Get help if you have to. Secondly, keep your word never to do anything mean again. Or small. Or dishonest --"
"Agreed, agreed, and?"
"And like my donkey."
"I do like it; I never said I didn't like it. I just said the yellow was shouting at you, which it is, but it suits the donkey, it's a nice drawing, better than I could ever do."

A Life in the Day of Me

{A National publishes potted biographies under this title. Write yours.}

I tossed about again, no use, 5.17 said the clock, I'd been awake for forty minutes, I wasn't going to get back to sleep, it was light, and the birds had been up for hours. Trying my best not to wake Herself, I slid out of bed and crept through to clean my teeth and do my relaxing exercises. Where would I go today? The wind had dropped so choose between Kenton Bar, and St James and St Basil.

"Doctors!" I muttered not meaning it, knowing full well that it was my sense of duty that drove me slavishly to obey their instructions.

I couldn't find my fleece. Then I remembered that Herself had washed it recently, so try the one place I'd never otherwise think of looking, the wardrobe, quietly. No. No use. Fortunately, it wasn't cold out. I locked the door behind me and remembered all about my fleece when I wheeled my bike past the car and saw it lying on the back seat, where I had left it two days previously.

I reset the trip computer to zero and pedalled off.

Suddenly I realised the bike had chosen Kenton Bar.

44 minutes 38 seconds of cycling later, my computer only records rotating wheel time, I wheeled my bike back into the house, wobbling on knackered knees.

Herself was still asleep.

Now came the first high point of a packed day. Weetabix Mini Bisks {Honey}, two naughty spoonfuls of luxury dried fruit, and an extra, wicked portion of glazed peel.

Yes, I could buy it with the fruit already embedded, but you get nuts too!

Black coffee sweetened with one Canderel tablet and one flat, evil spoonful of soft brown sugar. The Puritan inside bristled but I throttled him, I might have to wear a hair-shirt but refuse to have it glued on.

Check the plants, open the greenhouse and on your way back, feed the fish. Shiny scales! They looked even bigger than yesterday; I'll be able to walk across the pond on their backs next week.

With breakfast a lingering pleasant memory, I re-checked my Adult Education Class Homework, 'Anna's Ankh,' yet again, printed off the final, final copy, and rechecked that.

My Second Law of Computing states: You find your last mistake on your final printout!

Two final, final printouts later I was satisfied.

Activity in the bathroom, I retrieved the package from my bedside and went hunting for my girl. Some gentle face pleasuring was followed by,

"Happy Birthday."

"Thank you."

"I hope you like it, but you can change it if you don't. I've got the receipt."

The Crouching Tiger at Hawksley Halt could do us a Dinner for Two in the restaurant at seven, but not a birthday cake; they needed more notice, never mind, just squash in a trip to the supermarket.

Lunch.

Is it sad to regard a tin of soup, a yoghurt, and an orange as a high point?

After Lunch, I kissed Herself goodbye and left to my class. As arranged I parked on the site managers drive, and walked around to the front entrance where Suspiciously Officious guarding the gate halted my progress,

"Are you the gentleman who has just parked his car around the back?" He pointed with his radio aerial.

"Yes."

"You'll have to move it, sir; that's the site manager's drive."

"Oh, he was supposed to tell you he'd given permission."

Suspiciously tried to raise Derek on the radio, predictably failing.

"He might even have done it deliberately to play a joke on me; we're friends from way back."

Genially Helpful instantly waved me through to my class. He also knew Derek well.

The class had some casualties, some new blood, and some good little stories. When asked if I liked mine, I managed to tell the truth and reveal my vanity.

After the class, the reason for making the unusual parking arrangement with the notorious, practical-joke-playing, Site-Manager began. I performed a quick getaway to facilitate the frantic rush of too many arrangements in too little time.

Down to his school;	Pick up Grandson;
Back to hairdresser;	Drop Grandson;
Hustle to florist;	Pick up bouquet;
Return to hairdresser;	Get my hair done;
Grandson to home;	On to car showroom;
See to car;	Dash back for Herself;
Revisit showroom;	Finish buying the car.

The arrangements ticked like a Swiss Watch -- Filled with sand.

The intended pick up place for Grandson was full of road repairs, one-way traffic lights, cones, noise, bustle, fractious drivers and careless school-kids.

And Gareth wasn't there.

Frenzied searching.

Where is he?

Frantic calls on the mobile.

Where is he?

Change arrangements to me to get my hair done first.

Where is he? Did he just forget, or -- Don't go there -- Just don't!

The florist, about which Herself who is coordinating the search down telephone lines has no knowledge, will have to wait, might have to be scratched -- Don't.

In the middle of my hair, my mobile rang,

"Is this good news?" I said to Rachael as she paused in her cutting to let me answer it. It was; Grandson had just gone straight home. Forgot. "Okay send him straight up to get his hair done." I left the money for Gareth's hair with Rachael and collected the flowers from Jean Bullivant's, apologising for being later than arranged.

They were beautiful.

When I returned to the hairdresser, Gareth was waiting for me,

"Sorry."

"You can pay me back by guarding these." I settled him in the car, and he gently cuddled the flowers. Down at the showroom, we saw to the car. I dropped Gareth off at his house, on my way back to collect Herself.

"Have you got your car file?"

"I've got everything he asked for."

"The service history on the Nova?"

"Oh --"

"I'll get your car file. What he doesn't need can come back home with us."

Back down at the showroom, we sat through the rest of the paperwork, including the service history on the trade in, which Herself was entirely correct, he hadn't asked for. During a pause,

"Have you anything else arranged, for the rest of your birthday?"

"Well I haven't arranged anything, but you never know with this one." Herself waved at me: "He could have anything planned."

I gave the salesman full marks, his face never twitched. No hint that the new car that she had chosen three days ago, and now serviced and polished and waiting for her downstairs in the garage, was full of flowers, with a huge Happy Birthday banner, stretched across it.

Back home, primped and ready at six thirty we locked up to leave.

"What have you got a bag for?"

Not again! Will she ever learn not to ask pointless, nosy questions near Birthdays and Christmas?

I waved her handbag,

"You've got a bag. Drive."

She giggled and obediently drove.

It was a lovely country drive out to dinner, in her Birthday Present. At the Lion, we were shown to our table, and I settled the Birthday Girl into her seat,

"I need the loo."

"Leave your bag then."

Why? I only ask! If it weren't a vital player, she'd never have mentioned it!

I pretended not to hear, and trekked back through the bar, out of sight. I did need the loo, but more important needed to speak to the young waitresses. When I returned, the bag was empty.

The meal was well up to standard.

The youngsters cleared away our main course dishes and then, as arranged, appeared with the goodies, one carrying the cake topped by the single musical candle playing 'Happy Birthday to you', the other carrying a large cake knife with which to cut it.

As an extra little touch of class, unasked, they'd lovingly dressed the plate with sliced strawberries and a dusting of icing sugar.

Herself's face was a study,

"Thank You," she said.

The Flight of the Dyson

{You've got to laugh, if you didn't you'd --}

You may be aware that the expanding hose on a Dyson Cyclone Suction Cleaner reaches right up a normal household staircase. However, it is important to station the cleaner at the bottom of the flight of stairs. If the cleaner is already at the top, and you start there and work down, the cleaner does not remain on station, and the stairs become the flight of the Dyson.

A worker energetically vacuuming away several steps below it is, as I found out recently, unaware of the takeoff until the cleaner comes in to land on his head.

Grab the Dyson, and secure it from further adventures. Run through to the living room mirror, to examine the head for damage. The scalp is notorious for bleeding like a gusher.

Nothing!

Thank Goodness!

Unfortunately, things are not always so simple. Thick, luxurious hair may be a bonus on an older man, but it also acts as a reservoir for blood. As I relaxed in the knowledge that I'd got away with it, a red tide burst from my hairline and fell off my eyebrows onto the new green carpet.

I looked down to assess the damage.

A second huge splodge appeared beside the first small one. I recoiled away in panic; now the huge splodge had an impressive comet's tail behind it.

I grabbed a towel and held it to my head, while I tore reams of kitchen roll off and blotted the scarlet mainland and its chain of red islands strewn across the floor. Copious doses of cold water, followed by blotting had the carpet back to green, although, illuminated by ultraviolet light, the underlay will no doubt show enough evidence to convict an axe murderer.

I poured the water away and was preparing to go to the bathroom to clean myself up when I noticed a last small spot. Saliva is the best solvent there is for blood, so I wet a new piece of kitchen roll with a lot of it and wiped the spot.

As luck would have it, the red tide had seeped down my face, to my lips.

A large pink splodge replaced the small dark spot --

Whoomph!

{A story with three characters}

"I'm upside-over! Store me the right way up! Humans never do! Why? I only ask!"

The grouchy, low-pitched grumble reached her clearly through the cardboard.

"You're box is set up for display. It's the right way up; you must be upside-down inside it," replied the bright young thing.

"It was a rhetorical question! It did not require an answer! Anyway, how do you know?"

The clipped consonants of the crusty curmudgeon created a caricature; instantly she knew exactly the kind she was dealing with.

"They've taken me out of my box; I'm on display. I've been polished, and lights shone on me, I'm glittering."

"Huh."

"Why am I bumping about? Stop bumping me about!"

"We're bumping about because we've been bought. We're going home to cook."

"Oh no! Not to the same kitchen."

"I suppose so."

"Both of us together?"

"It would seem so."

"I could hardly stand your strutting about when I could not

52

see you. It will be unbearable to see it as well."

"Get used to it grumpy. I'm Pan by the way." There was an uncomfortable pause.

"My name is Fry."

The kitchen was a cheap post-war Council issue wasteland, long past its junk by date. The purchase of the two new pans was the first step in a tortuous replace-all process. They quickly found their place in the greater scheme. It was on the hob. Nor did it take long to suss out the basis of the system, Fanny Craddock's famous raw, rare or ruined, had been modified to begin at ruined, and head for Hades in a howdah from there. Other evidence warned Pan that the lack of care extended well beyond merely the fabric of the kitchen. She drew Fry's attention to it,

"Do you see that pile of greasy dust jammed near the floor, between the cooker and the cupboard?"

"Yes."

"It's a frying pan."

"It cannot be. Frying pans are elegant; they have claass. That is bent -- It is covered in dust and -- It is a dead frying pan, that is the difference."

"You'd better watch out, some of your clarse is chipping off when she hits her spoon on your rim."

"I know, I find the habit offensive. I am a precision instrument. I deserve better."

"And that dead frying pan has burnt on escutcheons, thick ones; they are just like the thin ones you're growing, but thick. Might be an idea to do something about them before it's too late."

"I would do something about them if I could, I assure you!"

"Oh look, flat-packs, and large boxes full of white goods. We're getting a new kitchen."

"And about time too."

"I like my new kitchen, white and pale blue. Plenty of light for me to glitter in." Pan was positively preening.

"There is not much of you left that can glitter, and anyway, for how long? The last kitchen was bright yellow -- underneath."

"Erm -- Hello?"

The chunky grill pan's black enamelled finish rippled with

macho might, totally at variance with the gentle greeting. Pan was entranced; she flicked her lid up outrageously,

"Hello, gorgeous, who are you?"

"Er, I'm Grill, I come with the cooker."

"I'm Pan, grumpy here is Fry, he's okay when you get to know him."

"Strumpet! Do not get ideas youngster; she flits after any cute butt that wanders past."

"Oh Fry, you do care, after all."

"Huh! Anyway, what are you doing up there? Anyone would think you're important."

"Just ignore him Grill; he lightens up if you don't take him seriously. But what are you doing up there? Are you a Flying Grill, the same as a Flying Saucer, but different?"

Grill looked down, smiling spontaneously as Pan fluttered her steamer vent at him,

"I live up here pet; this is where my burners are."

Fry was unimpressed,

"Huh, on the last cooker they were in the proper place, under me."

"It's called I-Level, that's what yon Human said."

"It is most likely that you are deaf, and it is High Level."

"No, I--"

"Ignore him, Grill, he's just an old grump, Uh huh, Humans."

"Oh no, you are not going to make Grey Soup again!"

"What's Grey Soup?" cried Grill in alarm: "It sounds less than charming!"

"I can only make soup with what she puts in me. Oh giblets, that's a good start. Can you see what else she's grabbling for, Grill?"

"Erm, nearly pet -- erm -- would it be Bacon Rinds?"

"Grey Soup!" exclaimed Pan and Fry together.

"She's turned me down low and left my lid off. Sorry Grill, I'll make lots of steam presently, which she won't notice, but you might."

"I assure you, you will notice it," sneered Fry: "Because the pungent aroma of greasy bacon rinds far past their use by date will be all pervasive. Oh, Pan! You are leaking again! I'm being splattered!"

"I always leak now. Ever since I was thrown at the milkman."

"I see what you mean, about yon pungent aroma. Pan pet, yon really is disgusting."

"Don't blame me; I'm just doing my job."

There was a firm bang.

"What was that?"

"Get used to it Grill; that was the door."

"But I'm still on." There was a note of hysteria in Pan's voice: "She's forgotten me, and I'm done, I've been done for a while, but I'm still on."

"You're not grey either pet, much darker. You're going black."

"And belching out foul smoke. For goodness sake, Pan, do not just sit there, do something!"

* * *

"Fry, I can see you, at last man."

"I am not looking. Not until those rough firemen have gone and it is safe to look."

"They've gone, Pan didn't think they were rough she was absolutely slavering. Didn't you hear what she said when yon big lad picked her up, made me positively blush."

"Common as muck, you should have heard what she said to the milkman when our Human threw her at him. She hit him, hit him in the -- you know where. Anyway, where is she?"

"Got taken away, garage I think."

* * *

Over the next few weeks, the remaining pair settled back into a life of furious charring punctuated by bouts of inactivity.

Then Pan was carried in from the garage and banged down on the hob.

"Hello," she murmured meekly.

"Oh, you are back I see. You didn't call, you never wrote, not a word!"

"Goodness, you're in a state pet. Bent, black, blue, green,

red, what ever happ--"

"Oh! Off again, sorry boys, bye!"

They never saw her battered, multi-coloured-relic persona again.

* * *

Sauce, held firmly in the hands of her Human, glided into the kitchen through the thick, choking smell of cremated toast and cinderised fat.

Her Human had to sway around drawers with knife handles protruding, and narrowly avoided an open unit door that was panting over the prospect of savaging her shin. The overloaded benches were already shedding items; there was no room for anything else, apart from on top of other stuff, which most likely would trigger another avalanche onto the littered floor. A tiny corner of the hob was available if one clung on tenaciously.

"The hob! The hob! Don't put me on the floor," Sauce pleaded as if her Human could hear her: "I'll stick to it."

"Why should you be any more special than the rest of us?" grouched Fry, barely bothering to glance Sauce's way: "We all stick to it, why cannot you?"

"Just ignore yon pet," said Grill as her Human eased him over to make room for her on the ring, and then departed "He's got a right grump on this morning."

"No change there then. I'll ignore him; I always did when he was like that," replied Sauce, while coyly nudging up to Grill.

"And I'm sorry about the floor, it's me," he owned up humiliated, but excitedly embarrassed at the gentle frottage from a dazzling female who hadn't even got her lid on: "I'm full of fat. Every time I get used, the surplus spills out, most of it goes on the floor."

"Doesn't she empty you anymore?"

"Empty is an adjective used to describe the state of her purse; it's not a verb in this house." Fry's original orange colour could just be seen peeping out from between chips and from under the deep brown stains. "What did you mean you always did?"

"I always ignored your grouches, even before she bought us,

back in the shop."

"She bought me with Pan."

"That's right, but I'm called Sauce now. Since my lid was lost in the garage, who burnt your handle? Silly question, how did she burn your handle?"

"Knocked me off the ring--"

"Many times man," murmured Grill.

"Quiet! As I was saying, she knocked me off the ring, spun me around, and always managed to end up with my handle over the flames."

"Many, many times--"

"I told you to be quiet!"

"I see your burnt on escutcheons are joining up," commented Sauce with a sniff: "It won't be long before you are as full of coal, as he is of fat. There's a chip off that big one; you can see the growth rings."

"You leave my growth rings alone! And you can't be Pan; she is long gone. She was burnt up and used for paint."

"Burnt up and used for paint, but not gone. I was cleaned up by my new Human and given a new lease of life. Her man straightened out my sagging bottom, and look at my handle. They're the same rivets, just straightened up and re-set. I don't even leak," Sauce primped and posed.

"Huh. Same old Pan, flaunting about with a hell of a strut on her, and you always leaked."

"Not at first and not anymore."

"So you do know her?" Grill was straining to see the newcomer from around the ragged sheet that hung from his handle like a greasy beard.

"So do you. She was boiling up giblets for soup--"

"And bacon rind, don't forget the bacon rind, that's what gave it its characteristic grey colour. This is the only house I've cooked in where I made Bacon Rind Soup. Grey soup."

"I remember pet. You caught fire, well not exactly fire, but you made a lot of smoke. They had to call the Fire Brigade."

"They all crouched down before they opened the door," said Fry: "They were really anxious in case they triggered a flash-over, and you went North in a single 'Whoomph', taking everything with you."

"The house stank like a yuckety-muckety burger joint for months pet, worse than Byker Bone Yard."

"It still does. Just with living in it all the time, you two don't notice."

"You thought all your Soufflé Days had come at once when yon big Fireman appeared."

"You were banished to the garage in disgrace, to be used to mix paint."

"That was a bit unfair Fry, yon disgrace bit."

"But true. It was entirely my fault that I boiled dry and burned the soup, she told me."

There was a pause while the logic behind Sauce's assertion was assimilated.

"So no doubt you will be delighted to be back pet?"

"Marginally less pleased to be back than I was to blame for burning the soup."

"So how come you are so clean?"

"My new Human, I think she must be the family Historian, she's called Daughter-in-Lore, she applied paint stripper to me, steeped me and scoured me, and her man gave me a bottom lift, and straightened out all the wrinkles--"

"Used that boswelox did he or was it yon Q10 plus?"

Sauce primped,

"No, a hammer and a block of wood, it hurt, but it worked, cured all the wobbles. I don't stagger about anymore." She had been surveying the plastic clad bones of the drowned trivet, sticking up out of Grill's fatty steppe; like the skeletons that lined Napoleon's retreat from Moscow. "But what happened to you, what's all that ragged plastic?"

"You might well ask pet. That's cooker. It's the housing from around yon grill burners. When it melted, it all fell down onto me. There's loads more under the fat."

"And then he let the rest fall off him, down onto me. No consideration for others, the youth of today, it is little wonder that I am filling up with coal."

"The cooker melted? Didn't your Human complain?"

"Oh she complained, at length, and do you know what she was told," Fry paused dramatically, he almost sniffed: "'That's because of the heat.' Apparently, when you use this type of grill, you must not allow it to get hot. If you do, it melts, and that is your fault, not that of the manufacturer."

Sauce bridled, drawing herself up to her full height, but then, as Grill made no comment,

"You're serious aren't you?"

"Yes he is pet," Grill was both resigned and cross about it: "'That's because of the heat!' the exact words."

"Our Human was so furious she banged Grill down on the bench, and all the hot fat in him sprayed up the curtains."

"That will have taken some washing out," Sauce gazed at the frayed and lank bottom of the nearest curtain, and then on upwards, the grease high tide mark could be clearly seen, high above: "Or not as the case may be."

"Not!" agreed the other two together.

"Oh, Humans about again," murmured Sauce.

The Humans were arguing politely but in a fiercely restrained manner. Sauce was grabbed and aggressively forced into the younger girl's hand; she promptly left, fastidiously peeling her feet off the floor with each step she took and taking Sauce with her.

"Bye," called the delighted little pan.

Distantly the front door closed.

"Our Human does not believe it is Pan either."

"But it was though; man wasn't it!"

The elder Human returned muttering and rammed Grill obliquely under the burners. He jumped out of his slide, twisted up and jammed firmly, cross-threaded in his slot.

"Wonderful," he muttered: "Now how are you going to get me out again pet?" A stray wisp of ragged curtain caught on the swinging cloth wrapped around his handle and stuck. Their Human lit the big gas ring, placed Fry on it, and slapped some grubby sausages into him. She grabbed her fork to compound the error by pricking them and turned the gas up full.

The Baker's van's horn blared from the front street.

With the sausages un-pricked, their Human laid her fork down and turned away to get bread and have her morning gossip with the delivery lady. She caught Fry with her arm, yet again, and turned him partly off the flame which now played on the already heavily charred handle.

Sometimes she noticed, but not today.

The door banged.

"Thanks! Thanks a bunch, I'm going to be burnt again! There is only so much retardant in me you know; it will run out eventually."

"That's the least of your worries, look at me; I'm right in the line of the flames."

"You're all metal, built to be burned."

"But yon cloth isn't. My fat's softening already, sliding out, joining up with that impregnated in the cloth--"

"And the curtains, with our Human off-site for half an hour. This is not going to be funny."

"But it might be final, man!"

"Do you fancy being recycled? This time next year being a car, or a bedstead, or landfill?"

"I don't think I'm about to be offered a choice."

The pair watched the flames lick around the fat soaked cloth, and burn through the wisp of ragged curtain. It fell away; like a severed rope bridge across a ravine. For just a moment it seemed as if that might be it, then a tiny flame glimmered.

Seconds later the hungry monster was leaping up the curtain along grease stains, decades old.

Dense-black, oily smoke spread over the ceiling.

Thick, oppressive, roasting-heat radiated down from it.

The ceiling tiles began to drip fire through it.

Plastic wrappers on the benches began to curl,
cardboard and paper blacken.

"Any second now," said Grill.

Whoomph!

Wishing for things intensely

{Precisely that}

Sometimes I wish for things so intensely that they happen. But the circumstances through which they come about, the ways chosen to let me have what I want, are invariably quite different from those I had in mind. It's as if fate cared only for the end, not the means.

I arrived at the Trafalgar Arms only ten minutes early because I'd walked slowly around the block. Twice I'd lined up for the door, but was unable to summon up the courage to enter.

The third time, I put my head down and walked straight in.

The sign to the Speed Dating session directed me upstairs to the ominous back room. Because I slid into the room quietly, avoiding eye contact, at first I thought most of the people there were like me. Only later, when I became aware of the flashy trousers and designer footwear, did I realise that my conservative attire picked me out as older.

"Ladies, please take your places. Gentlemen, your numbers are here. And don't forget everyone, there's a lot at stake tonight. One lucky couple will win a night out in London. A romantic dinner for two and tickets for a West End Show."

A drink and two dates later I found myself facing a Goddess. Dark hazel eyes looked out at me from a porcelain skin. Her beautiful smile was made even more captivating by the tiny midline diastema between her front teeth. The three allotted minutes were spent bathed in her soft Irish accent.

Joanne, her name was Joanne.

Fred and Joanne to win the night out. Please. Oh please!

Every girl I spoke to I called Joanne.

Fred and Joanne to win the night out, may the Gods choose Fred and Joanne.

Every girl that spoke to me did so from Joanne's face.

I willed intensely that Fred and Joanne would win the prize, repeating it like a Mantra in my head.

Fred and Joanne to win the night out.

* * *

I was waiting on the platform, I could hardly believe my luck. The London Train wasn't due for a long time yet, even so, my hand holding the flowers, was sweating. Then I saw her, a moment later she saw me.

Her smile lit up the station; fireworks exploded in my head.

I stepped towards her, my arms held wide inviting her in.

She stepped towards me.

Then she was running.

"Fred!" She called.

"Joanne!" He replied.

The oaf had called my girls name.

And stepped between us.

And captured her.

She was gazing into his eyes,

"Oh Fred, I love you," she said.

"I'm over here."

They didn't hear; I don't think I'd said it, merely thought it.

He was eating her face; she didn't seem to mind.

Fred and Joanne had indeed been given the prize, as I had willed.

But guess what?

I'd got the worst of the blush under control by the time she noticed me. A fleeting moment of vague recognition, like when you see the postman sunbathing on holiday, out of context.

"Oh hello. Erm -- nice to see you -- Erm --"

"Rufus."

"Oh -- Rufus, this is Fred."

"How do you do?"

"It's because of the complexion."

"Fred's my fiancé, er Rufus. You've probably not met, bit of a whirlwind romance. Rufus works in -- erm--"

Quick! Where? Dispatch is safe! Everyone has a Dispatch!

"Dispatch. The lads wanted to wish you a lovely trip; they sent these."

"Oh, thank you."

Fortunately, the train arrived then, and they boarded. They let the window down to speak to me.

"Please thank the lads for me, for the flowers."

"I will."

He had his arm around her shoulder, and they were smiling. We shook hands. Then they wished me good-bye.

As the train started moving, they waved. They were laughing, but I was blushing, disappointed, and it took a great effort for me to smile.

Negotiating The Rules Of Engagement

{Write a Radio Play with four characters; this was one of the last pieces of work submitted.}

Extract from the accompanying note to my tutor;

Mr Hughes,

In view of the fact that we are coming towards the end of our association, I thought that I'd better introduce myself to you. But even now he dare not reveal the unchained girl herself, so here I am, caged and muzzled.

The title character in Jennifer is -- {Deleted for a reason} --

She is also very much brighter than she realises, and although neither beautiful nor conventionally pretty, men find her attractive. One of several more very well kept secrets about her life is that she is promiscuous. She thinks of herself as the easiest lay in West Novochester, although the true situation is very much more complex.

In her story, Jennifer sets up a two-week long holiday orgy on board a narrow boat, in a thousand words or so of description and dialogue.

To give you a glimpse of my true style, I chose to try to rewrite these scenes for the radio play homework.

This was quite a challenge as, merely for example, although easy to do in a novel, neither Sylvie's blush, nor a fifteen-minute silence while Jennifer composes herself to ask her the crucial question, translate well to radio.

You wanted sixteen hundred words and four characters; I needed six, and over four thousand words.

Sorry!

During the subsequent holiday, where my Wild Child Self is allowed to roam unchecked, and which consequently is not part of this homework, the number of holiday-makers rises to a maximum of eight and then settles back down to six, the five principals and the missing third girl.[1]

At the moment this won't mean much, but read on, (nearly) all will be revealed.

{You have met Jennifer before, Dear True-Reader, in Jennifer Jackson's First Journey.}

Petra.

---

[1]   Jennifer And Sylvie, Flouting Convention, But Politely. *Petra Ceason.*

Negotiating The Rules Of Engagement

F/X CHINK OF CUPS RUSTLE OF CRISP PACKETS

TODD: You know this holiday idea we've been thinking about? During the long vac.

SPIKE: Let's go to Hawaii. Those dusky maidens. Coohr.

TODD: Shut up Spike, I'm serious.

STU: Leave him, Todd, he doesn't know any better.

SPIKE: But the great Stuart does?

RAY: [MURMURS] The anything-but-great Ray does!

SPIKE: [ANNOYED] What?

TODD: This holiday--

SPIKE: Or Tonga. The crew of the Bounty found out why they were called Friendly.

RAY: [MURMURS] The Bounty went to Tahiti.

STU: It's a non-starter Todd; all the caravans for hire are nowhere near any free fishing water.

RAY: [MURMURS] And vice versa.

SPIKE: [ANNOYED] Well it would be wouldn't--

STU: I don't mind roughing it in a tent for a weekend, but not two weeks. The idea of the caravan was to inject a touch of luxury.

TODD: What about a narrowboat?

RAY: That's a suggestion of genius Todd. A self-powered caravan that travels on free-fishing water. It's got my vote; if I'm allowed more than one vote, it's got them all!

STU: Are they heated?

TODD: They're everything, Stu. Everything you can get even on the most luxurious holiday home, you can have on a narrow boat, except width. They're only seven feet wide, but everything else. A caravan's limited to just a few tons, but a narrowboat isn't.

SPIKE: But you are restricted to Britain! I'm going abroad. Sun and Sex, that's my holiday.

TODD: Look I got a brochure--

SPIKE: Go abroad--

STU: Spike, right from the start you said you were not interested. We've made plans and costed it out for three paying. You're not going. It's our holiday! Todd has proposed a narrowboat holiday, Ray's seconded, and now I'm carrying it unanimously. We are no longer talking about whether, but small details like where! So either shut up or go or shut up and go.

SPIKE: Well in that case.

F/X SOUND OF DOOR CLOSING

STU: Right show me a heated one.

RAY: I've heard about narrowboat holidays. First, you must decide where you're going; then you look at what's available there.

TODD: We can go out and back, or there are a few circular tours.

STU: Circular, please.

RAY: Yes.

TODD: I hoped you might, I've been looking at something called the Avon Ring. Stratford upon Avon, the Stratford Canal to Birmingham.

RAY: [IN A BRUMMY ACCENT] Birmingham?

TODD: Just the outskirts, hardly into the city at all. The Birmingham and Worcester Canal to Worcester, down the Severn, almost to Tewkesbury, and back up the Avon to Stratford. It's supposed to be a strenuous week or relaxing fortnight.

STU: Sounds good. Ray?

RAY: Sounds great!

STU: Right let's look at what's available in Stratford.

RAY: Anywhere on the ring will do, because we come back again eventually.

STU: Yes of course we do.

TODD: What about the girls? Do you think they will mind changing?

STU: Dunno. What did they say about the caravan?

TODD: I thought you were going to ask them.

STU: We thought you were.

RAY: No we didn't Stu! Neither of those is true, is it? We all know that we want the girls to go, but we are scared that they think we're on the make, so we're all shovelling the ask onto somebody else. Yes? [PAUSE] Yes! I couldn't ask because, well you know why.

TODD: Because although they are both just very good friends, they are also dazzlingly bed-worthy, and if you bumped into either of them on board with the two of you in your smalls, you'd get hard immediately and die of embarrassment.

RAY: It would happen asking. I really want them to go with us; I could live with the possibility of death by accidental embarrassment; I just couldn't engineer it.

STU: How about this. Let's bang on and on about it. Make it sound great, like the adventure of a lifetime--

RAY: It is!

STU: Well let's make it sound like life will be incomplete if we don't go. Mebees be a bit iffy over the cost shared only among three. Hint that we need more bodies.

RAY: Or me feeling a bit dodgy about having to clean up after the pair of you for a fortnight.

TODD: What do you mean?

RAY: This room is a tip.

STU: It's no worse than yours.

RAY: That's down to Spike as you well know. I'll keep saying that I'd really like a girl to help me keep you two in line.

TODD: I'll bang on about the fishing. Jennifer's got a battered old copy of Brennand on her bookshelf, so she must at least be interested in it.

RAY: They're both fisher girls, I heard them talking about it last week.

STU: Right, I'll go on about the luxury, and the cost,

Todd, you plug the fishing, and Ray, you need help to make us keep the sty clean. Agreed?
RAY:		Agreed!
TODD:		Yeah, agreed.
STU:		Leave the brochures out open at possible boats, and lists. Lists showing the various advantages of the boats. Itinerary, places of interest, you know.
F/X TIME PASSING
STU:		They're luxurious. Honest Sylvie, they're heated, separate bedrooms, showers. Of course, luxury costs, but the cookers are gas fired, and the lights are electric.
SYLVIE:		Take a good look at the picture in the brochure, there are designs which have no stern rail of any kind, you can walk straight off them into the canal.
STU:		Part of the route is on rivers, the Avon and the Severn.
SYLVIE:		Taking an accidental walk off the Traditional Style Stern of a narrow boat into the Severn would not have much of a funny side. Hire one with a Cruiser Stern.
F/X TIME PASSING
TODD:		So I could literally be fishing from my tea table, Jennifer. Not that I would be, but I could. Of course, we'd have to wait until the fish settled. They'd be off their feed straight after we chugged over the top of them.
JENNIFER: No they wouldn't. By all means, give them a minute or two, but sling a little groundbait in while you're waiting. Good groundbait, laced with chopped worms and maggots. Fish are not the memory-less people that some scientists think they are, they're smart and used to boats, but they're hungry too.
TODD:		Do you fish often?
JENNIFER: When I can.
TODD:		What was your most memorable fish?
JENNIFER: My first. I'd only gone to keep some lads company. I borrowed some tackle from my brother.
TODD:		Brother?
JENNIFER: Adopted brother. Unofficial and not legal in any sense.

TODD: But he knows you think of him as your brother.
JENNIFER: Oh Yes. There is a brilliant fresher reading Chemistry at Nottingham who answers to the description. We adopted each other on December 13th in the Fifth Year. It turned out to be the best Christmas Present, of the best Christmas I ever had. Anyway, I cast out, made a complete cabbage of it, and was about to reel in for a second try. One of the lads told me to leave it for a few minutes.
TODD: You can only catch something if your lure is in the water.
JENNIFER: Quite. So I sat down, and when I looked back, my float had gone. Two, possibly three seconds, and it had gone. I thought that I just couldn't see it, my friend, of course, being a fisherman knew different. He told me to tighten my line, but be prepared for a shock.
TODD: And you got the shock?
JENNIFER: A three-pound tench. Quite a shock! I hooked it with my first cast; it hooked me for life!
TODD: Was the boy your boyfriend of the time?
JENNIFER: A very good friend who happens to be a boy, not a steady boyfriend. I've not got a steady, never have had. But keep that to yourself, if people think I have one, it eases the pressure.
F/X TIME PASSING
RAY: I'm really looking forward to it, almost all of it, all except one thing--
SYLVIE: The squalor?
RAY: Exactly!
JENNIFER: Start on day one, minute one. The moment either of them drops something at their bottom, ask nicely for them to pick it up.
SYLVIE: And don't get sick of asking and do it for them. They won't mean to, but if you clean up after them, they will let you.
RAY: You two are amazing! You've seen the mess I live in, but you made no comment.
JENNIFER: We've seen the mess you have to live in, but your bit is fine. Your desk is tidy; your clothes put away. The room is Spike.

RAY: He does tidy up once a week.
SYLVIE: For you, that would be enough, not for Spike.
RAY: I think I'll advertise for a maid, to go with us on the holiday.
SYLVIE: You're serious aren't you?
RAY: Yeah!
F/X TIME PASSING
STU: Anything?
TODD: Polite interest, some sensible advice. No hint of 'Can we come with you?'
STU: Same here.
TODD: It was actually even worse than no 'Can we come.' She made it clear that she's not interested in having a boyfriend.
STU: But that's not the mainstream, though, is it? I know you fancy her, and you love her as a friend, but you couldn't live with her permanently. Like me and Sylvie. I love her, as a friend, fancy her something rotten, but she terrifies me.
TODD: You couldn't live with that level of intellectual superiority.
STU: Yeah, mentally sprinting flat out just to keep your girl in sight. Recipe for disaster. With the best will in the World, she'd end up--
TODD: Thinking of you as the family pet, I know -- I know. Here's Ray, [CALLS] Any luck?
RAY: No. I even got so far as to tell them I was thinking of advertising for a maid. Jennifer suggested that I put the advert in Queen, or Vogue because we're more likely to get the sort of girl we need.
STU: Oh great! We're screaming 'Come with us!' as loud as we dare, and they suggest that we advertise for some upper crust tottie that would be willing to go for the chance of a bit of rough for two weeks. They've got us totally sussed!
F/X SOUND OF FOOTSTEPS APPROACHING, THEY STOP
SPIKE: Why the gum faces kiddies? The exams aren't this week.
STU: No, but my revision is Spike. I've got another three hours to do before bed--

TODD: And me. Better start now, or we will not be open for coffee before bed. See you at Dinner.
RAY: See you.
SPIKE: Where are you going?
RAY: I've still got two hours to do today, and you're way behind any realistic schedule, you should be coming with me.
SPIKE: Oh spheroids! I suppose I might as well.
F/X TIME PASSING
F/X DOOR OPENING
STU: Hi Ray, coffee's nearly ready. Spike at the pub?
RAY: No. He actually did some work today, quietly, real work, not just preparation.
F/X DOOR CLOSING
TODD: He's been watching you. There's hope yet.
STU: The girls are coming down later; we've put the map up and put some pretty dots on it. I know it's hopeless but--
TODD: I've discovered a couple of interesting oddities. It's just because we've chosen to do the Avon Ring. I didn't know about them before. I'll tell you what they are when the girls are here, play along, act interested.
RAY: I am interested!
STU: Cavy, they're coming.
F/X TIME PASSING
STU: What was it you were going to tell us, Todd? That you'd found?
TODD: Two things. Our route lies right through the outskirts of Birmingham, but a chunk of it is through a tunnel. A long tunnel, one and a half miles of it, a very long tunnel. It's the sixth longest in Britain. We go under a good slice of Birmingham.
RAY: If you have to go through a tunnel, it might as well be a long one, that's great.
TODD: But the other is a biggest!
STU: Yeah?
TODD: You know what the collective noun for locks is?
JENNIFER: A flight.
TODD: Give the lady a prize. A flight of locks. A flight of locks usually consists of anything from two to eight. Four, five or

six is the usual number. Eight's a lot. The point about a flight of locks is that you are not allowed to park overnight in the flight. You must take the whole lot, in one go, in one day.
SYLVIE: You've picked a route with a big flight of locks?
TODD: No Sylvie, massive. Seriously, I think it's the biggest flight in England. It's called the Tardebigge--
F/X DOOR BURSTING OPEN
SPIKE: You're not still on about that stupid holiday! I tell you what Sylvie, how about livening it up. We'll take you with us and give you a good gang-rogering every night. Fancy limping happily for a fortnight.
SYLVIE: I didn't know you were going!
F/X DOOR BANGING SHUT
JENNIFER: Nice one Spike! If you're ever wondering where all the girls have gone out of your life, just replay the last thirty seconds. Eventually, even you should realise.
F/X DOOR BANGING SHUT
STU: Thanks, Spike, you have just thoroughly upset my best friend on campus. You are not going on holiday with us, and if you had been before, you would not have been now!
RAY: No way!
TODD: Get out of our room and don't come back until you're invited, which won't be for a while, if ever!
SPIKE: What did I do?
STU: Get out before I beat the rhubarb out of you, and throw you out.
SPIKE: Ooh! I'm going.
F/X DOOR BANGING SHUT
TODD: That was a bitch!
STU: Did you see her face?
RAY: That wasn't just a blush, she was magenta. That was fury!
TODD: Well we've got absolutely no chance of them coming now.
STU: Coming on holiday with us, we'll be doing well if they ever speak to us again!
TODD: I can't leave it at that. I've got to go and apologise.

RAY: We'll all go!
STU: Yeah.
F/X SOUND OF QUICK FOOTSTEPS AND OTHERS RUNNING TO CATCH UP
JENNIFER: [CALLING FROM DISTANCE] Sylvie!
F/X QUICK FOOTSTEPS STOP, RUNNING ONES CLOSE UP
SYLVIE: I'm blushing, aren't I?
JENNIFER: Yes you are, and with that blonde hair framing it, you're glowing. But it's okay; I know why.
SYLVIE: Do you?
JENNIFER: Come into my room for a few minutes.
F/X SOUND OF DOOR OPENING
JENNIFER: You wanted to say yes!
F/X SOUND OF DOOR CLOSING
JENNIFER So did I! They've thrown Spike out, he wasn't going! Now you can go. We can! If you want.
F/X KNOCKING ON DOOR
TODD: [MUFFLED] Jennifer.
JENNIFER: Yes.
TODD: [MUFFLED] We've come to say sorry to Sylvie--
JENNIFER: She's here.
SYLVIE: Is Spike with you?
STU: [MUFFLED] No just us three.
F/X DOOR OPENING
SYLVIE: You have nothing to apologise for, it was obvious from your faces that you were as shocked as we were.
RAY: Sorry anyway.
SYLVIE: That's okay, and thanks. Can you leave it at that guys, we're in the middle of something in here. Goodnight, see you tomorrow.
BOYS: Goodnight.
F/X DOOR CLOSING
STU: [MUFFLED] She was still cross, you could see.
TODD: [MUFFLED] So was Jennifer!
F/X FOOTSTEPS
F/X TIME PASSING
JENNIFER: Are you still up for it?

SYLVIE:	Am I ever. I wasn't joking. I'd almost put up with Spike to get at the other three. Without him, I'm panting with anticipation.

JENNIFER: Just for the holiday, not for life?

SYLVIE:	Oh yes! Just the holiday. How are we going to wangle this, after last night, I mean they've never actually asked --.

JENNIFER: But the hints they are dropping are so broad now they might as well have. We push hard; boys usually need a lot of help to tread softly down the road that they secretly want to go. But they can't say no and go on the holiday that is. They're already top weight, and I've got the Ace of Trumps secreted up my sleeve.

SYLVIE:	Oh! Good!

JENNIFER: There's one other thing.

SYLVIE:	Yes.

JENNIFER: Erm -- At night -- Erm -- When the boys are finished with you -- Erm -- On the holiday -- Erm.

SYLVIE:	When the boys are finished with us on the holiday. Although he won't kick me out of it, given the choice, Todd would much prefer you in his bed.

JENNIFER: -- Erm --

SYLVIE:	Just say it, darling. If it's any help, I think I already know what you want.

JENNIFER: When they're finished -- Can I have you too?

SYLVIE:	Yes darling, of course, you can.

F/X TIME PASSING

F/X DOOR OPENING

SYLVIE:	Hi Guys, may we come in?

TODD:	Yes, please.

STU:	We took a chance and made coffee for you.

RAY:	We weren't that sure you'd come after yesterday.

JENNIFER: Yesterday's unpleasantness is finished and gone. Thanks, Ray, is it sugar or sweetener today?

RAY:	One brown sugar, and yours too Sylvie.

SYLVIE:	Thanks.

STU:	We're still sorry anyway.

RAY: Erm -- About Spike we mean.
SYLVIE: Well, we want to talk about that. It's opened up some outstanding business we want dealt with. No! Don't look like that. The unpleasantness is history; this is nice business, positive business.
JENNIFER: Spike was out of line. He was rude and offensive and patronising and in essence, everything that the rabid-feminist sisterhood hate most. He will probably make some poor cow a dreadful husband, and I am glad you cut him down to size because I suspect that is all he would understand. However, was he that wrong about the reason for going on the holiday, why are you going?
TODD: Fishing.
STU: Adventures. It's the trip of a lifetime.
RAY: Watch the Wildlife.
JENNIFER: Okay. Suppose you are berthed at a pub and some friendly young barmaid, who's between boyfriends, and whose feet are hurting, agrees to lie down on your bunk for an hour or so, would you partake of the goodies on offer?
STU: Erm --
JENNIFER Silence is taken for affirmative. How many nights is this going to happen out of the fourteen? No! Not want:
going to happen? [PAUSE] Yes I'd give long odds against three or more, long odds. To all three of you, look at that flock of pigs flying by. One of the main reasons for your trip is to get laid. Three boys, fourteen nights is forty-two boy nights, if you're lucky you'll get to share two exciting encounters between the three of you, am I right? -- Well? [SILENCE] Okay, I'm right. You would be much better off taking a girl with you as Spike so crudely suggested.
TODD: We --
STU: Well --
JENNIFER: There's one other thing, if you check the small print under the heading Conditions of Hire, halfway down this page here, you will see there is an entry about single-sex groups. They're not allowed.
TODD: Where?

STU: What d'y'mean?
RAY: Here it is. We're smashed! [READING] All parties must consist of responsible adults, and under no circumstances will a booking be accepted from a single-sex group.
TODD: We're done for.
STU: That's us sunk.
JENNIFER: Yes! You have a problem. I'm offering a solution, details to be hammered out later. Sylvie and I are applying for the posts of Ship's Doxy. That would solve your hire problem, and you would all get laid every night. No doubt you would like to talk it over. Sylvie and I are going to do my hair; we will see you after lunch to discuss any arrangements.
F/X TIME PASSING
SYLVIE: Come on girl, are you ready to force some boys down the path that they really want to go.
JENNIFER: Yes. Ready, charge!
F/X DOOR OPENING
SYLVIE: Hi Guys.
STU: Come in coffee's nearly ready.
JENNIFER: Never mind the coffee, as an idea is it Yes or No because if it's No, that's the end of that conversation, and we can talk about something else.
TODD: It's yes - Yes, please.
STU: Of course it's Yes! We've been wanting you to come the whole time.
RAY: We've been asking you to come for weeks. We've just been using funny words.
TODD: We didn't mean just as -- as --
JENNIFER: Acquiescent, cooperative, compliant warm bodies you could play doll with for two weeks.
RAY: We wanted you to come with us.
TODD: Yes, of course, we want the extras--
STU: Who wouldn't--
RAY: But it was you we wanted!
TODD: Are you serious about the extras, you repulsed boarders quite assertively, almost aggressively when we all came up in October.

JENNIFER: That was October, this is now, and the arrangement on offer is only for the holiday, not for life. The deal is that we come with you as equal partners in the expedition. We will contribute our share of the finances, housekeeping, tidying, bed making, etc., that is two-fifths. We will do the bulk of the cooking in exchange for you seeing to gas, water and sewerage because those can be physically demanding.

TODD: Okay.

SYLVIE: We want to do our share of steering and locking, and we each, all five of us, have our own lock key.

RAY: Never thought of that.

JENNIFER: It's just sense, then we won't always be bleating on about where is it?

STU: Okay.

JENNIFER: We want to be able to fish or visit places of interest in specified free time which basically means we all get up early and put the miles in before lunch, leaving afternoons and evenings free for leisure activities.

STU: That's fine; there are specific places I want to go.

RAY: There are places we all want to go, my guess.

JENNIFER: You can have us whenever you like, and we will hold still for you and do our level best to give us all a good time, with one proviso, neither of us is into being raped. So, if for whatever reason we are not in the mood, we'll still try to give you a good time, but then you leave us alone to go back to sleep or fish or whatever we are in the mood for. We'll go on the pill, make everything easy. Is there any problem with all that?

RAY: [DIFFIDENTLY] There's three boys, but only two girls.

JENNIFER: How many girls have you had, I mean properly?

TODD: We're all virgins.

SYLVIE: I'm impressed, you're coping well with us trying to organise a two-week orgy for virgins! How near have you got?

RAY: A few kisses under some mistletoe.

STU: I once tried to caress a girl's -- her breast. My hand was promptly removed.

TODD: I did a bit better when a cousin I was very friendly

with, came to stay. We were curious, and we liked each other, and we trusted each other, so we were happy to let each other do things. We were just getting to the interesting stage of removing some clothes when we were caught in flagranti delicto. Aunt arrived within the hour. My cousin was whisked off back home, and I was virtually locked up until I came up to University.
SYLVIE: And the establishment wonders why we have such a poor sexual record compared with other countries.
JENNIFER: I have a friend at home who is in a very happy, stable relationship, and has been for three and a half years. She was once asked by a pushy media bloke, who was trying to put her down, how she had lost her virginity. She replied, 'I don't know who got my cherry, I lost it when I was sixteen in a four-way, two-throw gang bang, and the other girl snogged me for most of the time. Follow that!'
TODD: Oh that it had been true!
JENNIFER: It was true, every word of it, I know for certain. The other girl, also enthusiastically cutting herself free of her virginity, was me. Ray, Sylvie and I will be more than happy to take you all on, every night, and I can't wait to get my hands on her, to snuffle her tits. I guarantee that you will roll over to go to sleep before we do. I've come on every boy that has had me, but never yet found a boy who could outlast me.
SYLVIE: We're not looking to start a long-term relationship, just some friendly frolics as the perfect finish to some perfect days. Another girl might be better, but it's how hundred per cent compares to Ninety-five. You won't **need** another girl; I promise you.
RAY: What about your boy back home Jennifer?
JENNIFER: My boy back home is slightly less substantial than my virginity, the main difference being that I **was** virgin once. The 'Boy back Home' is a figment of someone's imagination, not mine, I hasten to add, someone else's. He was such a useful idea that I never denied the rumour, but he never existed.
SYLVIE: Well! Are we on?

* * *

Dear Long suffering True-Reader,

The homework contained a further scene.

As a short story, the natural end is here, leaving you wanting more. If you really cannot do without the denouement and can stand holding pages that catch fire in your hands, it is all in Jennifer and Sylvie, who at the time of writing are/is unfinished, but I will sell you a rough-cut copy if you wish to read it,

but,

BUT,

BUT I warn you again, it's extremely hot in places, several places, me at my naughtiest!

Petra.

The Free Meal

{For Karen, who was there,
and witnessed what really happened}

The restaurant was crowded with office Christmas Parties.

"So what are you ordering?"

Tom Rigel winced. It was bad enough being stuck on the end of the long table, but being sat opposite his new young Head of Department, who had made a good start but was still an unknown quantity, and next to someone he didn't know, was the pits. Even worse the musak, from the speaker directly overhead, was so loud that all other chances of civilised conversation with folk further a-field, were destroyed. Worst of all, though, the stranger dominating his life from his left had a voice that overrode the P.A. system like a chainsaw.

Tom painted on a smile, however, because despite being on extended sick leave, which might yet result in retirement, his colleagues had still invited him to their party.

"Tom, this is Phil Stine," yelled Mary across the table. "He's on temporary appointment. Phil, Tom was my Senior Trouble Shooter." She had leaned forward to shout at him from close range.

Tom instantly linked the two words of the name with an i instead of a space, while nodding politely, and immediately felt much better.

"So what are you having?" Philistine bellowed again. "I think I'll have the soup. They can't make many mistakes with the soup." Halfway through, Tom rested his ear on his palm. The rest of the speech was reduced in loudness below the level of pain. From behind the safety of the menu, Mary gave Tom the eyes.

"I think I'll have the garlic mushrooms," she said.

"Prawn cocktail for me."

"No, no you want the soup, that's best. Now main courses, I'm having Steak Diane, and I'm having it cooked at the table so that I can oversee it, make sure they do it right. What are you having?"

"Grotty Pork with malice!" Mary's eyes were twinkling.

"What!" Exploded Philistine.

Tom covered both ears, but at last he began to enjoy himself, as his boss revealed a hitherto unsuspected playful streak.

"Huh! And I suppose you'll be having a chicken and chips?"

"Close."

Mary leaned forward again to speak,

"I know a restaurant where if that's what you order, that's what you get."

"The Waterford, yes," replied Tom nodding. "It's a big shock the first time you go, to find a whole chicken on your plate."

"Rubbish. It's Steak Diane for the three of us. Blue, of course, no other way to have it. Then you can leave half of it, claim it's overdone."

"No," said Tom mechanically.

"All you do is--"

"No!"

"Oh well that's what I'm having, and I won't pay for it, nor the wine. I eat free in restaurants all the time. Matter of principle, I'll show you."

"No you won't." murmured Tom into his menu. He glanced at his boss; she was gazing at him wide-eyed, disbelieving.

Presently the waiter arrived to take their order. Tom stood up to speak to him, and get in first,

"Mademoiselle will have Garlic mushrooms and Griots de Porc with Sauce ti-Malice. Can I have a steak grilled on a normal grill; I don't want it within ten feet of any charcoal."

"Certainly sir."

Tom spoke assertively straight through Philistines attempts to order soup and Steaks Diane for three,

"In that case, I will have prawn cocktail and rib-eye Surf and Turf, rare, please. Rare, not bleu. And can you turn the musak off?" The waiter grinned, leaned over and turned a knob discretely concealed among artificial plants. Other speakers continued to blare their message, although significantly muted, but a zone of calm developed around the end of their table. Tom sat down waving at the loudmouth. "And he'll have something else."

"Certainly sir."

* * *

Philistine surveyed his empty soup plate with satisfaction,

"Right, operation free meal. First, you praise the first course, which puts them off their guard."

Mary bridled,

"You are not seriously going to do this, are you?"

"Of course! Watch and learn. Waiter!"

Both Tom and his boss covered their ears.

"Waiter congratulations, this soup is excellent. I'll have a good wine with my steak. Have you got a really good claret?"

The waiter began to reply, but Philistine cut him off after the first name,

"Yeah, that'll do, bung it on."

A junior chef appeared and began preparing the loudmouth's steak Diane nearby. Naturally, this obstructed the way and caused severe local traffic chaos. The wine arrived, and when Philistine made to pout him a glass, Tom covered his glass,

"Not allowed, driving."

"So am I," bellowed Philistine. "One glass won't hurt."

"Not allowed!"

"He's on tablets too Phil; he's really not allowed." Then with more than a hint of steel, the Head of Department showed through. "Don't push it."

"Ah well, tablets, you should have said."

When Mary had taken her first drink of the wine, Tom raised his eyebrows at her.

"I'm glad you're not allowed; this is delicious."

"And free!"

"You are not going to claim that this is off?" Mary asked fiercely.

"Watch me, halfway down the bottle and halfway through the steak. Free meal. Just watch."

In very obvious disgust Mary turned her conversation more specifically to Tom, and it wasn't long before he began to enjoy the company of the much younger girl.

From time to time Philistine intruded. The other two ignored him when they could or acknowledged his contribution with a nod or a look.

"So what's Mr Mary doing tonight?"

"There isn't one--"

"I don't believe that for one second."

"There isn't. It's a control thing. I need to be the boss; it usually means that I have to say goodbye to the men I fancy. Those that want to lie down and let me walk all over them I don't want. If I wanted that, I'd buy a dog. Why am I telling you these personal secrets?"

"People always do, that's why they made me a Year Tutor. The wine's going down well, how are you getting home?"

"I'll have to ring for a taxi."

"Well in that case, may I give you a lift, I'd like to. I'd like to not take you straight home as well. We could go somewhere quiet, more quiet than this. You could do your boss thing, and if I felt footprints on my back I could do my spank thing, show you that you can be the boss completely, but this dog bites."

"Ha!" The involuntary laugh was slowly replaced by a shocked smile of dawning realisation. "You're serious aren't you?"

"Absolutely. In the few months, we had together before I had my stroke, I realised that I respected you enormously for being a good boss. In the last hour, I've grown to like you as a person too. Now I'm offering the next logical step. Like Dennis Thatcher, I'd have no problem with you running the country, just not me!"

"You're old enough to be my Dad. You're older than my Dad."

"No, you're completely wrong. The true situation is that you're young enough to be my daughter, but what the bunnies, nobody's perfect."

Mary burst out laughing, and their main meals arrived before she could reply.

Tom's prawn cocktail had been divine, and the first taste of the rare steak he was served exploded with flavour in his mouth and melted away virtually without chewing. How good chefs did this to dead cattle was beyond him, but it stiffened his resolve not to stand idly by.

"Well?" He asked Mary, as her face too showed that her meal was exquisite.

"Why not? I mean, if you don't come up to snuff I can always fire you, can't I."

"And if I try too hard to achieve snuff?"

"I've never fired anyone for trying."

Tom grinned and turned to address Philistine,

"How's the steak? I mean really, not how you are going to claim it is."

"Pretty good, not often had better."

"As praiseworthy as Mary's and my meal then?"

"Probably."

"And the wine?"

"Oh that's the real stuff, that's why it's so expensive. Sure you don't want some, it's free."

"No, can't."

At the kitchen door, the Chef and his staff could be seen anxiously looking out over their domain, apparently gauging the results of their efforts. Tom stood up and with unmistakable beckoning called them across. His voice, trained to capture the attention of six hundred unruly kids in assembly, effortlessly cut through the hubbub without shouting. Most of the clients stopped eating and turned to watch. As soon as the staff were within comfortable addressing range, he spoke, pitching his voice at a level which reached most of the room,

"My friends and I." He indicated Mary and Philistine. "Want

to congratulate the restaurant on this excellent claret, but you personally on these magnificent meals. I have never tasted better, and my friends agree with me." He clapped loudly triggering a healthy round of applause from the entire room. The staff thanked those around them as they withdrew smiling.

As Tom sat down,

"That should ensure that you are consuming the most expensive free meal of your life," he said, smiling benignly at Philistine.

* * *

Tom reached out and gently caressed the naked breast of the girl lying beside him.

"I still cannot believe I did this," Mary said without opening her eyes.

"That's what you said six months ago, in bed the morning after the Christmas Party. And believe me, Mrs Rigel, I can't believe it either, but I'm glad you did."

"So am I."

"Come on, get up, you can't spend the whole of your honeymoon in bed."

"I can if I want to, I'm the boss, and it's **my** honeymoon!"

"You get up, or you might have to be spanked!"

"Ooh!"

The Discovery

{Precisely that}

When Jet's timing was off, occasionally it was spectacularly off,

"Can I come over tonight? Discuss the Sixth Form Courses with you."

Karen's eyes rolled, as her knuckles on the hand holding the telephone whitened.

"No, not tonight please Jet." She was desperately groping for excuses: "Anyway there's nothing to discuss. You're doing Tourism. I'm doing Plumbing."

"There's General Studies; we're both doing that."

"General Studies is just to balance up the curriculum. It doesn't need discussing. I'll talk about it with you on Saturday."

"Saturday's shopping, I want a dress; we won't have time to talk about School."

Karen dropped the receiver onto the top of her desk with a clatter, picked it up and dropped it again.

"Oh. Sorry." She gave it another knock for good measure. "Look Jet; I've got problems. I've got to go. I'll see you on Saturday." And hung up. Her Dad looked up from the model car he was building,

"It's Thursday! It's Nine-o-clock! And it's Sailing!" He called, paraphrasing the famous introduction to Crackerjack.

"It's my one hour of the week. I know I'll never own a boat. But I can dream for one hour a week. Surely!"

"An hour and a half girl, never curtail your ambitions."

That night, the presenter completed varnishing the boat she was building as a centrepiece to the sequence of programmes and moved on to choice of sails, and sail care. The programme finished with a discussion with other Natural Earth Presenters on sailing expeditions. The other two girls endorsed the importance of care, especially in obeying the manufacturer's instructions with new sails.

In bed, Karen fell asleep dreaming of becoming such a successful plumber, that one day she might even consider owning a boat of her own.

* * *

On Saturday, she smoothed Jet's ruffled feathers by talking General Studies throughout the shopping morning.

* * *

Their introduction to the Sixth Form was as nice as the girls could have hoped it would be. There was a marked change in the way the staff treated the students, except for the few, like Mr Baques, who had always treated them as adults, since Year Seven. Equally marked was the lack of confrontation, due entirely to the lack of certain undesirables in the ranks.

Had Karen been asked her wishes, the vocational course would have matched them exactly. Several of her teachers had come to the profession late and illustrated their lessons with anecdotes from the factory floor. She didn't mind being the only girl in the room because the staff made a point of not mentioning the fact, almost as if they hadn't realised it. English, Maths and General Studies they were taught as a Form Class, and of these only General Studies carried an examination. The other two were there merely to maintain an acceptable standard of literacy and numeracy.

Mr Smith took them for General Studies and illustrated his lessons with anecdotes from Canoeing.

"Life's a constant compromise, like canoe design. The ideal canoe is long, short, wide, narrow, and flat-bottomed with a sharp keel." He shrugged at the grinning youths in front of him: "My experience of life is something similar, and I bet yours is too."

Jet had gushed at length about how they would join West Wild Water, and learn a new sport.

"Let's go canoeing, it seems like fun, nobody else does it in our form, they're all football and hockey, we won't have to put up with Trevor and Maggie fighting. We'll go on Thursday. Start canoeing, start a whole new phase in our lives."

There was quite a bit more.

When Karen managed to get some words in,

"Have you considered sailing? Rather than canoeing."

"Don't be silly, we've never considered anything like this before, and now we've got a Heaven-sent opportunity to do something new and different, and straight away you want to try something off the wall. We'll go and join Llew Smith's absolute beginners class; they're Year Sevens so that nobody will know us, we'll be the only people we know who do canoeing and --" Jet was thrusting the error of her ways so forcibly down her throat that the possibility of a hidden agenda occurred.

In her mind Karen had to agree, their General Studies teacher was more than just a passably attractive man.

Consequently, on Thursday, the Globe-Trotter dragged the reluctantly acquiescing Plumber down to the swimming baths, to learn Canoeing.

After warming up, they performed exercises, Press-ups, Squat thrusts, and Vee-ups.

"You start with only five of each. I know you could probably do ten, or even fifteen, but you wouldn't be able to get out of bed tomorrow." Said Mr Smith to the assembled kids. "We'll work up to a big score over the year."

They learned how to get into the tiny one-girl boat, that sat so serenely while empty, but wobbled like a ball on a stick with someone in it.

Then how to eject correctly after a capsize, and soon after

that, how to paddle, feathering between strokes.

Karen leaned forward, dipped her paddle into the water on her right and pulled, flick of the right wrist, and dip into the other side, pull, un-flick and repeat.

Dip, pull, flick, dip, pull, un-flick, repeat in a controlled sequence.

The end of the bath was approaching fast.

Almost without conscious thought,

she exaggerated the slight snaking of her canoe's course through the water.

The bow came around in an accelerating curve.

With a controlled power stroke,

she straightened up,

and sped back up the bath.

All around her youngsters were travelling in circles, or bumping into each other, {a neat extra dip on one side avoided a collision of her own,} or swimming towards the side of the bath towing an upturned canoe behind them.

Jet surfaced scowling with her hair rats-tailing down her face. She was struggling with her capsized boat, as Karen watched, it submerged beneath the surface and began to sink away. Chuckling as he did it, Mr Smith was going to her aid.

Karen weaved her course among the wreckage, swapping chit chat with bobbing heads, and testing ideas that occurred to her, for steering and turning.

Mr Smith called time.

Time?

In disbelief, she glanced at the clock. An hour had gone, gone from her life, leaving the warmest glow she had ever known.

They stored the canoes away and showered off the heavily chlorinated water. Jet managed a discreet silence until they were safely back inside the girls changing room, then she savagely heaved her bather off and began furiously towelling herself dry,

"We're never doing that again!" She said, punishing her skin, which was covered in a purple network: "I don't mind being cold, or wet, or even a little frightened, but all three together! We are never doing that again!"

Karen said nothing, all calls of sails plucking at her heart's strings forgotten.

The Globetrotter could hump and grump as she pleased, but the Plumber had discovered Canoeing.

A New Start For Annabelle

{Write a Story with a twist in the ta(i)l(e)}

Annabelle skipped down the stairs, "I'll get it," she called to save her sister, who was making the coffees, from coming too. She opened the door to the visitor and stood pleased, but surprised. It was a huge bunch of flowers. Peeping around from behind it was her secret love.

"Hello," he said.

"Oh -- Donald -- What are you doing here?"

"Making like a dove. Complete with Olive Branch." He offered the bouquet.

"You don't need to offer me an Olive Branch. You always treated me right."

"The Olive Branch is from the one who didn't, your ex. But he's sent me to mediate -- Ask you to forgive him, and have him back."

He couldn't even come himself.

"And Miriam? Couldn't he even see it out to the end?"

"He did. Miriam's dead. She only ever had five to seven months from diagnosis. Turned out to be five."

"That means she's hardly cold yet Donald."

"I know, I'm just the messenger, I'd prefer it if you didn't shoot me."

"Was he with her at the end?"

"Oh yes. Yes, yes."

"Was -- Bonneville -- With -- Her?"

"He was on his way. It took a couple of days to find him when the crisis hit."

"Where was he?"

"Dunno."

"Las Vegas or Monte Carlo?" She waited, her eyes boring into him in an unblinking stare.

Donald twitched, shuffled, and shrugged, but eventually,

"Vegas." Almost like changing the subject, he proffered an envelope: "I've brought a letter. As well as the flowers."

She pulled the door wide and ushered him in,

"Coffee?"

"Please."

"Charlie," called Annabelle: "It's coffee for three."

* * *

Charlene fumed but waited until their guest had gone before she cut loose.

"The rat! The total mangy rat!"

"It's dogs that get mange, but rat, yes. Minging rat, yes, oh yes! The question is what am I going to do about it?"

"Do? Nothing! You're going to tear up that." She gesticulated wildly in the general direction of the letter. "That -- Disgusting assumption that you would be prepared to go with him on a -- a -- Dirty Weekend. You're going to -- Telephone him and give him a piece of your min--"

"That's two not-nothings that I'm not going to do! They are what Bonneville expects me to do. My guess is he's already got phase two in place. I'll save him the bother."

"You're not going?"

"That's exactly what I'm doing Charlie. Now be a good supportive little sister and keep out of my way. I'd like you to accompany me on a shopping trip, and help with my packing, but no more instructions which I'll have to ignore. Pretty please."

Annabelle leafed through her wardrobe, checking items and making notes. From time to time Charlene reached an item out and tried it up against herself.

"Your mountain gear is lovely you know. I'd wear this to a disco."

"You'd boil. I'm getting new for the weekend; no don't say anything, I'm getting new, not the boots obviously, but everything else."

"Annabelle! It's--"

Annabelle thrust the credit card under her sister's nose,

"The account is in Bonneville's name, not mine, but I was careful never to use it, so my card's still valid. If he wants my presence, he can have my presence, but it's going to cost him --"

"Oh -- I see. Well, he can pay for the transport too, get the bus ticket on it as well."

"Bus? No child, chauffeur-driven limousine. Not a stretched one, not for Lake District roads, but a Bentley, or Daimler, that will do lunch nicely."

* * *

The elegant, black Bentley scrunched to a halt in front of Patterdale House. A moment later Donald appeared to welcome her.

"He said you were coming, I didn't believe it, but I'm glad to see you." He hugged her. "This is a bit swish. Have you won the lottery?"

"No. I still have access to a credit card with a high limit. And before you ask, no, he doesn't know, not yet."

Donald's eyes opened wide, and he pulled a wry face,

"Dibbs on telling him."

"Not until after the weekend, please Donald."

"Okay."

Annabelle dismissed the chauffeur and Donald helped her in with her bags. Her room was a pleasant one overlooking Ullswater. Donald stayed with her chatting until dinner, when his cousin, at last, deigned to put in an appearance.

Bonneville's greeting was,

"I didn't think you'd come."

"I wouldn't miss this for the World, a free weekend in lovely surroundings. I reckon you owe me at least that."

"Don't be like that Belle--"

"Annabelle! You've got several bridges to repair before diminutives will be permitted." She smiled as she offered her arm: "But a decent dinner could lay the foundations for the first one."

Bonneville took the proffered arm and guided her in to the prime table beside the window. He released her and sat down.

"Now then, tell me what you have been doing with yourself."

There was no answer. He looked up, Annabelle; was still standing beside her chair, waiting, looking at him. He scowled, got up, and pulled her chair out for her. She smiled as she spoke,

"Thank you. This and that you know. I took a leaf out of your book. It's really amazing how much human beings will part with, in return for friendly acquiescence."

"You've been sleeping your way through somebody's bank account?"

"Oh, is that what you were doing?"

"No! I didn't mean me! You!"

"Oh no, just being pleasant, and friendly, so far anyway."

"Who is it?"

"You don't want to know. Tell me about Miriam; I hope you made sure that her last few months were good ones."

"Yes of course I did. That's why I married h--"

"And left her to die alone."

"I wouldn't do that! I want to talk about us. I never stopped loving you, but she needed me, you didn't. Now that I've given her a good send-off, we can pick up again where we left off."

"Are you ready to order, Sir?"

"Yes. The chef has my special order, Mr Chatti, just ask him for it."

"And Madame?"

"Miss will have the lobster," interjected Annabelle: "And the fillet steak, rare please, rare, not bleu, with a Rockhopper Salad."

The waiter smiled,

"Very good Miss."

"And a bottle of your best sweet white, with the lobster, and one of red with the steak.”

“I’m not allowed sweet wine.”

“I know, it’s for me. Your best, please.”

“Very good Miss.”

“And Mr Chatti will have bottled water. Unless--”

“Bottled water will do fine.”

The waiter took their menus and departed.

“So no easing of restrictions on the diabetic front then?”

“Quite the reverse. It’s got more aggressive; I’m on a special diet, maximum safe dosage. Well, it’s actually well beyond the maximum safe dose, but it’s keeping me alive.” He produced a tooled leather case. “Present from Miriam.”

Annabelle nodded. They talked about neutral topics until starters began arriving nearby, then Bonneville, without fuss, retrieved the syringe from the case, and gave himself an insulin injection, which, to most people, including normal diabetics would be lethal.

* * *

“Well, goodnight then.”

“I’m not getting anything for the slap-up dinner then?”

“No. It paid off a bit of the debt, but you’re not in credit yet. We’ll see how tomorrow goes. How gentlemanly you are on our walk.”

“I’m always a gentleman.”

“Never, Bonneville dear, but you’re transparent too. The good weather will have the top of Helvellyn like Harrods sale tomorrow. You chose Place Fell because up there, we will be totally alone, and you can have your wicked way with me on top of the mountain and no-one will disturb you. Well, we’ll see, you might or you might not, we’ll see.”

* * *

Bonneville unslung the rucksack and dropped it down beside the summit cairn. He produced the tooled leather case and prepared the injection. Annabelle watched him administer it.

“So I’m to be seduced after lunch, am I? I was rather hoping it would be before."

His face showed his shock at her suggestion.

"Erm -- Well I've got ten minutes."

"Ten minutes was usually more than you needed."

"Cheeky baggage! Come here."

Despite the statements, Annabelle's concentration on favouring her right thumb while disrobing her partner, and quite aggressive insistence on some degree of foreplay, extended the time well beyond the safety zone.

"I'm sorry! I'll have to stop and eat; I'll faint in a minute if I don't."

"Okay, you won't be much good to me floppy."

Grinning, Bonneville opened the rucksack and then began tearing things out of it, specimen bags and small field-microscope, a first aid kit, but his searching produced no food.

"Where's the food? There's no food! You've picked the wrong ruck up!"

"Not me, you picked it up. That is my gear, not yours, but you picked it up."

"Give me a choc bar quick!"

Annabelle indicated her naked form, shaking her head,

"I've got nothing. You planned this whole day; you told me not to bother with anything."

With a panic-stricken look at her, Bonneville took out his mobile phone and switched it on.

Nothing happened.

"I charged this up overnight! What's the matter with it?" He pulled open the battery compartment and touched the terminals with his tongue. "It's dead! I'm done for."

"Can't you eat some grass or something?"

The withering look he gave her was the last thing he did before slipping into hypoglycaemia-coma.

Annabelle got dressed,

"Don't go anywhere; I'll get help."

There was no response.

She set off, trotting back towards Boardale Hause, but when she missed her step on an erratic and rolled it, and turned her left ankle, reducing her progress to a slow hobble, Bonneville's fate was sealed.

* * *

The inquest returned a verdict of death by misadventure. The coroner commended Annabelle for her bravery in walking on the twisted ankle, and when that became impossible, crawling, in her attempt to save her lover. Her ankle and knees had required serious medical attention.

* * *

For the next few weeks, Donald supported Annabelle through her convalescence. After the reading of Bonneville's will he turned up at her house, she welcomed him in, and he brought her up to speed over coffee.

"Miriam's daughter by her first husband gets all her money."

"The money Bonneville married her for?"

"Well, yes, I suppose so."

"No, suppose about it."

"But I get the Chatti Family Estate, of course, it's entailed, but he left it to me anyway, any child of Bonneville's would have inherited before me. He didn't get you pregnant on the Fell by any chance?"

"We didn't get that far."

"Good. But my guess is you made sure of that."

Annabelle looked blankly at him for a moment then,

"What are you saying?"

"I'm saying that I love you, I always did."

"Oh."

"I used to hurt when Bonneville mistreated you."

"Are you planning to do anything about it?"

"Marry you. I have enough love for both of us, to begin with. You like me; I'll turn that to love eventually." He silenced her with his fingers across her lips in a tender, delicate gesture. "And no! You don't have any choice in the matter because the only person they can't force me to testify against is my wife."

Although she blanked him again, she didn't recoil from the intimacy of the fingers.

"The rucks were in a row, he really did pick it up; I saw him do it, but he got the wrong one only because you rearranged them, my guess."

Still, she gave no response.

"The ankle? That was a masterstroke, I don't know how you managed it, but it put you out of the frame."

"But obviously not as far as you are concerned."

He reached out and took her hand, holding it up for her inspection. The deep purple bar across the ball of her thumb had a neat line of paler small squares punctuating it.

"A straight short across the terminals of a fully-charged NiCad-battery can theoretically generate up to sixty amps. It must have hurt like sixty." He snorted at his own joke: "Like sixty amps! I don't know how you got to his telephone, but I know you used a silver teaspoon, you can still see the hallmarks in the burn. I don't know that a burn that deep will ever heal without trace. I know what you did and that you did it for Miriam, not yourself. I don't blame you at all. You probably beat me to it."

"He left his telephone in his room, he always forgot. He ordered me to get it, despatched like a Victorian scullery maid."

"He always did. I don't know how you stuck it."

Annabelle shrugged,

"It wasn't a teaspoon; it was a mustard-spoon. I turned the ankle as a kid; I knew exactly how to do it again. But apparently, it's weak now, a permanent reminder. My answer is yes! If you are willing to take on a murderess, the least I can do is say yes Mr Chatti, I will marry you. But it is willingly. I like you enough for that, but I love you quite a lot too, more than you seem to suspect. I stuck it with the late unlamented because it kept me close to you. I was waiting for you to intervene. I didn't realise the lengths I would have to go to, to force your hand. You can have me in sixteen days with a special licence."[2]

---

2   When 'Annabelle' was written, but these requirements change without notice, please check. *P.C.*

"I got the licence a month ago; I've arranged it for this afternoon. Tonight when I take you to bed, it will be as my wife."

"Okay, to protect me. But I'll have a proper Church do as soon as we can arrange it."

"Fine."

Preparing for Winter

{Story suggested by a picture of a parsimoniously dressed, elderly man sitting in a gaunt, bleak and threadbare room, but looking towards the window in an eager manner. Amongst the doom and gloom, there were a few gems.}

He'd nearly made it. It had been a very tight call. The threadbare tablecloth and chipped pot-plates had been cleared even of crumbs; the larder had been empty for several days. Children's laughter from outside had bought him passage to the door, but even now he wasn't free, not quite yet.

The view was dismal. It was of a narrow, brooding, oppressive, grey-and-damp-until-out-of-sight, tenement street. The dank smell of incontinent dog offended his nostrils; he shut his mind to it all and listened.

The gurgling laugh of a baby eased the arthritis in his joints and allowed him to take a few steps towards the sound.

The walls drew back revealing a group of children playing in an alleyway.

A little girl, in a stained, ragged, hand-me-down dress, looked up, saw him, and smiled.

Gathering speed, the glowering, grey walls withdrew ghost-like from around him, like a camera trick.

The cold dampness underfoot gave way to warm dry dust as the street widened.

The walls sloughed off the grey sadness of winter, and melted away revealing trees. Their shadows spilled suddenly across the neat lawns, in front of the starkly sunlit houses bordering the wide boulevard.

The little girl, in her trend-setting pink bikini, was still smiling at him. Suddenly she jumped and squealed, as her brother splashed her from the paddling pool on their lawn.

Giggling, she ran off to retaliate.

He collected the glow of a primrose in the morning, and spent it immediately; his gait became positive and thrusting.

The joy of the spring flowers along the way closed over him as he plunged into it.

The colours in his scarf took up their hues while his clothes gathered their smooth, flawless texture into his elegantly cut, lightweight suit and matching designer sunglasses.

He now cut a fine figure, strolling through Summer and on into Autumn.

His knapsack was filling up.

Among many of the delights it contained lay the wispiness of morning mist rising from a lake, and the promise of seedlings straining upwards through warm summer rain. He was particularly pleased to have collected the elation of a rainbow and the sigh of a lover.

The euphoria of the crowd, cheering home their victorious team, took up a lot of space; he only had a few small pouches left. He'd specifically kept some back for the smell of cherry tomatoes and the taste of wild blackberries straight from the vine.

He delayed his return until Christmas Eve, waiting outside Fenwick to fill his pockets with the shine in the eyes of the children gazing into the window; finally, he slipped into the store, and wallowed in the emotions generated, as the staff choir walked by, singing carols.

Back home, in his neat little cottage, the man unpacked his treasures and stored them away to see him through the winter.

He glanced up at the Staffordshire dogs; it was three years

since he'd had enough joy left over by the following spring, to fix them forever.

After two poor years, this one had been good, with a bountiful harvest.

It would see him through comfortably.

He smoothed out the richly embroidered tablecloth, and arranged the solid silver cutlery around his Wedgwood dinner service; with a bit of luck, he might even have enough pleasure left over in April, to make them permanent.

He stoked the fire to a friendly blaze; the cheerful flames illuminated his tasteful and elegant furnishings perfectly. Then he glanced at the window, grinned at the deepening gloom barricaded outside, took one last look around, and settled down in his comfy chair.

Winter was far from his favourite season, but this one would be good.

All A Square Peg Needs Is A Square Hole

Hilda woke up,

"Not again. Please not again." She plucked her alarm clock out of the air as it dived off her bedside table. A quick check showed no more treasures in danger, but smaller items of furniture were on the march, although her wardrobe and ottoman were just vibrating gently.

Outside on the landing, as usual, all was still, not exactly quiet, but under control. It was a total freak of acoustic dynamics that her bedroom amplified his snores, while her landing cancelled them out. Another night on the stairs, she thought, I can't stand much more of this.

The following day she began researching a solution. She had no wish to cause Justin permanent harm, so neither cyanide nor arsenic, just something to cause him to leave quietly of his own choice. An uncontrollable need to use the toilet after every meal she prepared for him would get the message across. Phenolthaleine would do fine. Fortunately, she stayed her hand before the final, irrevocable step, deciding to do further research first. The second volume on drugs and poisons halted her with the words, 'the most powerful laxative known. One drop is enough to --' She had been going to sprinkle it about.

"Bust beads! I might have killed him." It was only when Aunt Augusta asked,

"Killed who?" That she realised she'd spoken aloud.

"Nothing -- Nobody."

Too late Hilda realised, who was talking to her,

"Sit down. Tell all to Auntie."

Hilda heaved a big sigh and told all.

"So he's no longer a candidate? For the other half of your bed?"

"He never was; I chose wrongly there too. Oh, you might as well know; he's more of your persuasion, the male version."

"In that case. Rather than you going to jail. For manslaughter. Introduce me. I may be able to solve your problem."

* * *

"Justin, this is a friend of mine, Augusta, my best friend. She's also my Aunt, but don't let that put you off, she's friendly too."

"Her nosiest friend Justin. How do you do?"

He shook hands while returning her greeting.

"Hilda. Go into the garden. Hunt scorpions for a while. Justin and I need to discuss business."

Augusta called her back in a while later,

"Congratulate me. I'm getting married. Fastest we can do it. Sixteen days by special licence.[3] Justin's busy packing. I'm taking him home now. You can sleep in your bed tonight. That's what you wanted. Isn't it?"

"But all that means is he'll keep you awake all night with his snoring, instead of me. Especially in that cardboard box, you inhabit."

"No dear. He won't. I've just got a new job and a new place. It is a solid, well built Victorian house with bedrooms at opposite ends of the building. The job's good money. But not quite good enough to pay the mortgage, not properly. Justin's contribution will make all the difference.

"Oh. But you're a -- You hate men."

"No dear. I like men. They're so funny. I just don't want a

---

3   Again: when this story was written, please check. *P.C.*

man with me in my bed. Justin will be in the other room. With his boyfriend overnight if he wants. And Jane. Or Jessica. Or Emily, or whoever can be with me in mine. We've done a deal. We're each other's cover."

Road Rage

{Precisely that}

Sebastian watched Tamsin escort the doctor to the front door of the little semi, and then return to his other self. She uncovered his face, and smoothed the sheet,

"I promise I'll try to be brave. But for now. Just for now. I need to get it out. Please forgive me." She knelt down, covered his hand with hers, and began to pray. Presently the prayers became a confession,

"You always thought I was with you because I liked you. Because I respected you. Because I was flattered. A young girl flattered by the attention of an older man. But it wasn't that. They were all true. But I loved you, Sebastian. Loved you! And I'm late, and you know I'm never late. Yes, it's only a few hours, nearly one day. But I'm never late. The gift I wanted from you most of all. I'm sure I've got it, and I never got to tell you." The first tears didn't even make it to her cheeks before they were shoved unceremoniously into obeying the pull of gravity by those pressing in from behind. Her claim that she had loved him in life was confirmed by her reaction to his death. The sobs grew louder and shook her shoulders, and for a few moments her whole body.

"I know you're not here anymore --"

He reached out, caressing her arms, and stroking her hair. The sobs lessened and presently ceased. She rose and turned looking straight at him,

"You are here. Still. I know it. You are here aren't you?"

Yes.

"We're having a baby."

I heard.

"There are things I have to do. I'll tell you all about it in bed tonight."

Okay.

"What do I do first?"

It's all on your list.

"My list yes. In the dresser."

The top drawer, on the right.

"Yes."

She went downstairs walking straight through him on her way. He followed, guiding her, comforting her and supporting her. She found the list, took it to the telephone, and began.

The undertakers arrived while she was still working systematically through the items. She let them get on. Presently,

"Right Miss, we're done. It's Tuesday 21st at eleven-o-clock, procession from our Chapel of Rest to the Crematorium, followed by the Wake back here at one-o-clock."

"And no changes from the agreed programme."

"None Miss. We rarely do The Diamond Service, so I confirmed all the arrangements before I came out to you. It's all set up exactly how Sebastian wanted it."

"And the cost?"

"Will be within the budget, only just I'm afraid but within it."

"That's fine. If there are any problems, don't cut back on the level of service. Check with me."

"Yes, Miss, we understand that."

"Me. Not the sisters!"

"Yes, Miss. You're the executor."

"And it's Mrs, since a month ago."

"Oh. Congratulations, and condolences."

Sebastian stayed close by his girl for the next few days supporting her while she carried out his wishes. The attacks of his sisters when they discovered the terms of his will were vitriolic,

"Equal shares? What do you mean equal shares?"

"We're his only relatives! Just because you wormed your way into his bed a few years ago--"

"When it was illegal--"

"Doesn't make you a relative!"

"We'll go to court, you'll get nothing, and we're cancelling this travesty of a funeral!"

"It's a frivolous waste of money!"

"Horse-drawn hearse indeed! What next?"

Tamsin didn't reply; she just raised her eyebrows at the solicitor.

"I wouldn't go to court if I were you. You're correct; Tamsin is not a sister, and therefore you would not expect her to inherit a sister's share. She is your brother's widow."

"Widow!"

"Don't be stupid she's only seventeen!"

"It's a trick!"

"She is your brother's widow, and as such the court will award her much more of the estate than specified in the will. Especially when it becomes clear that it was she who asked that the bequests be made equal. It's up to you, but you cannot cancel the funeral because your brother's executor will not allow it."

Sebastian left them to it. He had believed that Tamsin was perfectly capable of ensuring his instructions were carried out; the exchange had merely confirmed it. He drifted off to witness the beginnings of his dying wish being realised.

The hearse, already beautiful, was having a last extra sheen polished into it. He was surprised at just how big it was, as he had been when he saw it for the first time. Of course, it had to be big; it had to accommodate anyone, not just his Mr Average frame. The glass box, with its black supporting columns, shone. The gilded fittings gleamed. The paintwork had recently been renewed and showed it. Not even the wheels had any chips or scratches in their flawless surfaces. All his life Sebastian had made do and mended, coped, muddled through. His final send-off was going to be everything that, Tamsin apart, his life had not been.

On the Tuesday morning, the hearse was decked out with black plumes. The matching pair of black horses also had an impressive headdress each. A coachman in livery climbed onto the seat high above the road, and sedately walked the carriage out onto the highway, down towards the Chapel of Rest.

The horses stepped out, knees high, displaying their pride at the occasion. The coachman stared straight ahead while soaking up the admiring glances with his peripheral vision.

The muffled hooves of the horses and rubber tyres of the wheels gave little warning of their approach along the road.

Sebastian suddenly realised that while concentrating on their image, and the effect it was having on the populace, neither coachman nor horses had seen the hole in the road ahead. Nor had they seen the men who were working down it.

He tried, he really tried to warn them, but Tamsin wasn't around to pick up the transmissions.

The nearside horse trod on a worker's shoulder, took fright and bolted.

The front wheels dived into the hole, and bucked the coachman off and forwards over his horses' heads, into the road.

The commotion panicked the second horse which also bolted, plucking the hearse out of the hole like a cork from a bottle.

One of the abused wheels promptly parted company from the axel, leaped over the tables on the nearby pavement café, in through the doorway, and on up to the counter, which it hit with a loud bang.

The harassed waitress, with three orders stacked up already, didn't look to see who was demanding attention, just shouted,

"It's no good thumping on the counter, wait your turn like everyone else."

From his elevated vantage point, Sebastian watched.

How the A&E staff would react when the workman arrived claiming to have been run over by a horse-drawn hearse was anybody's guess.

And, of course, his Diamond Service send-off, was off! Sadly he watched his dream career off down the road, faster and faster, as the increasingly terrified horses were erratically pulled and pushed from behind by the one-legged, three-wheeler, noisily exploding into small pieces behind them.

His top of the range, splash do, send-off, his one and only indulgence, had become his life's usual handcart-and-blackout-curtains, muddle through.

His sisters would crow like cockerels.

Even worse, Tamsin would be upset on his account.

His anger and frustration boiled over, bringing a whole new dimension to the concept of Road Rage.

"Oh Bother!" he said.

Dear True Reader,

I regret to record that the accident involving a horse-drawn hearse, the central incident, on which Road Rage is based, is fact. There were two workers down the hole, one of them told us what happened while he was being treated in A&E. When I wrote the incident up in my usual, slightly wonky, way, I believed the second man to be uninjured; I never saw him at the hospital, and, apart from existing in the other worker's narrative, he was never mentioned.

Sadly I learned later that, far from being uninjured, he had subsequently died from his injuries.

After much thought, I have specifically chosen to leave the story in the collection.

I hope no-one minds.

Petra.

Birthday Present/Birthday Future

{Sequel to Enforcing The Deal -- Page 20}

The telephone was picked up at the other end,
"Hello?"

His heart thumped, as it always did when he heard her voice.
"Happy Birthday!"

"Oh, John. I got your card, thank you. Is it still on to pick the kids and me up from my interview?"

"Yes, no problem."

"Good. I'll be able to thank you properly."

"What presents did you get?"

"I got a lovely teak handled barbecue set from Bovin. Stink from Jill, and pillows from Mum and Dad." Her voice was lively and enthusiastic. "I got a card from Bovin's Mum; she's bringing me something back off holiday."

"You're having a lovely day then?"

"Yes. I'll see you at four. Bye."

He looked sadly at the dead receiver,

"A present for you but bought with himself in mind from your husband, a promise from your Ma-in-law, a half-personal present from your sister. Otherwise a blizzard! You didn't even expect anything of your children or Father-in-law. You're having a rotten birthday Vera. You just don't know the difference."

At four o'clock, John Mason left his office and went next door to collect Vera's children. The in-house crèche was the main reason for choosing the legal conglomerate as her place of work. That was assuming that she passed the interview of course, but he had no doubts that she would. Four-year-old Mandy was watching for him. She picked Tina up onto her hip, waded out of the ball pool, and met him at the door.

"Did you get them?" The children's big brown eyes were gazing up at him, rapt, expectant.

"Yes. They gift wrapped them. Just like you wanted."

Big grins broke out on both faces.

"We've never said. Tina never said. It's still a surprise. Here's Mummy."

The trio turned towards Vera who approached grinning and holding her thumbs up.

"Congratulations," said John, while taking care to hug only Vera's shoulders, and kiss only her cheek. Even so, he was scared she'd detect the pounding heart. A few minutes later they had returned to his car.

"You strap Tina in. I'll see to Mandy."

While Vera was busy strapping Tina in the child's car seat, he slid the big parcel out from the boot and gave it to the elder child.

"Mummy. This is from Me and Tina and John. Happy Birthday."

She allowed the children to help her remove the wrapper from the gift, and then went ecstatic over the set-of-three, different-sized, soft-toy Racoons it contained.

If I'd had to wait until my twenty-first birthday for my first ever cuddly-toy, I'd be crying too, thought John.

"They're lovely, how did you know?"

"John told us."

"That was so lovely and thoughtful, thank you."

John turned away to avoid contact; he didn't know which was more hurtful, not kissing, or stopping after one.

"Come on. We have to pick Bovin up."

When they arrived at West Novochester, John pulled up beside the Sixth Form Suite to wait for Bovin. Even now the building brought back the bittersweet memories of sharing a classroom with Vera, and quietly adoring her from afar. It only became apparent that she had fallen for their Chemistry teacher when, early in their Sixth Form course, she suddenly left and married him. Mandy was born barely six months later.

The mental pain the memory caused hit John hard. He visibly winced.

Two students emerged talking. John had seen them before on previous visits and automatically looked for the lift that would be waiting for them.

"Dad we need to stop off at the Supermarket on the way home." called the brunette as she approached the car. The driver nodded.

Bovin appeared and bundled clothes through the open passenger window onto his wife's lap. He was dressed in running gear, and, although addressing Vera, he was looking at the students.

"That Pealleovbelles Tumpkins, such a stupid name! She's put down the Robinson's address on her Record of Achievement forms. Typical dumb blonde! She's written her friend's address, and that she wants to be an electrician! I'll have something to say to her tomorrow. Fancy deliberately ruining them by writing the wrong address, and stupidly pointless career targets."

By now the daughter had already got into the back of her Dad's car, and John watched the blonde climb into the front passenger seat, and meet the driver halfway, in a lovers kiss. The third finger of her left hand guiding his face into hers sparkled in the sunlight.

She didn't put the wrong address, he thought, but, as usual, he said nothing, because, again, as usual, Vera was already losing her first argument of the night with her husband.

"But it's my Birthday."

"I'm going for a run."

"My Twenty-First!"

"I'm going for my run! Your birthday's got nothing to do with it."

"And then you're going out; I'll not have seen you all day, on my Twenty-First."

"You're being childish. Have my suit laid out ready when I come home, with that new shirt and tie, and make sure my shoes are really clean, no finger-marks this time."

Bovin had gone, running away from them up through the School grounds towards the top gate.

During the entire exchange he had not greeted his wife, he had not spoken to his kids, nor had he said goodbye. He hadn't even asked about the interview. John let in the clutch, and drove Vera home, not looking at her. He chatted with the kids, calling through to the back, putting up a smoke screen for her to hide behind.

* * *

The telephone rang, echoing through his sparsely furnished bachelor pad. Already on his way to the kitchen, and with his hands full of dirty dishes from his Chinese takeaway, John vacillated for a moment, and then replaced them on the table.

"Hello."

"John! Bovin's not back. He should have been home an hour ago. At first I was cross, but now I'm getting worried."

John didn't have to decide, Bovin was well over an hour late, and there was no way he would willingly miss the chance to strut his stuff at a night out with the boys.

"I'll come over."

Vera met him at the door,

"He's still not back."

On her behalf, John telephoned the A&E departments of the local hospitals.

"Nothing," he said. "They'll ring us if they get any news."

The relayed message wasn't entirely accurate. The first hospital had asked for the address and said they would get in touch if they heard anything. The others had no-one answering Bovin's description. John thought he already knew, so he was not surprised when the police knocked on the door, a few minutes

115

later.

"Mrs Bovin?"

Vera nodded.

"Can we come in, would you show me through please?" asked the lovely young policewoman gently. Vera turned and led the way. The policeman detained John in the hallway and quickly verified that it was he that had telephoned.

"I take it he is in the General?"

"A jogger answering his description is, certainly. Heart attack, what is Mr Bovin's full name?"

"Bovin B. Bovin."

The policeman's pen wavered.

"No, you heard right, the B stands for Bovin too, his Dad's strange."

"We need a formal identification, did he have any distinguishing marks, to give us an indication beforehand."

"He has a prominent mole on his neck. Here." John illustrated graphically. "Dark brown. Big. Stands unusually proud."

The policeman nodded sadly, giving him the eyes,

"I'll get Susan to babysit. From next door."

* * *

John returned the young widow to her home and put her to bed. She obeyed his instructions zombie-like. After a short time; he checked up on her. Her eyes were shining in the darkness.

"Vera. Close your eyes."

She did so.

"Keep them closed until tomorrow."

He found some bedclothes and made up a camp bed in Mandy's room, but he didn't sleep much. Three times he checked on Vera and twice more told her to close her eyes. The third time he suspected she'd heard him coming.

The next few days, packed with appointments all over the city, lumbered by. It seemed as if death caught everyone out to a picnic. Everybody needed to be seen before anyone else could do anything, and everybody needed a copy of the death certificate.

John remembered the unwashed dishes in his flat only when desperation forced him to visit for more clothes.

* * *

A couple of years later, with Vera now settled in her new job and being seriously considered for promotion, John's Uncle Culp began building a new exclusive little housing estate in a nearby village. Quality homes, in large gardens, slowly emerged from the ground, and John watched the development with interest. One, in particular, satisfied all requirements for a permanent nest in which to raise chicks. His Uncle accepted his offer, and he, and the mother of his, as yet, unborn chicks, visited frequently to consult over details.

On one such visit, John discussed the electrics with the assistant electrician. Although he knew her by sight, there was no reason for her to have recognised him.

"These are the five separate rings you asked for, lower storey, upper, kitchen, garage, and garden." She was tapping along the breakers in the consumer unit as she spoke to him. "Then the shower, and the oven, and there are two spares. The lights and the alarm are split from the rest."

"So when the main RCD protects us from harm. We'll still have our lights?"

"Yes. But they have MCB protection too. When I'm finished, you shouldn't be able to get a shock from this system." She paused, as her eyes slid over John's shoulder. "Excuse me a moment --" The youngster stepped past John to greet Vera, with genuine warmth: "Hello Mrs Bovin. How are you?"

"I've told you, it's Vera, and I'm very well thank you."

"You're looking really good. It's lovely to see you looking so well." The girls hugged. "What are you doing on a building site, dressed for a ball?"

"I'm obediently celebrating my birthday in the manner that I have been told I must from now on. Cinders is on her way to the ball; she's just stopped off to collect Prince Charming. You can congratulate me. It's Vera Mason now. This is my husband,

John. John this is Pealle Tumpkins, Bovin used to teach her."

John plucked the blonde's left hand up; the diamonds glittered and the plain gold band was very new.

"I think you'll find it's Pealle Robinson now, darling. You can congratulate each other."

Retirement

{Enforced!}

A Maths teacher writes a letter to his Year Ten Class.

Dear 10_2b,

Thank you for your Get Well Soon card, it was much appreciated.

Firstly,

The Facts:-

That first Monday that I was off, I set out to come to School normally.

I backed the car out of the garage as usual and was just about to get out of it; when I felt what I can only describe as a thump in the eyes.

I felt very dizzy, and I couldn't see properly. My garage looked like what I imagine a painting of it by a demented, cubist-impressionist would look like, on a bad day.

I tried to get out of the car and discovered I couldn't look down. I didn't know that I glanced down as I got out of cars, until the moment that I couldn't do so. I was sitting in the car telling myself out loud,

"Look at your knees." It was as useless as telling Boris to shut up. I couldn't look down.

I remember being out of the car, leaning back against the door and slowly falling over to my left. I had to straighten up, and then I had to straighten up again from falling over to my left. Silly thoughts go through your head in crises,

I'll get some stick when my wife sees the state of my shirt from the car! {As I straightened up from falling over to my left again.}

Inside my house, and don't ask me how I got there, because I don't know, I sat in my chair, and began to eat my cereal, and dropped the bowl out of my lifeless left hand into my lap.

Yes me!

Renowned eater of this parish, allowed a bowl of food to escape, into my lap.

It's a good job the cereal's absorbed all the milk; I thought: Or my lap could be covered in milk and cereal by now.

Still unable to look down, I felt around, found the bowl, picked it up, and promptly dropped it into my lap again. The second time, I held it supported by both hands and, with great difficulty, spooned the food into my mouth.

The first suspicions of what might have happened to me were strengthened a few minutes later.

My wife found me sitting in my chair, my breakfast bowl, now largely empty, was on the trolley at my side, I was sprawled to my left, my left leg was out at a strange angle, and my left arm draped over the side of my chair onto the floor. The left side of my face was hanging down as if invisible weights were pulling it towards the floor, and there were two large splodges of milk and cereal, in my lap.

I had had a stroke. In my case, a tiny blood vessel in my mid-brain broke, and damaged, or killed, a part of my brain that controls my eyes. After detaining me for nearly a week in hospital, the medics know almost everything about it. When; Where; Severity; Effects; except Why? This, as you can imagine, is a particular item of knowledge, which interests me.

I am hoping that the mini-blood-bank that they took from me will provide the answer to: 'Why?'

They were always taking blood samples, from everybody, a purple phial here, a yellow one there, and then the nurse arrived with a suitcase full of sample tubes, all colours, and sizes. I looked, and demonstrating perceptive, deductive-powers, said,

"Ah, bloodletting time, you're doing me first I see."

"No, just doing you." She proceeded to fill all of the bottles from just me, one after the other, Tony Hancock's proverbial armful.

They stabilised me, scanned me, twice, once in the CT and once in the MRI, and sent me home patched up when I was able to walk again, which was after a week. It will be some time before the doctors will release me back into Society.

I am on tablets for the rest of my life, but I am very much better and telling myself that I am getting better all the time. {The truth-value of this statement is a variable!}

I won't be back to School for a very long time. The Consultant laid it on the line, Three Months, for starters, then we will look at it, and the condition is enforcing his instructions. This rebellious spirit of mine may be willing to shortcut, but the weak flesh has already said 'on your bike'! My wings have not so much been clipped, as surgically removed!

The rest: -

Hospital food was a revelation. School Dinners nearly all is forgiven. Even now, at home, my taste buds have not recovered, food does not taste as it should. I'm assuming it's my taste buds; the food doesn't look like cheaply-buttered, carpet-tiles. All those jobs at home, which I have been feeling guilty about not doing, are still not going to be done. The only difference is that I no longer feel guilty about not doing them! The ones that can't wait, like the garden, someone else has to do, and money changes hands - the wrong way.

My symptoms are almost permanent double vision, a list to the left when I walk, and a regrettable tendency to fall asleep in the middle of a sente -- zzzzz -- zzzzzzz.

The brain, well my brain anyway, copes with these situations by not acknowledging that anything untoward has happened, so I quietly force the two pictures that I see to make sense for me, but the family, of course, are confronted by the irrefutable evidence of my list to the left. That is, people tell me that I list to the left, but I know different!

The truth is much simpler; an evil spell has been placed upon my surroundings. I get lined up to hit the middle of a doorway, go for it, and at the last moment it jumps sideways, and I walk into the left upright.

As this cannot possibly be my fault, I don't worry about it, I've just asked my wife to buy me some garlic; also a cauldron, newt's eyes, a few other ingredients, and to blast the heath --

To put it in context for you, if I was standing at my desk and finally lost it with Boris and set off to the back of the room to scud his lug. Instead of getting near to his nibs, I would stagger off to my left, past Jason and Fiona, and end up next to Alix, facing the door. {Mind you, this would be only a minor inconvenience to me, after all, Alix is female, polite and good looking. Boris is male, -- zzzzz -- zzzzzzz.}

Negotiating the path around my pond carries with it the ever-present possibility of an early bath. {NO exaggeration!!} My wife tells me that watching me near it leaves teeth marks on her heart.

My double vision is more of a problem for me. While teaching you, I would see two Waynes, two Lisas, four Daniels, two Louises. Watching Jimmy's amorous advances on Tara is bad enough at the best of times, but to be forced to see him stealthily surround her in stereo!

Seriously, {and sadly} I am under the strictest medical instructions to stay away from School, and all school work.

I may not have been at Death's Door, but I have been given a long, hard look at the garden gate, and I must obey the instructions, so it will be a long time before we meet again.

You have probably guessed by now, what I have been working up to telling you.

What I have been plucking up the courage to tell you.

Seriously to misquote the Bard, some people are born to retirement; some people achieve retirement, and some people have retirement thrust upon them. I decided a while back not to take on a Year Ten in the September before I retired the following August, so I would not have chosen to desert you half way through your final two years run up to the examination, sadly, the choice was made for me. The fine details of the test results yet to be disclosed are largely irrelevant, we have already been told that the damage is sufficiently serious to force me to retire on medical grounds. The brain still works reasonably well, but the performance of the body is a liability to me, and inside School, also to you.

In a crisis, although I would know what to do, I would be unable to do it.

The consequences could be tragic.

If we ever meet again, it will not be as teacher and pupil.

Sorry, our times together were the high points of my week.

The future:-

I always knew that when I retired, I would have no problem filling my day, all those questions about pond capacities, electronics projects' truth tables, pricing the wood needed to build a wardrobe, were, as you may have guessed, based on my hobbies. I have already restarted the main one, gardening. The other day I decided to pot up some fuchsias. I carried a bag of compost, from the store to the bench, a distance of about five metres. Then, for half an hour, I sat looking at two identical bags, lying side by side, rapt.

Well, actually, more like wrapped -- in a cocoon of exhaustion the like of which I have never known. However, it was ecstatic exhaustion, last week I couldn't lift the bag, never mind carry it, so things at my end are definitely on the up.

But things at your end are full of promise too. Together we have given you a solid foundation from which to achieve good results next year. Work for Miss Box like you worked for me, and we will all be rejoicing in your success next summer, I promise you.

Once again, I'm truly sorry I have to leave you, but at least fate was kind enough to give me the opportunity to tell you so!

On a lighter note to end with, I am improving, I tell myself so every day, so it must be true, and I'm really looking forward to applauding your triumphs next year,

Yours etc.,

Dear True-Reader,

I have much pleasure in recording that 11_2b worked for 'Miss Box' as hard as 10_2b had for me, and performed way beyond the level that their lowly placing would suggest. They were a terrific bunch of kids, and I am delighted for them, *M. W.*

The Hungry Box

{The Box}

It was the appearance of the box that startled Melanie. Not its shimmering, vibrant colours, or dazzling perfection, because she'd recently learned that a cube is one of only six perfect-solids. The shock was that it wasn't there, and then suddenly it was falling out of the dry stone wall, from a gryke far too narrow to have concealed it.o

Although not that large, she knew it was heavy, because of the smashed grass and deep muddy gouges where its corners had cut right through the turf to the damp soil underneath. The little girl didn't try to pick it up but walked around it instead. Each face was self-coloured and all different. The entire spectrum was present, and several colours more, pink and brown, and some for which she had no name.

It did strike her as strange that she had to walk three times around it, to see all the colours. At first, she thought it a trick of the light but soon discovered that it was three times around, every time.

"Smelly Mellie! What's that you've got?"

A handle set in the top of the box invited the curious to open it and look within. She ignored the call from the obnoxious bully while accepting the invitation. The view inside explained everything; she slammed it back shut and held it closed, shaking.

"What is it Smelly."

"It's Melanie! Melanie Ratchett! I'm not the one called Boggs!"

"Ooh! Temper! Temper!" George Boggs ran at her. Melanie dodged, but he still managed to push her down.

"You're not to look in."

"Why not?"

"It's bigger inside than it is outside."

With a snort and a sneer, the bully plucked the top open and looked inside.

"It's a trick."

"It's not. It was on the Christmas Lectures on BBC Two. But you wouldn't know; you wouldn't have watched them."

George groped deep inside, desperately clutching at the scintillating, glowing-gold interior, that seemed to be always only just out of reach. Melanie watched transfixed as he leaned in that little bit too far. His foot slipped on the muddy grass. He lost his balance and fell forward. The small box took him in one gulp like an anglerfish, and the lid closed with a soft kiss.

A moment later the box shrank to a line, and the line to a dot and the dot disappeared.

When she was interviewed, days later, about the boy's disappearance, the arrogant, young, know-it-all police-cadet who took her statement didn't even bother to file it.

* * *

In due course, the little girl that watched lectures for grown ups, grew up herself, and far from losing any, developed and honed her acumen on the way.

* * *

Melanie finished her lecture and dismissed her students.

"Doctor Ratchett!"

She turned giving him the eyes.

"Sorry -- Melanie."

Her star pupil had stayed behind.

"Yes."

"I just want to say thank you. For your analysis of my Time Travel Theory. My mates think I'm mad. But you can see the possibilities."

"You're as mad as those that bay at the Moon, Richard, Dear. That doesn't say you're wrong; you just won't be believed. Take me to lunch, while we discuss it. Don't panic; I'm paying."

The lunch was delicious, and the conversation erudite. Eventually, Richard had to ask.

"Why are you so sure that my theories are right? On the right lines."

"Because they require the existence of a fourth spatial dimension."

"But that's the flaw. As everyone else points out."

"But I've known it exists for nearly two decades, I've seen a four-dimensional cube. Seen it, touched it, and even looked inside it. Not for long, I grant you, but I've done it!" She took his hand and gently caressed it in a manner far removed from professional. "Reverend Charles Dodgson's Hatter, meet his March Hare! Hello."

'-- upon the stair,
I met a girl --'

{A ghost story}

Dear True-Reader,
This is the very best I can do, I hope you like it - it has a SMOG readability grade of less than eight - and neither a nipple nor an orgasm in sight!

Petra.

The knock, from several metres beyond the back door, was polite but firm. George ignored it, concentrating on his meal.

A few minutes later the knock was repeated. Again, he ignored it.

He carried his tray through to the kitchen and fastidiously washed up the dishes, accompanied by the regular Rat-Tat-Tat of a heavy metal knocker, which his modern, double-glazed, metal re-enforced, poly-laminate back door, didn't have.

Only when he had finished, made his cocoa, and tidied everything away, did he step over to the door and comply with the Countess's summons to let her enter.

There was the usual pause while she stepped across from where the door used to be, centuries ago, and then glided by him in the familiar cold swirl and cloud of stale sweat.

The disturbance in the time-space-continuum was as substantial as it was invisible.

"I don't know why you wait over there. Or have to knock. Or even need someone to open the door for you -- Just come in. I know you could if you wan--" He stopped; he was talking to an empty kitchen. Shaking his head sadly, he followed her through to the living room.

"And, I'm not being rude. But could you have a wash?" He tracked her progress, round and round the table, from the rustling that her clothes made as she walked. She seemed to like the unique table that George had designed and built himself, specifically to match the stairs which curled around the sides and across the back of the dazzling-white, feature chimney-stack. He pointedly followed the rustling sound with his eyes, as if to increase his chances of communicating with his visitor.

"I'm going to bed." With the sound-picture in his mind, he thought he knew what her clothes had looked like in life. "Straight to bed. I'm not stopping on the landing. I've got things to think about. Decisions to make."

Although the fire was collapsing safely in on itself, he still erected the spark-proof guard and clipped it in place. Carrying his cocoa, he made his way to bed, quietly to ponder the proposal his bosses had given him.

As usual, the Countess followed him up the russet hardwood stairs. The chimney, the walls, and the stairs between them were the only feature of the modern house that had also been part of the ancient Peel Tower. Astonishingly they had survived through two rebuilds. Silently she urged him to stop half way. Resolutely he turned at the top of the first flight, crossed the half landing behind the chimney, turned again, and plodded on up the second flight. He ignored her polite, friendly, but mute appeals, knowing that when he reached the top, she would be gone.

* * *

The Running Pheasant had a dozen or so locals in the lounge, enjoying quiet pints. The costs of maintaining the genteel, Olde-Worlde aura were being met largely by the profitable restaurant, sited in a barn conversion, at the other end of the building. His enjoyment of the quiet country pub was going to be the pleasure George missed most if he accepted the offer of the new job in the city. The conversation, mainly about farming topics, eventually touched on the price of feed, which, as the local supplier, involved George directly.

"You'm be putting t'price up again this winter I 'spect?"

"Not me personally Fred."

"I know not you'm personally. You'm Company."

"Mebees. But it might not be me. They want me to go to Novochester. Head office. It's a big opportunity. I'm thinking about it."

"You'll be selling the Grange then?" said the landlord: "Or are you going to, like, spend half your day commuting?"

"I'd have to sell."

"You will have to declare the Countess," said the Police Sergeant, in her precise, cultured tones, while sipping her on-duty mineral-water. "You have to declare such things now."

"I would have anyway, Janet. Mr Baker declared her to me."

"That's why his wife left, he, like, used to say not, but I'll bet it was."

"Yer'm never came back; he'm be living with another girl over Hardwick way."

"The Countess isn't threatening, you know. Friendly, she's quite nice. She smells a bit. But just walks around the table."

"I know, t'were young Mrs Baker were t'strange one. You'm don't wear a man's watch if you'm a girl."

"They wear men's everything these days Fred. My two empty my wardrobe, like, on a Saturday night. But I agree, the Countess isn't threatening. Just go to bed, she disappears at the top of the stairs."

"On the half landing."

"Oh, really? I always understood she went to the top of the stairs."

George smiled involuntarily as he looked at the young Sergeant, the other reason why he didn't really want to leave,

"That's what I was told too. But she stops on the half landing.

She disappears when I get to the top."

"Yer'm used to go all the way t'top. For hunneds of years. All through two rebuilds. You'm affecting yer'm behaviour."

* * *

The Estate Agent was philosophical,

"You've lasted longer than most. The Grange has been my most consistent source of income since I started. I'm pleased to see it back earning for me, but I'm sorry it means we lose you."

"It's not certain yet. Just an elbow in the water job."

"Okay."

"I'll declare the Countess of course."

"Yes, it's a requirement now."

"Is it true that she used to go all the way up the stairs? At one time."

"Yes."

"She doesn't now, only half way. She stops on the half landing behind the chimney. And stays there until I reach the top. Then she's gone of course."

* * *

The prospective purchasers were a bluff, jovial pair, too full of in-your-face bonhomie for George's taste. They said they were definitely interested, and would be putting in an offer within a few days, and left, still gushing with bonhomie.

As soon as they were out of hearing range, George, already having a rethink, turned to the agent,

"Did you tell them about the Countess? As well as showing it on the sheet?"

"Yes. They Pooh Poohed it like all outsiders, like you quietly did, eighteen months ago."

"I might invite them overnight."

"Or just a late meal."

George nodded, brightening,

"I can almost see her now you know. Not very tall. Hair in a bun. Huge dress, with twenty underskirts, standing way out from her hips. It's dark red, or possibly maroon. With a shawl, a lace shawl over her shoulders. She's pretty and busty. And quite young."

"You've seen the picture of her in the Library?"

"No. I didn't know there was one."

"You've described her exactly!"

* * *

The knock on the back door was peremptory, quite unlike her usual friendly request for admittance. For a moment he thought he might have a different visitor, but when he opened up, it was the Countess's cold but now sweet smelling presence which glided in past him.

Her gown was rustling louder than usual, her unease as tangible as her new scent of Roses.

"Oh, it **is** you. You're early tonight." He closed the door. She had stopped in the doorway to the living room, blocking his return. George didn't like walking through her; it was their only interaction that made him feel uncomfortable.

"I know what's wrong. You don't want me to sell. It's not certain. I still haven't decided."

The uncomfortable vibes were very strong; whatever was troubling the Countess, selling her home was secondary to it.

"Let me through." He waved at the living room, and she retreated and began her circuits of the table. "Thanks for getting washed, by the way."

The skirts swished in an agitated manner. He caught her thoughts. Frustratingly, the brittle strands kept snapping, like water weed,

"You want me to stay. Because I'll -- do it? Yes. If I knew what you wanted. I'd do it for you."

The perambulations were not her usual serene progress.

"All right. You have my undivided attention. What do you want me to do?"

The Countess turned, her skirts swished as she strode to the stairs. She stopped.

"You want me to go to bed?"

Swish. He could almost see the tiny foot stamping in

frustration into the deep carpet.

"Obviously not! Do you want me to follow?"

Swish. Swish. Swish. This time he'd got it right, she'd turned, and mounted the first stair. He followed, she was calm now, and he felt good, in contact. They climbed the first flight in tandem; he could sense her glancing over her shoulder, checking on his progress. They reached the top of the first flight and turned to cross behind the chimney stack. She stopped blocking his way at the bottom of the second flight. She wanted him to stay on the half landing.

"What?" He asked. "I'm here. Now what?"

Nothing, she was waiting.

"Do I go back down stairs?"

The angry, frustrated swish.

"It's no good stamping your feet at me! I can stamp my foot too."

He did so, in carpet slippers, on an oak deck, decimetres thick. The consequent noise, as a reproof, was a pusillanimous fiasco. Embarrassed, and beginning to get annoyed, he turned to the chimney stack,

"Or smack a wall." He matched deed to word, with a powerful slap of his slightly concave-cupped hand, designed to redeem his reputation with decibels.

The resultant sharp CRACK was all that George could desire for reputation redemption and the effect of the blow exactly what the Countess had wanted.

With a soft crunch a large, Africa-shaped piece of plaster, detached from the chimney stack and fell away. It broke up on the landing and cascaded down the stairs.

George fumbled in his pocket for his mobile phone, leaning sideways as he did so to get a better view.

"You can relax. I'll not be selling now."

The Countess swished up the second flight and departed, but George was still not alone.

Well preserved by the lime in the plaster, a girl's left arm wearing a dark-red, short-sleeved dress, was now in full view.

Judging by the scraps peeping through from behind further

loose plaster, there seemed little doubt that the rest of the girl was most likely still attached to her arm.

The telephone was answered at the fourth ring by the Police Sergeant's familiar voice --

"Hello Janet, it's George. You'd better get over here. Come in the back way; it's open. You've got a crime scene to secure. I don't want to move until you tell me I can. And where to, and how." --

"I've found what the Countess was trying to get me to find." --

"A body. Well, an arm. But I think the rest of her is here too." --

"In the chimney wall. On the half landing." --

"No! No, it's not. I am pretty sure it's a girl. With the clothes 'n that. And she's wearing Engagement and Wedding rings. But it's definitely not the Countess. Not with a gent's digital watch on her wrist, showing the correct time. And today's date."

Notes: -

My acknowledgements to the Sutherland Family whose true-life, haunting-experiences provided the inspiration for this fictional story.

My apologies for misquoting Ogden Nash for the title.

Petra.

Wet

{Done in Class. Write for twenty minutes or so about
two people who meet at a cross-roads.}

"Roger! There you are! I've been looking all over for you."

The man turned and looked behind him to see who was being addressed.

There was no-one there.

Nor was there anyone down either of the bridleways crossing the one in which he was standing. The speaker approached, she was an attractive girl in her twenties and very obviously homing in on himself.

"They sent me to find you when you didn't turn up."

She took his arm and guided him away along the side lane to the right, towards a steeple in the middle distance. The girl began feeling the arm she was holding, and then the rest of the coat.

"You're wet! You're all wet, Roger. How are you all wet?"

Roger looked down at his coat and squeezed it. Water ran out.

"How long have you been all wet like this?"

The man being called Roger paused, and thought,

"Always. I've always been wet."

"Oh very funny! You're late, which means we're late, you're

134

wet, and now we're wet! Have you got the ring?"

Roger patted his pockets; one of them contained a small hard object, a ring box.

"Well, that's something I suppose. At least you're only the best man. You'll have to stay well clear of Miriam. If you get her dress wet, she'll kill you. What is it anyway? You stink! That suit's only on hire. This is water weed! Well, it's too late now. Miriam's been sent around the village once already. And your shoes are filthy, and I spent all yesterday afternoon making sure you polished them properly."

"Sorry."

"Honestly I don't know what I'm going to do with you. Mother said I should never have married you. Quick! Into the Church before Miriam gets back."

"Who's Miriam?"

"What?"

"And who are you?"

The Creation of Chicago Lynes

{Chicago Lynes is a minor but vitally important character in our novel 'Karen, The Girl That Would Be A Plumber'. She is present in person, in only one short scene. This story does not appear in the book, but Petra had to have complete knowledge of it to write the scene in which Chicago appears.}

James was frightened.

He stood before Mummy in their bare living room, shielding her, fighting his fear, her hands resting on his shoulders. She'd pushed him into the corner to protect him, but he'd wriggled out and stood in front of her.

The rough men were stripping the house, not that there was that much left to take anyway, wardrobes empty, cupboards bare. They'd pawned his Playstation for food last week and had already eaten the proceeds. Hannah's personal stereo had followed, two nights before.

Mummy had been worried even before the rough men arrived. There had been problems for months, ever since Daddy left.

Since long before Daddy left. He rejected the thought, not wanting to go there. His angry hunger intensified, as he watched the prospect of his next meal vanish, with the departure of the portable TV out to the van.

"I'll have your watch!" Demanded the Nastiest Villain. Mummy passed it over above her son's head. "Coat!"

"Not the coat, it is worthless, I will need it for the children, and it is wet outside."

"What makes you think you're going outside?"

He grabbed.

James fought him.

The brute dispatched him across the bare room, with contemptuous ease.

He lay, his body trying to rise.

His brain screaming in terrorised pain.

Get up! Help Mummy!

"No Wilf. Ay-Jay said not." While speaking the Tall Villain reached out to restrain him.

"He said not the litter; we can have this one. We can do what we like to this one. We could have the cub too; he'd never know. Stiffs don't squeal."

"Not me. I said not to. I'm going out to the van. Whatever you do, you answer for."

"Me neither!" Said Smaller Villain, and followed his mate out to the van.

"Coat!" Nastiest Villain repeated, and then getting no response he grabbed it from Mummy's shoulder, ripping it from her.

Mummy fought him, in silence.

She stabbed with her sharp claws.

Her hands hurt him with basic Karate.

He couldn't close with her.

Crying, but desperate to assist, James got to his knees.

Mummy was fighting for her life, delaying her violation, not allowing the beast to take her, as well as her belongings.

"What's going on?"

Hannah's call distracted the thug, whose eyes gleamed with lust, as he saw the tempting, younger, nubile girl in the doorway.

The change of objective ensured his failure.

Mummy delivered a vicious chop across his throat, on full

power.

It landed just far enough off target not to be fatal.

The man called Wilf crumpled.

"Run! Run for the street!" Cried Mummy, as she leaped over, grabbed James, and then she too took off, hooking her coat up as she did so.

Hannah, already outside, glanced behind once to confirm the others were following and fled.

The men in the van saw they were escaping but made no attempt to stop them, merely surveying the house.

The trio ran, and scurried, and ran some more until the suburban shopping centre came into view, and with it, the relative protection of Friday's last-minute, shopping-crowds.

While sitting clustered around one of the tiny tables of the pavement café, the three pooled their resources.

Mummy had three pens and the spare key to her repossessed car.

Hannah had yesterday's knickers, her nightie and some toiletries from last night's sleepover, thirty-eight pence, her school-bag and her Artist's Folder.

James's contribution was a grubby hanky, a piece of string, a strange-shaped foreign coin with a hole in it, and two pieces of chewing gum without their wrapper.

"We will have to go to Uncle Bob and Aunt Grace, and throw ourselves on their mercy."

"I'd rather not," replied Hannah: "Leonard gives me the creeps."

"I cannot see any other option."

"Mummy, I know what he wants to do to me, and I don't want him to."

Mummy glanced at James, after a moment he looked down, he knew what his lecherous cousin wanted too, and if Hannah didn't want him to do it, that was fine. He agreed with his elder sister; Leonard was a creep.

"In three hours time, it will be getting dark. We will still be hungry, we will still have nowhere to go, and we will be getting wet. Think about it, if you can come up with a better alternative, let me know. Meanwhile, thirty-eight pence is neither here nor there, ask Luigi if he will trade it for a pot of tea, for three?" The enquiry was directed at her son.

"Yes please," murmured James, and Hannah, already on her feet, crossed over into the café.

"Luigi, we've only got thirty-eight pence, can we have a pot of tea, three cups?"

"Pot of tea, three cups, extra water and three scones is two pounds fifty. Pay me when you sell your first painting or sketch me an original Hannah Snowdon-Lynes now. Signed and dated." He waved at several framed sketches behind the counter: "Some of these are worth more now than the bill I waived for them then. Some of them a lot more."

"I'll do you a sketch. What do you want?"

"The Cathedral, looking down the road, from where you're sitting. Do it in the rain, deserted, forlorn, dark." He cocked an eyebrow. "Can you?"

"Oh, I can do that." Replied Hannah with a twisted face. "The way I'm feeling now, no problem."

By the time the scones had been consumed, and the group were well down their second cups of tea; the sketch of the eerily half-lit Cathedral was gathering gloom and menace in the rainwater reflections pooling the forlorn, deserted, darkening street.

"So that's why you're not, like, answering your 'phone."

The trio looked up. The trimly plump young woman addressing Mummy was quite pretty. "It is Mary Lynes, isn't it?"

"Yes," agreed Mummy looking hard at the girl, who held out her hand.

"Stevie--"

"Oh," interrupted Mummy rising to her feet, the look of welcome banishing that of pain, for the first time in weeks. "Stevie Bollard, of course. Children, this is--"

"The famous designer, I'm Hannah, this is James," interrupted Hannah also rising to shake hands. James found himself doing likewise, with a lifting hand each from Mummy and Hannah grasping his shoulders.

"This is a stroke of luck, I've been, like, 'phoning you for days. Janie gave me your number." Stevie sat down in response to Mummy's gesture to do so. "Janie Thompson, used to be Janie Jones?"

"Oh, yes."

"You acted in the plays at School, you were good, like, really good, have you thought about doing it professionally?"

"I have not thought about much of anything beyond survival recently," explained Mummy. "You could not contact me by telephone because we pawned it three weeks ago, for food."

"Oh. I'm sorry to hear that. But not that sorry, because I want to employ you. If you're, like, a bit short, you're more likely to say yes."

"I am already saying yes. But on one condition, that you advance me enough money now, to buy food and lodging for the three of us until my first pay cheque clears."

"You don't want to know what the job is first?" Asked Stevie, her eyebrows raised. "It's legal, but something the vicar's wife wouldn't, like, approve of, not in public anyway."

"Stevie in about two hours time I will need to start soliciting, and I have nowhere to take clients, other than that cold, wet, back alley over there, but I'm fully prepared to do it. What you have planned for me cannot be worse than that."

"No soliciting, no cold, no wet, no back alley, no dangerous car ride, or, like, seedy hotel. No dangerous maniacs, but no difference in the fundamental activity either mind, other than it being in front of a camera."

Hannah gasped but said nothing.

"What you see is what we have got. Hannah has not even got a top coat to wear. You are spearing fish in a bucket."

"Okay. I'll advance you food and, like, shelter at least for tonight. Then I'll show you some scripts, and you can tell me how you feel about performing. Come on."

The three girls stood, Mummy and Stevie moved away a short distance, waiting while Hannah paid for their tea with her sketch. James followed, stopped and turned away. He was looking from side to side, scowling, his thoughts racing,

My own mother, and my sister not objecting. But she'd objected about Leonard doing it to her. He searched in vain for a way of escape, then a hunger pang evaded the scone, and hit him deep.

Hannah returned, asking something about where it was they were going, and the girls set off, without even checking to see if he was coming.

He decided, he'd pretend to go along with it, eat and sleep tonight, but tomorrow he'd tell Daddy. Everything would be alright when Daddy came back. Everything was always alright when Daddy came back.

No, it's not, not since-- He crushed the unwelcome thought back in its box. Everything would be alright.

Stevie's car was a big, bland but reliable, Japanese jeep. She began outlining the plan as they climbed in,

"We'll stop off at the supermarket and pick up some groceries. The Film Studio has a little flat attached, all facilities, fully self-contained. It's for a night watchman, caretaker person, but, like, there's nothing there worth stealing as yet, so it's vacant."

Stevie paid for the groceries and drove the family out to the Industrial Estate. They slowed outside the building with the blue light and stopped at the next one.

"This is the studio, next door to the Police Station, so it's quiet, and, like, safe."

"You work next to the Police Station? Isn't that a bit daft, with the kind of films you make?" Asked Hannah, saucer-eyed.

"Quite the reverse. Next to the Police Station we don't get bother from, like, the ungodly, or even worse, the Crusading Godly!"

Hannah was still unsure,

"But aren't you breaking the law?"

"No, there are things I can't show, not yet. The edited versions are, like, perfectly legal to make and sell."

"Oh! The troll's always going on about sex and violence in her assemblies!"

"She always did. She always confused the two. Nobody gets hurt in my films Hannah, not even pretend hurt. No rape scenes, no violence. You'll see much worse, happening for real, like, on the news almost any week."

The youngsters face relaxed, almost to a smile,

"Oh. Good."

"It's just my films wouldn't get a certificate for public showing. But it's okay to show them, like, in private, or in a film club." Stevie parked the car, and led the way down a short side path, carrying the groceries.

"Let me do that," called Hannah.

"It's okay; we're, like, here. Get the key from my coat pocket; it's this red door here."

Stevie showed them around the little flat, and then left them to settle for the night,

"There's, like, only one bedroom I'm afraid, but it'll do until you get something better. Everything works, even the telephone, just don't call Hong Kong please."

Mummy laughed,

"We promise we will not call Hong Kong."

Making up the double-bed and the narrow, emergency, single-bed, and preparing and consuming their first square meal for several weeks, took up most of the evening, and trying to make plans for the future, the rest of it. James was sent to bed at his usual time, while Mummy and Hannah tidied the flat and finished the dishes.

The living room light went out, and they came through, feeling their way in the darkness. Presently their movements became less tentative, as their eyes adjusted to the dim light smuggled in from outside.

"Are you awake James?" Murmured Mummy.

He chose not to answer, preferring to see his sister undress, without hiding from him as she would normally do.

He was disappointed, however; she kept her back to him, revealing the spectacular hourglass curves, and pert bottom, but not the bits he really wanted to see. The bits of his sister that Leonard and his friends drooled over remained a mystery.

He could hear murmured conversation, after they got into bed, and lifted his head fractionally, to eavesdrop.

"-- and that was an unexpected reaction earlier, Miss Snowdon-Lynes, 'Oh. Good,' that there was no violence in Stevie's films. Would you be so kind as to explain?"

Hannah shifted uncomfortably, looking across at her brother. James stayed immobile, still feigning sleep; he could see her dimly through his slit-opened eyes. When she leaned towards him, to get a better look, he closed them. The covers rustled as she withdrew back into her own bed.

"I don't want to act out violent scenes. I don't mind the other, but--"

"You are only fourteen young lady; you are not acting out any scenes. Goodnight."

The following morning, just after breakfast, there was a knocking from behind a curtain in an alcove in the kitchen. Hannah pulled it back to reveal the Caretaker's own entrance door to the Film Studio. She turned the rim latch and opened it.

"Good morning. Like, may I please come in?" Asked Stevie, a bottle of milk in one hand, and several scripts in the other.

Hannah waved her through.

"Mummy, it's Ms Bollard."

"Stevie please Hannah." Then addressing Mummy: "Morning Mary, I've got a few scenes to show you. Is now, like, a good time?"

"As good as any time is. James if you would wash up, and Hannah see to the bedroom. Then you can do your homework for Monday."

Despite creating as little noise as possible, and straining to listen, James only managed to catch tantalising snippets of his Mummy's conversation. It did, however, give him confirmation of his fears of the night before.

"-- do appreciate it's everything, like, every way possible? And with me too, lesbian scenes."

"The lesbian bit is fine, but you said you were legal. There are ways that are illegal, between man and woman. I have no problem with doing them, but you cannot show them, even in a film club."

"Yes, but not for much longer, like, that sort of stupid

anomaly usually gets put right.[4] We'll keep it in the can, and re-cut it when it's no longer --."

And,

"-- are very nice boys, and Jim is a terrific Director. You'll, like, get on fine. Will your husband --"

"-- so with a history of affairs as long and varied as his, he cannot object if I play the game by his rules --"

After lunch, Mummy called the family together and told them.

"I have signed the contracts with Stevie. I am to become a film actress, beginning on Monday. They are adult films about sex education, but they are erotic too."

All James worst fears clumped upon him.

What would his friends say?

Visions of the School Bullies,

"I had your mother last night; she was lovely."

The pain and embarrassment were excruciating.

As the red mist cleared, James realised that he was screaming his complaints at his Mummy, who was sitting hands clasped in her lap, eyes cast down. Hannah, however, was regarding him with utter contempt.

"You blazing hypocrite. Ever since I grew these." She waved across her front: "You have been creeping up on me, spying on me, trying to get a glimpse of them. Not once in your tirade did you mention the problems of anyone but yourself. It was Me! Me! Me! All the way. Now Shut Up! Unless you have something constructive to say, some positive contribution to make, you say nowt. You've had your turn." She turned her back, shutting him out, and addressed Mummy. "I'm Hannah Snowdon at School. I never write the double barrel, most people have forgotten it exists. James starts Secondary School in a couple of months; he can be James Snowdon too. If you performed under your middle and Maiden name? Mary Snowdon of the School run wouldn't obviously be Chicago Lynes, the naked girl on the television."

"It is a thought, but I have a fairly distinctive face, not to mention the appalling way I speak. Elocution lessons have to

4   It was; Criminal Justice Act 1994. *P.C.*

answer for a lot."

"You could practise speaking differently, but the looks are easy. If you're going to be a Porn Queen, why not be a real Queen?"

"What?"

"Imagine that I slung the bra, and put a small man's, tight-waistcoat on under a loose bomber jacket with a pair of jeans. If I completed the ensemble with a short scarlet wig and a baseball cap and held up a bank, every witness would remember my red hair, but at least half of them would get my sex wrong."

"What are you saying?"

Hannah pulled her sketch pad over and flung a score or so of lines across it.

"Who is that?"

The picture was an almost photographic likeness of Mummy. Even in the deepest cups of his bottled up rage, James had to acknowledge the facts; his sister was good.

"Me, on the School run."

Another half minute of additional sketching followed,

"Now who is it?

Mary Snowdon had disappeared.

In her place was Cleopatra, Queen of Egypt, not renowned as a classic beauty by all accounts, but as a Sex Goddess, a good bet for high on most men's Top-Ten-of-All-Time list.

"Chicago Lynes. Yes, dear, you might have a point."

The day job of the male lead, who also directed the films, was Company Accountant to one of the big local firms. Jim Teale was average height, not spectacularly good-looking, but he worked out relentlessly every day. The elegant clothes hid a photogenic body, and he moved gracefully because his hobby was The Ballet, performing, not watching. Last week, James would have liked him, taken to him, and even more so because they shared the given name. Now he regarded the approach with suspicion,

"May I please talk to you, about your Mummy's new job?"

"No."

His sister didn't even raise her voice,

"Yes he can, and you have just been rude, and for that, you will apologise-"

Jim interrupted,

"I'd like to waive the apology for permission to talk."

There was no reply, but permission had been given.

"Being a good actress is not easy, anyone can be a bad actress, but to be good, needs talent. Your Mummy has got it."

No reply, so he pressed on.

"Also, she is doing something that is notoriously difficult to do at all, never mind do it with conviction. Have you ever stood up and spoken in assembly?"

The switch slipped through the youngster's guard,

"No."

"Do you think you could? There were three hundred and fifty students in my year, do you think you could speak to that sea of faces."

James tried to shout that he could, anytime, but the gentle, friendly face in front of his commanded respect, not lies. Silence was all he could shout.

"While undressing? And do it without any vibes, as if you were in your bedroom at home?"

"It's the undressing that's the trouble!"

"I know. Could you do it?"

"No."

"No -- It takes massive bottle, but your Mummy could, and nobody would laugh, or be embarrassed because she makes it so natural. She is very good you know."

"It's wrong, dirty."

"Not when your Mummy does it. I have seen it done wrong. Rough. Without feeling. People watching it done that wrong way, might go away and do it wrong. They won't know any better, but if they see the lovely, loving way your Mummy does it, they will understand how to do it properly."

"What do you mean, do it properly? Nobody should do it; it's disgusting."

"Ah, I understand. My Dad was brought up like that. You won't have got that attitude from Mummy."

James blushed.

"From Grandma, possibly?"

The set of the boy's jaw was the answer. Jim pressed on,

"Believe me, James; sex is normal, and natural, and lovely, and nice. How often do you think a nice, young-married couple make sexual love?"

"Never, not if they're nice, it's disgusting."

"Think of your favourite young married teacher."

The boy's expression softened.

"Is it a man or a woman?"

"Mrs Cart."

"How long has she been married?"

"A few weeks."

"She will be making sexual love with her husband every day. If they are trying for a baby, several times a day, it's how you make babies. If they are not trying for a baby, it still might be more than once a day, because it is one of the nicest, most loving things a man and wife can do together."

Horrified, James began his rebuttal,

"That's--"

"He's right James." Hannah's voice was gentle and concerned as if she knew she was causing pain: "It's not wrong, or dirty, or disgusting. Nanna was twisted about sex; you know that, yourself. Loving sex is lovely, it's just about the nicest physical experience you can have, but you have to learn that for yourself. All Mummy is doing is writing the textbook for it."

James ran out with his hands over his ears, squealing inarticulate sounds to drown out her words. It was a while before he realised that the noise he was making was to drown out the smell of Nanna.

He was unsuccessful.

If a Holiday programme had shown a girl in a bikini or a Natural Earth programme featured mild, pair-bonding behaviour, he could still see the slight figure switching off the television. The smell of Nanna was of righteously indignant disgust.

Could Jim be right, that sex was nice, and that it was how you made babies? How Mummy and Daddy had made Hannah, and --

Only another onslaught of howling with his hands over his

ears was good enough to dispel that thought.

And yet another, when he realised the full implications of Hannah's words.

It was many hours before he realised that Jim couldn't be lying about babies, it would be too easy to prove him wrong.

Unless it's a double bluff, that I wouldn't dare ask!

Well, that's tough because I dare!

At School, he sought her out, the fount of all knowledge, the one who didn't pull the punches.

"Mrs Cart?"

"Yes."

Someone had opened a hole a decimetre wide in the bottom of his confidence; it ran out without even a gurgle.

"Oh, it doesn't matter."

"James, come back. What is it? Here, write it down on this paper. It's often easier to write difficult things down, rather than say them."

"Oh -- Yes -- Alright."

James wrote, went to push the paper over, remembered she was a teacher, pulled it back and added a question mark.

Does sex make babies?

"Yes."

"Oh -- Oh!" That was the one answer he had not been expecting. "How else can you get them?"

"That's the only way."

"Under gooseberry bushes?" He pleaded desperately.

"No, I'm afraid not. Not gooseberry bushes, storks or bargain offers in the supermarket, just sex."

His final confirmation was the sadness in her eyes, revealing just how much she didn't want to explode his myth.

Nanna lied to me. If she lied about that, what else did she lie about? Where's Daddy? He turned and fled, ignoring the call of,

"James, are you okay?" from behind him.

There was no-one in when he got back to the flat. He rang his Daddy's sister.

"Hello?"

"Oh, hello Uncle Bob, it's James."

"Oh, hello James, there's nobody in I'm afraid -- Unless I can help?"

"Er -- Why did my Daddy go away?"

"He lost some money, nasty men were looking for him; it was best they didn't find him."

But they found us!

"Has he found the money?"

"It wasn't that kind of lost. People are in business to make money; usually, everybody makes a little money on a deal, and everyone ends up happy."

"How can everybody make money?"

Daddy didn't use to say that.

"When Hannah sells a drawing, is she happy?"

"Yes."

"So is the buyer of the drawing, he has something priceless, an original, by a good Artist. Hannah has money; she feels good too. D'y'see?"

"Oh -- Yes."

"What if somebody said they had a drawing, and sold it to the buyer for big money, but sent them a sheet of newspaper instead?"

"One gets the money, but the other doesn't get the drawing."

"Aaron made a lot of deals where he paid the money, but he didn't get the drawing. A lot of deals James, eventually the money ran out. Got lost."

"Oh. Is that a killing?"

"For somebody to make a killing, somebody else gets killed. Occasionally it was your Daddy." There was a pause then Bob added softly: "Often, it was your Daddy."

"Oh -- I see. Thanks, Uncle Bob. Bye."

If anything the telephone call had only made matters worse. James desperately needed his Daddy to explain that things were not as they seemed, he was sure that that was all that was needed, a new view of the facts. It would give a totally different interpretation.

Mummy's new housekeeping box was on the table, full of the filthy money from her new job. James took a pound; she wouldn't miss a pound,

She owes it to me anyway, he thought, rationalising the crime away.

Now all he had to do was find Daddy; then everything would be alright.

He took the bus across town and began searching. He asked the first familiar face he saw,

"Is Aaron around, please?"

"He's around, I saw him earlier; you're his kid, aren't you. Try the Horse; he might be there."

The Bay Horse and the Red Lion both failed him, but another vaguely recognised street trader delivered.

"I saw his van in Jake's Garage, if the van's there, your Dad'll be close by."

The van was still in Jake's, and James walked in past the cars on the forecourt, confidently calling for his Daddy. There was no-one about. He walked on through to the back of the garage, to the service hut, where the men had their breaks. He climbed up, opened the door and called out. When there was no reply, he went inside. There was no-one in, he even checked the toilet at the back, just in case, but as he came back out, he heard feet approaching. When they stopped, Daddy's voice said,

"I said you could have the sow, but not to touch the whelps."

Smiling now, the boy hurried to the door.

Standing in the middle of the garage floor was Nastiest Villain, the man called Wilf.

On either side, the other two, with pick-axe handles.

James ducked back, out of sight, as Nastiest Villain spoke,

"I didn't touch anybody."

Daddy's reply was calm,

"You were going to; that is enough."

The sickening sound of snapping carrot was accompanied by a scream.

"And the other one!"

The sounds were repeated. Daddy spoke through the screams as he would through silence,

"When they've mended I'm going to break them again,

several times. Take him away, sling him through the doors at A&E, we don't want him dying before we've done him again."

The voices and screams faded.

James risked a look; the garage was empty. Daddy's van still filled most of the view. The royal blue lettering on the side of it, which he had looked at for years, but never really seen, stood out boldly from the white background.

Aaron **J**oshua
Snowdon-Lynes
If you want it
I've got it or I can get it for you

The youngster slid across to the door and looked out. Daddy was nowhere to be seen. Nastiest Villain was being bundled into the back of a car by the other two. His legs hung at odd angles. He screamed when they knocked against the seat. The car was driven off. There was no-one else on the forecourt. The boy flitted from car to car, slid out of the gate, and made time for the nearest horizon.

* * *

"I want to apologise." James had had to wait until he could get his Mummy and sister alone together. He stood before them, nervous and penitent: "I was wrong. I've been beastly to you both. I've been blaming you for the break-up Mummy."

"I know."

"And it wasn't your fault. And I have been trying to sneak looks at your breasts, Hannah. And that was wrong, and I'm sorry."

Hannah stood up and cuddled her brother in, pressing his face gently into the objects of his desire.

"All you had to do was ask nicely," she said, caressing his hair: "I'd show them to you."

Mummy joined the pair, and when Hannah released him, she kissed her son.

"It's all right, don't cry." She wiped his eyes. "But I still need to work, and I'm very good at my new job, even if you don't like it."

"That's okay too. I don't like it, but Jim says you're really good too. You're my Mummy, and I should let you do what you want, without making a fuss. And it would be a shame not to do something when you're so good at it."

"You've changed," said Hannah softly.

"All grown up, in just a few hours," added Mummy. "What happened?"

"I've realised who Ay-Jay is, and what he had said that Wilfman could do, and who he could do it to."

This time Mummy cuddled him to her bosom,

"Oh, my poor baby -- Don't stop loving him; he'll never stop loving you."

Discovery

An apartment near:
The Large Hadron Collider,
Cern,
Geneva,
Switzerland.
2006:

"I've started to worry about this research we're doing," murmured Ingrid.

Senior Engineer Robert Davison put down one of the London papers that were flown into Cern especially every morning for the British ex-pats, and regarded his wife sadly,

"Not you as well. The money saved if we gave up would not be spent on humanitarian projects. We wouldn't cure the common cold with it, or find a vaccine for HIV."

"I know that; it's not the cost. Money spent gaining knowledge for mankind is never wasted. It is the particular boundary we're pushing back that's the problem."

"It's just a question of getting the magnets on the approach to Atlas a few degrees cooler. It's just a design problem; we'll sort it."

"You mean I'll sort it, not we, me! It's the kind of design problem that turns you men to jellies overnight. You can only suck heat from something to something colder, **or** by making it work very hard indeed. The Atlas Particle Detector that you built, that you're so proud of, weighs the same as the Eiffel Tower. I've got the temperature of its particle accelerating magnets down to four degrees Kelvin, but it's the next two degrees that are the real problem, as you well know."

Robert returned to his paper and Ingrid, a little nettled, continued the complaint.

"And it's not the technical problems; I'll solve them, it's what we are doing. The ethics of what we're doing."

"We're discovering the Higgs b--"

"Proving the existence of --"

"We're proving the existence of," he replied laboriously. "The Higgs boson particle. There are those who want it disproved because it will make life more interesting for them, but--"

"It's not the Higgs! It's what we're doing! We are going to re-create the conditions in the universe a few nanoseconds after it began." Interrupted his wife as she always did when he became just a little too patronising: "What if we miss by that few vital nanoseconds, and recreate the universe instead?"

"Don't be silly! We cannot do that. Where's it going to come from?"

"The same place the current one did. Nothing, no space, no matter, no time, no shape, no size -- BANG, and the clock starts ticking. How do we know that thirteen and a half billion years ago two scientists of the day were not having this very conversation?"

"Now you're being ridiculous!"

"Is this the way the World ends, not with a whimper, but a very Big Bang caused by two very small hydrogen nuclei travelling at ninety-nine per cent the speed of light, but in opposite directions, colliding head on?"

Again he thrashed the paper into submission,

"With that level of paranoia bouncing around inside you, I don't know how you sleep at night."

"I don't; haven't done so for a while. I get up and walk the walls."

"I sometimes wondered where you'd got to."

"But you never asked," she replied softly, as she turned away.

The Large Hadron Collider Control Centre,

Cern,
Geneva,
Switzerland.
2007:
A man and a girl, each wearing headphones, sat in a soundproof booth listening to a countdown.
TWENTY-FIVE
TWENTY-FOUR
TWENTY-THREE
Signalling for silence to the brilliant young physicist with whom he walked the walls at night, the technician said,

"There's something I want you to know before, just in case. I know it's hopeless because you're married, and chaste, and honourable, but I want you to know that I love you." With a wry smile, he reached over and switched on the microphone in front of her. When the count fell to ten in his headphones, he pointed at her.

Professor Ingrid Davison, with a deep breath, took up the count into the microphone. Her voice echoed hollowly throughout the building,

"FIVE SECONDS"
--
"FOUR"
--
"THREE"
--
"TWO"
--
"ONE"
--

BANG

Somewhere Else,
Somewhen Else:
"The Earthlings did it again I see. That's fifteen experiments back to back!"

"If you give them curiosity, it does look as if they eventually press the kill all button, just to see if it does."

The other looked at the nearby button marked,

"Yes, well I won't do ours just yet if you don't mind. Are you going to give the sixteenth lot curiosity?"

FACT

In mid-2007 the Large Hadron Collider, in Cern, Geneva, came on stream.

At 27 kilometres around its perimeter, it is the World's largest particle accelerator and has four particle detectors of which Atlas is only one. It will have the ability to recreate the conditions a few nanoseconds after the Big Bang. Among many other experiments; they really **are** looking for the Higgs boson particle. This is a predicted, but, at the time of writing, missing piece in the particle physics jigsaw.[5]

What if they miss?

By just a few nanoseconds?

Well at least there's no point in worrying about that,--

-- and Global Warming!

---

5 On 4 July 2012, it was announced that a new particle had been detected in the mass region around 126 GeV. i.e. where the Higgs is expected to be. Subsequent work has tended to confirm the discovery, as the particle does have properties that predictions say it ought to have. The Higgs is associated with the fact that certain other particles, predicted to be, and which should be massless, surprisingly, have mass.

Investigations are ongoing. *P.C.*

Pirate

{Another ghost story, written with contributions from several classmates.}

"'W-W-W--" her Boss gave up, yet again leaving his brother to complete the speech.

"We're having a lock-in, after the Charity Midsummer Party tomorrow. Can you work it?"

"No sorry. But I'll come in early, help to clear up."

The two men nodded and returned to sorting the decorations for the party.

How the locals ever did a days work after a Lock-in was a mystery to Gladys, but they did, some working the vast prairie of the Hotch Pudding, which stretched from the pub's lonely meander, a full two miles along the Severn to their farmhouse base. The popular inn's nearest neighbour any other way was three miles, mostly by river.

Lock-ins apart, Gladys really liked working at the Pirate's Tuns. Specifically, she really liked her boss and had already measured him for curtains. The only problem was, although John North could overcome his impediment with most other people, his pretty young barmaid turned him dumb.

The Party had been fun, and going as her several-times-great-grandfather, Pirate Trevellyan had been a masterstroke.

"Hey, Gladys, what a great outfit, give uz a twirl girl." Gladys did so: "And put that in your pot, for the stunning outfit." 'That' was mostly coin, but occasionally paper. "Can I have a look at the earring?"

"It's real gold, and very heavy. I had to clip it to the headscarf. It's too heavy for my ear."

"Where's the other one?"

"Dunno. I've only ever had one. It was supposed to be Pirate Trevellyan's. And half of a pair. You can see." She leaned even further over the bar: "There are clips and bits for a partner, but I've never had it."

"Let me have a look?" She moved to his friend and offered the ear. "That looks like half a heart, with writing on it. O, Ce, d?"

"That's what it looks like. But what it means I haven't a clue. My guess is the rest of the words are on the other half."

When the third punter had wanted a closer look at her earring, she'd had the brilliant idea to charge fifty pence a look.

The Gloucester Cancer Care fund was consequently several hundred pounds better off.

But now time had been called, the tour buses had loaded and left, and the locals, having decamped out of the front door under the watchful eye of the Inspector; had been joined by the Sergeant as they made their way back in, through the rear.

And her taxi had arrived, except it hadn't, just another punter to relieve of fifty pence.

The landlord's brother and his friends had monopolised the telephone, to make nuisance calls to their friends and enemies alike, so she had to trek across the car park, to the public telephone box, to remind her cousin he was picking her up.

Automatically, while waiting for him to answer, she checked her appearance in the flyblown mirror on the back wall of the kiosk, turning her head to view the earring more clearly. The punters were right; it was worth fifty pence a look, enhancing the seductive swirl of the rest of her ear, by extending the lobe dramatically.

"Hello?"

"Hello, Mark? Remember me? Your stranded cousin?"

"Oh! Gladys -- sorry. Miranda came around, we, er--"

"Get dressed and get out here please, I want to go home."

"Cheeky baggage, can you see down 'phones? I'm on my way."

Mark found her waiting in the car-park, promenading the outline of the ancient building that stood there before the Pirates Tuns was built to replace it.

"Why are you waiting out here?"

"Hiding. All this crugg on my face. I wasn't going back in there. Not with black smudges on."

"What black smudges?"

"Just get me home, please. I'll deal with them at home."

At home, black smudges were prominent by their absence. Gladys, tired, and now confused, washed herself and went to bed, she'd worry about it tomorrow.

At three twenty-eight in the morning, she sat up in bed, suddenly wide-awake.

It wasn't just missing black smudges; the girl in the mirror had been wearing the earring in her ear.

Which had been on full show.

Anxious and breathing hard Gladys replaced the headscarf and earring and examined herself in her mirror.

The view was nothing like what she'd seen in the telephone kiosk.

She rearranged the headscarf and clipped the earring on, delicately curling her hair behind her ear as the girl in the mirror had done.

Goosebumps flushed all over her, now she knew, the goosebumps pulsed. She also knew what she had to do about it.

"I'll do it today." Her skin relaxed and smoothed out. "Today before work." Calmly she returned to bed and slept soundly until the alarm.

* * *

The girl in the mirror, sporting the same black smudges as yesterday, smiled silently through all the automatic responses like 'Who are you?' but obediently turned her head, and kept it there while Gladys matched up the earring with its partner. The earrings were a pair, not a reflection; there wasn't even any lateral inversion.

"Oh, it's not an O."

The girl shook her head minutely.

"It's the left one of the Three Tuns."

Her eyes widened as she nodded.

"The Three Tuns Logo, and underneath, Cellar door."

Again the girl smiled and nodded, turning to face her.

"There isn't a Cellar Door. Just trapdoors. In the floor. I mean the ceiling."

In erm wall, you'm not been looking hard enough, 'ole be there, marked with erm Tuns.

"The cellar wall?"

You'm find erm, stand close, push the Tuns, make you'msel rich, you'm call your first girl Pirate, after erm.

"Fat chance. The only man I ever wanted never talks to me."

Ee'm never talks to you'm because 'ee'm can't. You'm grab 'ee'm under mistletoe, and you'm snog 'ee'm good and tell 'ee'm stutter don't matter, tell 'ee'm to write it down. You'm snog 'ee'm good enough, and 'ee'm'll do the rest.

* * *

Her cousin answered on the fourth ring,

"Hello."

"Hello, Mark. Do me a favour, please? The family Bible, Pirate Trevellyan. I know it says Vicar Trevellyan married Pirate Trevellyan. Our ancestor with the dodgy reputation, the one that vanished. Can you find out to whom?"

"Hold the line -- It doesn't say, just Vicar Trevellyan married Pirate Trevellyan of Tinport Head, the date, and a couple of kids. It's the only entry that doesn't say who to."

"What if Pirate Trevellyan was a girl?"

"Wha-- Oh, I see what you mean."

* * *

"John is there a door in the cellar? In the wall?" Gladys

pressed a notepad and pencil into his hand: "Just write it."

No

"Is the pub logo anywhere? The Three Tuns? In the cellar?"

Yes

"Would you show me please?"

Need cleaner. Wrote John and dragged it over to the hatch.

Down in the cellar, he led the way to the far corner, far out under the car-park. The telephone box had to be nearly overhead.

The picture, crudely carved into an otherwise blank, dressed stone wall, was heavily obliterated with the dust and cobwebs of ages. John revealed it with the powerful cleaner's brush attachment. Gladys took the vacuum from him, and cleaned up a larger section of the wall, searching the grykes for clues. Her boss drew her attention to a significantly deep one, tracing out a complete, roughly oblong shape for her. She nodded and pushed the Tuns. Despite remaining immobile, there was a distinct sense of desire to move,

"Hang on. She said stand close." She stepped as near as she could; the flag nearest the wall sank minutely under her weight. She looked up at him, shocked. He stepped in close, next to her, adding his weight to hers.

Together they pushed the Tuns.

With the thresh no longer impeding its progress, silky-smoothly, and with a slight sigh, the door rotated on its central brass spindle.

The pair gasped in shock, and John reached out and enfolded her.

The room revealed was quite shallow, no more than three metres deep.

In the centre stood a small table, with a round-topped wooden chest upon it.

Seated at the table, looking straight at them along a cocked, double-barrelled horse pistol, was the girl in the mirror.

She had been sitting there for a long time. Although all that was left was air dried mummified remains, there was none of the rictus sardonicus grimace, her skin was taught and brown, but for the empty eyes, she could still be alive.

Although there was no light to be seen, there had to be a substantial ventilation passage.

The air was cool and sweet.

"Wait." The first word he'd ever managed to say to her.

John eased her out of the line of fire, leaned in and gently raised the lid of the chest. Gold glinted softly. Lying among other treasures, Gladys could see her earring's other half. Taking equal care, John retrieved the earring, replaced the lid, and shut the door. He pressed the earring into her hand, and spoke as if the stammer had never been,

"Come on." He took her arm and guided her away: "We need help with this. Not a word to anyone until we get the cavalry on site."

* * *

The couple left the Police and Museum staff to sort out among themselves, who could do what, and to whom, or what it could be done, while Gladys checked up on their rights on finding hidden treasure. Although the process would take time, and rested on several points of law, it did look as if John, as the owner of the pub, and she, as the finder of the treasure, would benefit eventually. Gladys wasn't really bothered one way or another; she got what she wanted, later that night.

When they closed up, she confronted her Boss.

"Well?"

"Th-Th-Th-" He stopped, desperately he reached for the pad,

Thank You!

"Is that all?"

He just looked at her, his eyes telling her that it was not all, not by leagues, but --

"John. A thank you kiss might be in order. And I'd like one. If you could manage it." With eyes full of panic, he tentatively reached for her.

She moved in, matching him, right arms over left shoulders, left arms around waists, heads tipped slightly to the left to avoid bumped noses, and smooched him the very best she could, from toes to scalp. His impressive noble reflex was instantly apparent, as was his embarrassment as a result of it; he eased gently away. She followed him in, holding tight and snuggling close. He stopped retreating, and snuggled back, assuaging her fears that her feelings were not reciprocated, they obviously were. After a while, slowly, reluctantly, they came up for air.

"You can thank me like that whenever you like." She kept a tight hold, while she spoke: "A permanent arrangement would be nice."

"Oh Gladys, I w-w-w-want that so much."

Later she went to thank her girl, the black smudges were still there, but the earring wasn't. Presently Gladys mentioned her plight,

"What happened to you?"

Revenue men raided erm, erm stayed to guard the gold. They killed Vicar. 'Ee'm were only one who knew about 'ole, knew erm were in 'ole.

"Can I help you? Do you need exorcising? Or something?"

No, erm be fine now, now you'm found erm, erm can join Vicar, rest in peace now.

"You're still beautiful you know; as if you died only this morning."

Erm be Milkmaid at dawn, Smuggler at dusk and Tanner most of in between.

"Ah, so you avoided the pox, became rich, and kept your looks in death. I'm sorry you're dead, I think we could have been great friends."

But erm not dead any more. Erm'll live on in you'm beautiful daughter now. Friends for life.

Technology is wonderful; when it works

The closing credits began to roll. The programme had been good, but then most OU stuff was. As the couple went looking for the Radio Times, the trailer for the next programme caught their attention.

"-- who now run a 'Find that missing piece of porcelain' service."

They looked at each other and Cindy winced as usual as she prepared to struggle out of her seat and into her wheelchair. Ash waved her back and performed the chore himself.

The cracked gravy boat was in easy reach, near the front of the cupboard. He lifted it out tenderly, and read the legends underneath.

"It says Mayfield -- that's all, Oh Wedgwood, Made in England, Barlaston, of course, but I can't read the impressed numbers, there's a pink W and a green 2, that might be it."

"Maybe, if that's all there is, it's always worth a try. Nobody else has got one." And the couple had asked at a lot of likely sources, including Wedgwood themselves, over a timescale spanning more than a decade.

The presenter finished his introduction of the magazine programme about collecting and collectables and moved on to the first item

"-- but first, are you missing a cup from that service that Aunty Betty left you, or a figurine to complete a set? Two ladies might be able --"

They sat captivated by the story of how two friends had needed bits to complete tea sets and having exhausted themselves, as well as the obvious possibilities, began to ask around among an ever-widening circle of friends of friends, and relations of relations.

"I haven't got that, but if you happen to stumble across a Peter Rabbit, nobody wants while you're looking, I'm interested, and I've got a spare Mrs Tiggywinkle. If you want it, you can have it," or similar, became a frequent reply.

"You know about Topsy? Well, take a look at this." The camera panned past the ends of deep, tightly packed racks of crockery, figurines and decorative objects. The many ladies busy between them had to slide in and out sideways they were so close.

"Impressed? Well it's only one of four warehouses that the China Detectives as they now call their company --"

Ash was already writing the letter in his mind while enjoying the programme, but not making any attempt to remember the details, relying on the Mac's ability to surf the Net later.

At nine when the news started, he made his customary escape into the arms of the other woman and logged onto the BBC website, to chase up the small detail of where to send his letter.

He hadn't anticipated being able to communicate immediately by sending an e-mail, for instance, so he hadn't told Cindy what he was doing before escaping from all that comment and speculation the TV companies transmit instead of news.

The names and addresses of several firms who had contributed to the programme were listed, and among them were some fax numbers. Ash grabbed the screen with Shift F3, logged off to conserve his precious dial-up connection minutes, and wrote his letter.

The cistern in the bathroom began to fill, so dishes were being washed in the kitchen. He would be needed soon. He checked his letter, corrected it and saved it, just in case, and loaded it up into his Apple-fax application. He retrieved the number from the screen-grab and typed it in.

Failure.

Technology is wonderful; when it works.

In fairness, the fax application was the only flaky link in an otherwise impressive bit of gear.

Ash restarted Mac and tried faxing his letter again, typing in the number for two ladies who now owned four warehouses.

Beeps and static!

Yes!

Mac was talking to another machine, sending and verifying, presently her screen cleared, and the dialogue box, announcing that his fax had been sent and received, flashed before him. Ash pulled down the Special menu and closed her down.

Power-Macs close down sequentially, application by application, and you can watch them if there is no drying paint handy.

Part way through the closedown procedure she began her American-style telephone ringing. He laughed,

"It's the China Detectives," he said, childishly pointing at the screen, which promptly blanked, cutting the speakers. British Telecom's double ring reached him faintly from the other end of the house.

Only one person rang at 10 o'clock at night.

As he cleared away, Ash wondered what it was that his mother-in-law wanted this time.

He turned to go along to dry the dishes and tell Cindy that he'd found a fax number, composed an enquiry, and sent it off.

The kitchen door flew open and Cindy's voice, shocked, incredulous, almost fearful, called along the hall,

"Ash! It's the China Detectives!"

Her expression was comical, traumatised, disbelieving.

Ash couldn't help it, he giggled.

He walked through to the kitchen plucked up the telephone and said,

"I've just sent you a fax."

"Yes, we know, our machine has been spitting faxes all over the floor since nine o'clock, we are ringing you because we've got what you want."

Diced, floured and gold-fishing with shock and with Cindy still staring up at him wide-eyed, Ash exclaimed,

"How do I get it?"

"We'll send it to you first class post tomorrow, if you like what you get, send us a cheque for £25?"

"As simple as that?"

"Yes, can I just check the delivery address?"

Saturday found him writing a cheque for £25 and hurrying to catch the post. Their Wedgwood dinner service was still complete, but now perfect.

Technology is wonderful; when it works!

On Being Nine Next June
{Written Late 2007}

{The antidote to all the moaners in the World! Every Monday Himself joins the queue in our local Post Office to draw pensions. Every Monday we have to listen to a tirade of criticism 'that's the trouble with this country' by an unkempt, unshaven, threadbare, grouse. One day soon, we're going to tell him!}

I will be nine next June.

The World is a wonderful place, and every day is a beautiful day. There is wet weather; cold weather; windy weather; but there's no such thing as **bad** weather.

I remember my birth clearly.

It was Mid-Summer's Day, a Monday.

I got up, showered and dressed in the clean shirt for the day, and newly washed trousers for the week. I tied my tie and studded it with Charities badges. That week I chose people; children, clowns, an Angel. Few people notice the duplicate among the dozen badges, a little girl for the N.S.P.C.C. Even less commented that animals rate Royal societies while children don't.

I opened the greenhouse and fed the fish in the pond; the golden rudd took the flakes from my fingers. My car started first kick, as always, and I reversed it out onto the road and returned for Joan's.

I backed it onto the drive.

Whack!

My eyeballs hurled out of my skull a metre or so sideways to the left. They hadn't actually moved, there had been no pain, they didn't even feel uncomfortable, but that yank had been viscously hard.

Just wait, I thought, the dizziness will pass, and then you'll be fine.

The dizziness persisted.

The view through the windscreen didn't make sense. I knew I was looking through my open garage door, into the garage. What I could see was a Cubist Painters impression of the garage, sliced up eccentrically and the pieces rearranged in the wrong order, and the whole view spiced up with double vision. I glanced down in preparation for getting out of the car; I didn't know that I did that. I only became aware of it, because my eyes didn't move.

Look at your knees! I thought. My eyes didn't move.

"Look at your knees!" I insisted out loud. My eyes didn't move.

"Look at your knees you daft bugger," I said sternly. My eyes stubbornly refused to obey. I could tip my head forward and look at my knees, but the eyes were fixed in a horizontal plane.

I remember being out of the car and leaning back against it. I had to straighten up from leaning over to my left; then I had to straighten up again from leaning over to my left.

I'll get some stick when Joan sees the state of my clean shirt off the car! I thought as I straightened up from leaning over to my left again.

I must have shut the garage door, and carried my breakfast through to the living room, but I don't know how. Everything looked strange, and walking seemed a problem; crabwise to the left, my feet crisscrossing like a dancer's, seemed to be the only way that I could progress. I tried to walk forward, crabwise to the left, turn around, crabwise to the left, anything, crabwise to the left, so I just did it that way.

I sat down in my favourite chair, a sideways crash landing to the left, and began to eat my cereal. The bowl, still largely full, dropped from my left hand and slid sideways into my lap. I picked it up confused,

How did that happen? It's a good job that the milk has been absorbed by the cereal, I thought. Or I would have a lap full of breakfast by now.

The bowl plunged into my lap again.

Come on get a grip, what's the matter with you today? I concentrated hard on my left hand holding onto the bowl, but now my right thumb wouldn't readjust the spoon automatically. It obeyed the instructions to hold the spoon only with great reluctance.

The first thoughts of what might have happened to me, and that I might actually be in a spot of bother, surfaced like an unwelcome beneficiary at the reading of a Will. I tried to look around my room,

No.

To readjust my seating position.

No.

To anything.

No.

It was no use; the spirit might be willing, but the flesh wasn't weak, it was very strong, and it wasn't having any.

Don't be silly; I'm only 58, strokes happen to other people!

There, I'd thought it, even if in the negative, the word had been caressed.

Stroke.

The little that I knew of the condition matched the more obvious symptoms, the weak left side; the confusion; the fact that I'd dumped my breakfast out of my left hand into my lap twice. There were friends who would have refused to believe that food would have been allowed even a partial reprieve once! Better have a word with Joan, but do it without alarming her.

"Joan, can you give me a hand pet?" I called firmly, to project through the closed door and up the stairs.

"Yes, I'll be down in a minute."

Presently the lounge door opened, "Yes, what -- What's happened?"

I tipped my head back to raise my level of view from Joan's thighs to her eyes. No need to say anything I could read it all in her face.

I had tried not to alarm her, but I couldn't see what she could. I was sitting in my chair with my lap covered in milk and cereal. The empty bowl was on the trolley at my side; I was sprawled to my left, my left leg out at a strange angle and my left arm draped over the side of my chair onto the floor. The left side of my face was hanging down; invisible weights were pulling it towards the floor.

Joan wasn't assessing the probabilities of 'Stroke? Yes, or No?' she was trying to guess how serious it was, and was she about to lose the man she'd loved, ever since she first set eyes on me, 40 years ago, almost to the day.

"I think I need to go to hospital," I said, but it came out of the right-hand side of my mouth as phluph talk.

"Sit there, don't move, I'll get an ambulance."

"No just phut ee in thur far an tfae ee, amphulanssess fare for sich pheophle."

Oh Lord give me strength, she told me her thoughts, weeks later: My man is dying in front of my eyes and doesn't want an ambulance because they are for sick people.

"I'll get ready, don't move."

Somehow Joan got herself ready and she and me into my car, with the sturdy help of a passing neighbour. I had also created more chaos by insisting on ringing School to warn them that I would be off. Joan had been frantic with worry but had accepted that I needed to ring, for my own peace of mind.

Although most of it is hazy, I remember bits of the rest of that day clearly, like the sultanas in a teacake.

Joan got me to the A & E department of the building that had most terrified me as an adolescent, and the time in the morning, plus one glimpse of my face signalling something seriously wrong, got me transferred straight through to the doctor. By the time she had parked the car and rejoined me, arrangements were in place to transfer me to Neuro at the Infirmary, and the migraine had started.

It was a real migraine with head cleaving pain, but even worse, vomiting from the heels only alleviated by crouching on the floor, and moving limbs to their central position to prevent serious muscle damage. I tried to get up off the trolley and was jumped on by several nurses, doctors, technicians and sundry cleaning staff.

"I need shu be shick," I called plaintively: "I need shu fouch on shu four." The rails were hauled up into place either side of me, and I was firmly held down. Joan supported me telling the staff that I would be sick, but also restraining me, calming me and helping to hold me on the trolley, desperate for me not to do something that would finish the job I'd started an hour ago.

"We'll get you a dish," someone said, but Joan had seen the wild look in my eyes and said,

"Quick, he needs it now!"

A kidney bowl was presented to me, but it was too late to point out that I could fill a kidney bowl twice over, with fire hose power, so I just proved it instead, and everyone got a bit.

"I'm shorry, sho shorry."

"Don't worry about it; we'll clean it up." The staff forgiving the patient close to death, who's vomiting was due to no action of his own.

But nobody seemed to learn from my ability to regurgitate.

I was sick in the ambulance transferring me to the Infirmary, and everyone got a bit.

I was sick on the trolley taking me between departments, and everyone got a bit.

I was sick in the transit ward and everyone got a bit, twice!

Especially my named nurse, who scurried around, trying hard to help,

"Oor are yuz being sick again Marvin?" He was utterly hampered by the hospital's standard issue kidney bowls being too small by approximately an order of magnitude.

The mistake over my name made the temptation to misquote Adams' Hitch Hiker's Guide to the Galaxy too strong, so I did it,

"Brain the size of a planet, and all I'm asked to do is lie here covering everyone with sick."

My ignominious spraying of the landscape was only stemmed when the doctors finally listened to Joan and me telling them that only a nausea killing injection would work.

I had my first Hospital shower, the morning after I was admitted, just before I was transferred to Neuro. I was asked if there was anything that I needed and asked if I could possibly have a shower. An attractive, and very young nurse told me apologetically that she would have to stay with me. I was amazed at my indifference. It was this very necessity to parade my nudity, and very average equipment, that had so terrified me as a kid.

Different circumstances, different attitudes, I thought.

It was still only Tuesday morning, and I was still dancing crabwise to the left, and, half soaped and straining to reach the parts that only that beer can, I nearly fell over. My nurse had to dive in and hold me up. When she apologised, I told her it was OK,

"Just dive in and grab hold of whatever you have to." It wasn't until later I realised why she looked at me with wide eyes when I said that.

When my colleagues came to visit, I told them to quash the rumour that I had had a nurse in the shower,

"The truth is that I have had an attractive young nurse with me in the shower!" The colleagues returned to School and reported back that whatever else had gone, my sense of humour was still intact.

My control of my eyes was in tatters, with double vision the most intrusive characteristic.

When I attempted to focus on something, my eyelids rolled back out of sight, just leaving the lashes in view and the eyes bulged clear out of their sockets.

Maiden aunts swooned, ladies screamed, strong men quivered and children cowered behind skirts, as an Alien from Outer Space with Protruding Hairy Eyeballs glowered unintentionally at them from the hospital bed. It was many days before I got the wayward right eye under control and I stopped seeing two distinct pictures.

I never did get back to School; Dr Burn was quite clear,
    "You'll kill yourself if you go back!"
    So I retired, and when I discovered Petra, allotted her some time to write.
    Sometimes she even tries Poetry, fails and produces Pomes.
    Here's one, it shows how I feel about my escape.

        'So I took the gypsy's warning,
        'Death's call would be ignored.
        'When bitter, angry, scything wind
        'Cuts me with razor chill,
        'And sleet lashing across my face,
        'Soaks melt into my soul.
        'Know I nearly was protected
        'By six deep feet of earth
        'And I give thanks, rejoicing in
        'The cold, wet, proof of life.'

I will be nine next June.
    Second time around?
    Yes. Oh Yes!
    But plaited halliards, most folks only get one shot.
    Believe me; there's no such thing as BAD weather.

Summer

*{Write a poem about Summer, (wince) but do not
mention any summery thing}*

The Garden Centre's Discount Day,
Patio chairs, when we've no Patio?
Clumpy heavyweights, hard to lift.
Bottled lustre comes expensive.
A thieves' target, demanding to clean.
Sumptuous covers add to the cost.

I tap the tingling, tactile, tangible:
Tough temptation,
That Teak alone supplies.
All sins forgiven by loving touches:
Worry later,
How to pay the plastic.

The Indian Restaurant

{Brief:

Given the introduction to a story, and the choice of two alternative endings:-

One; the couple united and joyous, planning their future life together.

The other; the pair sadly resigned to separate lives, parting for ever.

Join them up.}

Comment:

Guess which ending we chose!

(Opening paragraphs)

'The Indian Restaurant was packed, every table occupied, and the noise-level meant that conversation had become far from easy.

Jill looked across the table at Mark as he applied himself to his favourite Vindaloo. They had been friends for several years. Two intelligent people at the top of their respective professions. But although they had a close friendship and enjoyed each others company, their relationship remained just that - friendship

Jill had always been a little shy and reserved in his company, out of respect for his intelligence and his achievements, and Mark had never made any romantic advances to her - because of a chance remark he once overheard, by another female colleague - that suggested that Jill's sexual proclivities leaned towards the female of the species. And she certainly had a lot of female friends. Suddenly Jill reached across the table and touched his hand. Then as loudly as she dared in the noise around her, she said, "I love you!"

She was taken aback by the shocked look on his face, and quickly withdrew her hand.

Mark stopped eating, and as though he had not heard, removed his glasses, took a handkerchief from his pocket and dabbed his eyes.

"Telemarks, this curry is hot," he said: "It's making my eyes water."

"Did you hear what I said?"

"Yes. Please don't say it again or you'll make me cry.'"

* * *

And;

as it is nicely buried halfway through the book;

so that only the True-Reader will read it --

I'd like to add a comment,

while Standing On A Soap Box --

In the original, Mark broke the second commandment in his opening speech. People who would neither lie nor steal often do it gratuitously. I changed it to 'Telemarks.' There are some things I feel strongly about, that's one; Sex-And-Violence is another.

Why one of life's greatest joys is usually lumped with one of its worst woes beats me. There is not much of either in my short stories, and, apart from the odd murder or hundred, very little violence in my novels, and what there is, is usually 'off stage.' My novels, however, are stuffed with sex!

Centre Stage.

In the spotlight.

And as explicitly erotic as I can make it!

It's often there just because two characters who like each other happen to bump into each other! The critics will refer to it as 'gratuitous,' to my great joy, Dear True Reader!

If you think I'm making a statement, you're so right!

You will also probably notice that some of the text and formatting of 'The Indian Restaurant' has changed, other than drawing your attention to this; I make no comment.

Petra.

The Indian Restaurant

The Indian Restaurant was packed, every table occupied, and the noise-level meant that conversation had become far from easy.

Jill looked across the table at Mark as he applied himself to his favourite Vindaloo. They had been friends for several years, two intelligent people at the top of their respective professions, but although they had a close friendship and enjoyed each others company, their relationship remained just that - friendship.

Jill had always been a little shy and reserved in his company, out of respect for his intelligence and his achievements.

Mark had never made any romantic advances to her - because of a chance remark he once overheard, by another female colleague - that suggested that Jill's sexual proclivities leaned towards the female of the species, and she certainly had a lot of female friends. Suddenly Jill reached across the table and touched his hand. Then as loudly as she dared in the noise around her, she said,

"I love you!"

She was taken aback by the shocked look on his face, and quickly withdrew her hand.

Mark stopped eating, and as though he had not heard, removed his glasses, took a handkerchief from his pocket and dabbed his eyes.

"Telemarks, this curry is hot," he said: "It's making my eyes water.”

“Did you hear what I said?”

“Yes. Please don’t say it again or you’ll make me cry.”

Cry! Of all the responses he could have given, that one packed her in a box. She stared at her plate. What now? The direct approach had exploded in her face. Jill folded her napkin and picked up her bag,

“Excuse me for a minute.” She stood up and made her way to the Ladies room. Fortunately, it was empty. She retrieved tissues from her bag and repaired her face. Her reflection finished the restoration and looked steadily at her.

Try again next week?

“No! That’s what you told yourself last week,” replied the girl in the mirror.

But CRY!

“Call the bluff!”

It will hurt him.

“So? You’re bubbling your heart out inside. You cannot end up any worse off than you are now. Even if it becomes the end of your friendship, it’s the end of the pain too. You’ve been there before; you’ll survive.”

Go back in there fighting? Call the bluff?

This time the reflection merely nodded.

He was watching for her, nervously apprehensive, worried. Well that was something, at least he cared that much.

“Right Mister! If it makes you cry, it makes you cry. I have just said the nicest thing I’ve ever said to you and had it ignored and rejected. You are going to have to explain what I did wrong, and you are going to do it now.”

“Couldn’t it wait un--”

“Now!”

“I didn’t ignore it, or reject it. I didn’t mean to hurt you.”

“Well, you did, and for that, you will provide an explanation.”

“There’s really nothing to explain.”

“And don’t think you can change the subject because you can’t.”

“I never change the subject.”

"You just did. I know you'll try, you always do, but I won't let you this time. Nor will I will listen to twaddle, explain!"

"My sister had a friend who was a lovely person, but whose dress sense was a joke. I set out to change all that -- not the lovely, the joke bit."

"And you succeeded."

"Then she went off and married someone else."

"Which was a mistake, mandated, but he asked me. Nobody else did."

"But then you did something else, and I understood." He paused, and opened his hands depreciatingly: "So it's a defence mechanism, self-preservation sort of thing."

"But why? What did I do wrong?"

"Nothing. Well, nothing apart from the one tiny little detail, and that's not wrong."

"What tiny little detail? Come on. I've been there before with you, JFK's visit to Dallas was perfect, 'apart from the one tiny little detail' --"

"Well, two tiny little details."

"Mark!"

"You did nothing wrong; you're perfect, including the flaw which makes you human, the fact that you don't like yourself very much. No that's overstating the case, the fact that there are things about yourself you don't like." He stopped and resumed eating his meal.

Jill stared at him across the table. Presently she reached out and intercepted his hand on its way to his mouth. When he looked up, she tipped her head and gave him the eyes.

"You know what," he said assertively. "You know! You've got a gorgeous figure; stunning legs; an attractive face; lovely hair. You could give the girl from Ipanema deportment lessons, and you drape it all in frump to hide yourself in the background."

"That was then. I listened to you and did what you suggested, even though at times it makes me feel uncomfortable. I dressed spec--" She flung herself back in her chair. "You've done it again -- again. And I fell for it again -- again. You've changed the subject. Mark, what did I do wrong?"

There was a long pause, and then Mark laid his irons down,
"Dymphna?"
Jill's eyes hardened,
"What about Dymphna?"
"You love Dymphna -- Well you do, don't you?"
"Yes. So do you."
"Of course I do."
"You are going to have to explain because I am confused. I met you through knowing your sister, and it turns out that that was a mistake, I did wrong. Explain."
"You didn't do anything wrong. That holiday with Dymphna, after your marriage broke up. When I came to pick the pair of you up from the airport; Dimp was radiant. She'd had a wonderful holiday. You were glowing; you had too. I know what she is; I know she's a lesbian. I've known all the time; she came out to me before she came out to anyone else. I've got a sister, Jill, the sister I want; I don't need another."
"She'd clip you for describing her as lesbian. She's an aggressive big bull dyke, according to her. She's not; though, she's lovely. Did you think that I'd spent the holiday in her bed?"
"Well -- Yes -- I mean I've seen the pictures." There was a pause: "Were you cold?"
"Ah -- Those pictures. No, the little bolero top was blisteringly hot down the back, a feather mask and the body paint was quite enough down the front to keep me from boiling up. Does 'seen the pictures' mean the video too?"
"Yes."
"So you watched me kiss some girls, at a wild street party, and drew your own conclusions."
"Snog! Not kiss, and it wasn't 'some girls,' it was a street-full of girls. I watched you fondle--"
"Get fondled by!"
"Get fondled, caressed and snogged by a street-full of girls, one after the other. And you loved it. And I drew my own conclusions."
"I wouldn't have thought my being gay would have bothered you, you've been friends with Peter and James for years, you

introduced them.”

“Peter and James being gay doesn’t bother me a snip. My long-term plans include neither of them nor theirs me I dare say.”

“Ah -- But me being gay disrupts long term-plans of yours?” She couldn’t keep the hope out of her voice.

Mark regarded her steadily without replying.

“You’ve changed the subject again Mr Slippery, but this time I choose to run with the change. If you had studied the video carefully--”

“I did. Having spent years trying to shorten your skirts and render your blouses less opaque, I wasn’t going to pass up the chance of ogling your naked form being groped, albeit wearing a layer of paint. I just pretended it wasn’t their hands doing the groping.”

“Had you studied the body language more carefully, you would have noticed that every single girl was offered to me, mostly by her boyfriend, in a few cases her girlfriend. They were holding her firmly from behind, and mostly groping her too, and Dimp was holding me still so that we had to go through with it. It was far easier for both of us just to kiss the face in front of you, although after the first the rest were a lot easier. I just shut my eyes and thought of who I would like it to be, and that was not the girl in front of me. It wasn’t any girl. And then I enjoyed it; I admit it.”

“Are you saying you’re not gay or are you?”

“I’m not gay. I had a shamefully long list of heterosexual lovers at school; I suspect even longer than yours.” His eyes opened wide. “Yes, not many people know about that, apart from the boys involved of course, because I only said yes to the quiet ones. That was followed by a disastrous, but thankfully short marriage. Goodbye! Good Luck! No hard feelings! A dozen or so girls over the years have propositioned pome, and I chose to let a couple share my bed. For one of those, once was once too many, but the other was very nice. Dimp put me back together again after the divorce. I needed to say a seriously big and sincere thank you, and there was only one thing she wanted. I’m not gay, a soupçon of bisexual possibly, but no more than most of the population."

"Who did you think of, when you shut your eyes? On the video."

"Are you saying it matters?"

"Now who's changing the subject?"

"Me, there's no copyright on being devious and slippery, and don't you ever forget it -- Well?"

"Of course it matters, in the context of this conversation."

"Who do you think it was? I've only ever told two people that I love them, my ex-husband and you. I believed what I was saying at the time, but I now know that only one of them was really true. My ex was just a memory even before he walked out of my life into Marjorie's bed. I am a heterosexual, ex-frump, and I love you. What are you going to do about it?"

* * *

They had become aware that the noise level had lessened considerably, allowing their own voices to be much quieter and more private, and as they left the restaurant arm in arm, both their hearts were filled with hope for a beautiful future, together.

The Disappearing Duvet

{A summer ghost story. When I let him read it, Gareth didn't say a word; he just smiled at me ruefully!}

Granddad strode into the bedroom and drew Gareth's curtains wide with a flourish. Sunlight speared in; it was already hotly burning off the dewy mist outside,

"Gareth, up, ready, we leave in an hour. We're going over the water, just because you reached your teens a month ago doesn't say you can lie in bed all day." Gareth smiled at the reminder that he had passed that important milestone and peered at his Granddad through sleep-slitty eyes.

"You see this" he pointed to the huge, fluffy, overkill, winter duvet surrounding him. "It wasn't in this room last night. I woke up chilly. My duvet had gone. I've searched everywhere for it, it's gone. I had to get this one out of the back bedroom. And it's too hot."

"I knew you were paddling about with lights on. And doors open."

The youngster was miffed, "I had lights on and doors shut. And after all the care I took to shut the doors as well, and anyway that isn't the point, where's my duvet? It's not anywhere." He followed his Granddad from room to room looking at him, not the room. He knew it wasn't there.

"I can't find it either, you must have eaten it, go on get ready, or we'll be late."

A few minutes later, washed, dressed and downstairs he told his Grandma, stealing himself for the withering fire.

"Don't be silly. It will be in your room."

"It's not."

"In full view."

"It's not."

"It's got to be somewhere unless you have eaten it." There was more, but it prickled too much.

Granddad was much easier to deal with. He accepted things as they are, you'd find out days later, that he'd been mulling them over sorting through how he felt, and if he'd been badly done to, or especially if you'd thoughtlessly hurt Grandma, look out! Forget withering fire; expect to be blasted out of the water. But as far as spells and wizardry were concerned he was quite amenable.

Miracles were the norm in Granddad's world; he grew plants from seed.

Grandma returned from her search and addressed her husband, "I think he's eaten it."

"Would I be eating breakfast cereal if I'd already had duvet?"

The reply was merely to chivvy him to get ready.

In town, the two bought Gareth's Mum her birthday present from him. After a search, they found a 3 for 2 offer on bath gel which pleased. An attractive girl accosted them and gave them each a blister pack,

"I've got aftershave." The youngster proudly announced. "What've you got? It'll be the same; I'll use that when I get home. Can I borrow your razor?"

"No."

"You don't need to have shaved to use aftershave. I'll call it 'No shave.' That'll do it." Several other items were gathered and then the eggs.

"How you keeping?" The stallholder's usual greeting to elderly and therefore frail customers.

"Fine thanks - Getting there." He turned aside to Gareth,

"The duck eggs are too small, much smaller than the jumbos." Then addressing the merchant again, "A dozen of your Roc eggs please." He waved at the jumbo pile. The little woman looked as confused as she always did at this request, but obediently sorted them out, and the pair continued on their way

"Where are we going now?"

"Over the water, I told you earlier."

"Where, though?"

"Riverside Office Supplies, to buy office furniture."

Sometimes Granddad was as infuriating as all the other adults combined, and what was even worse, he told the truth. Gareth had never got over being told he was to have Wooden Potatoes for lunch, only to discover that that was exactly how the produce of Wooden Farm was labelled on the sack, so his retired Granddad was likely to be buying office furniture despite obviously not needing any. He fingered his phial of aftershave expectantly. There seemed to be something not quite right.

"Look!" he was holding the empty container up in front of his Granddad's face.

"You've pulled the top off."

"It wasn't me. I don't need to shave inside my pockets." His Granddad grinned at the peeved expression.

When they pulled into the parking lot in front of a building announcing a sale of office furniture, Gareth jumped out of the car, and headed for the small entrance beneath the notice, smiling ruefully to himself. Granddad went the other way and rang the bell on the grand entrance. Gareth hurried back pointing

"It's that one surely."

"No, this one, I hope."

On the door, a notice announced that visitors would be issued with passes and that they must wear them at all times.

"Will I get a pass too?"

"Everyone gets a pass."

"Will I have to wear it?"

"Yes, of course."

Security opened the door to them.

"I was hoping to buy some office furniture in your sale." A

couple of minutes later they were back in the car. Security had been jovially polite, it was next door, and they were shut on Saturdays. Gareth had been correct, but the taste was bitter,

"I'm having a bad day's haunting. Duvet missing. Duck eggs too small, exploding aftershave in my pocket and now I'm not even going to get to wear my pass."

Back home, the withering fire restarted, with Gareth vainly protesting his innocence.

"I found the duvet. It was in the airing cupboard. Did you wet it?

"No!"

"I think you must have wet it."

"I didn't!"

"I didn't put it in."

"Nor did I."

"Granddad didn't."

"Well--"

"That only leaves you. You must have put it in."

Gareth gave up. Grandma was lovely, but she just didn't--

"Runs in the family." Murmured Granddad: "None of them listens, Nanna Cook was the worst, just accept it."

But that still left how the duvet got into the airing cupboard.

Gareth tackled the real culprit that night.

"Why did you do it?"

"You were hot."

"But you could have just dropped on the floor. Instead of hiding in the airing cupboard."

"You'd trip up."

"I spent all day taking the blame. Use some common sense, some brainpower. Put some thought into things."

"I can't. I haven't got a brain. I haven't got a head, never mind a brain. Duvet's can't think."

The revenge of the inanimate object

{Written with Alix and Frederick.}

er husband died of relief, you know?" Betty whispered from behind her tray.

Freshly pensioned, and now safely in the tea shop, Les Girls moved over to join Brenda, who, once again, had claimed the coveted seat next to the radiator, and was already munching through the only éclair.

"Betty, when exactly is this, like, trip to Bournemouth?" Asked Winifred.

"The one I want us to go on is next weekend; it's got free excursions, you know?"

Brenda chirped up with,

"What trip?" through a fine mist of chocolate and cream.

"She'd have known if she wasn't so keen to get to the front, like, in the Post Office!" Snarled Winifred but under her breath.

"It's an Institute Weekend Trip to Bournemouth, with excursions, you know?"

"Oh good!" Said Brenda: "When are we going."

"Next weekend, long weekend, but you'll have to be quick, there's been an influx of pensioner interest, with it being the bingo, you know?"

"I'm in!" Said Brenda: "I'm due a big win."

"Please don't leave me out, my dear." Said Emily: "I need to go to the ladies, but I would like to go on the trip, as well." She eased herself out, and set off for the toilet, but had to brake hard, as Brenda barged in front, yet again.

"Brenda, you nearly knocked yon Emily over!" Agnes got no reply; Brenda had dived through the door; lest a loo-lingerer was lurking inside, and got sat sooner.

"Which excursions are we, like, going on?"

"The National Bingo Bonanza is a must, you know? There's Museum, Art Gallery, even a Mine."

"We'll have to be careful not to get on the wrong bus, my dear. Go on the wrong trip, like we did, two years ago was it?" Said Emily, waiting disconsolately for Brenda to reappear, and herald a seat available.

"And that was just a local prize; this one's the National. Big folding, you know? It would be tragic."

"Who's, like, the caller?"

"It's him on the Tele. That does the holiday programme, you know?"

"Oh, yon with the hair?" Said Agnes, perking up noticeably.

"Yes, him."

There was a collective sigh of adulation for their idol.

"Will we get on it?"

"Yes, I've already got the tickets, but don't tell Awisqjay just yet, you know?"

Winifred smiled,

"Let her, like, stew a bit?" She said, nodding.

"Yes, I got six tickets. I was thinking we might invite young Jean, get her out of her widow's weeds, it's been six months since, you know?"

"She likes yon with the hair. It would do her good."

* * *

"No buts, you're coming. I've seen your mother, and she'll take the kids. We go down on Friday; it's a long weekend, you know? Back on Monday."

"But--"

"And bring that nice dress, with the scoop neck, the short

one. I want to see yon with the hair's face when he sees you in that."

"Well--"

"Maud will do you a makeover at ClipArtistes on Thursday. Saturday, the big day. Wouldn't surprise me if you had a date by the night, you know?"

Jean gave in gracefully.

"Alright, I'm coming, makeover, posh frock, and glass slipper."

* * *

"Stand back Jean; you're in Awisqjay's way, you know?"

"What--"

"The bus is due, back here girl -- There, that's safe now, out of yon's way."

A few moments later, the long distance coach swept majestically into the bus park, matched by the equally military precision of Brenda's surge through the swell of people washing towards it. Only the driver's timely opening of the door prevented a collision with her face. The other five girls boarded, like everyone else, with northern decorum.

The group worked hard on Jean during the long trip down south, and by the evening had succeeded in getting her to lighten up, and even laugh occasionally.

* * *

It was on Saturday morning that events took their turn down Unkindness Avenue, although at first, everything appeared normal. One moment Brenda was sitting quietly with the rest, checking her bag for her lucky marker, the next, folk were bouncing off her like a bow wave.

"Oh, Awisqjay's off, seen somebody move, you know."

"Who's Awiskjay?" Asked Jean, bemused.

"A-W-I-S-Q-J, Amble Women's Institute's Serial Queue Jumper. Now, who might yon be, do you think?"

"Oh, I see."

The remaining women wound their way slowly through the

throng, and outside to the waiting buses. 'Bingo', read a retiring notice, discretely tucked away in a corner of the destination board of the fourth bus in the line. Betty checked carefully with the pretty young thing, resplendent in her driver's uniform that it was indeed the excursion to the National Bonanza, {"Absolutely, I'm going too!"}, before shepherding the rest of her flock aboard.

The bench seat at the back was still vacant, and the group spread out along it, growing together and feeling good.

*　*　*

The Bingo session was notable for lots of gentle, humorous banter, and no sweating, as card after card failed to anticipate the numbers called.

"Where's yon with the hair then?" asked Agnes.

"They'll be saving him, like, for the big event," replied Winifred.

"He is my big event, my dear." murmured Emily, to the amusement of the others.

"You're old enough to be his mother, you know?" Chided Betty: "It's Jean we're parading for his delectation girl."

"You make me sound like a prize cow." The others laughed.

"Prize yes, any man would be proud to hang you on his arm, you know. Cow, now--"

"That's enough Betty. The modern code's infinitely better than the one we were, like, brought up in."

"I agree absolutely, just tiptoe quietly past Brenda's room when you drag him off to bed, my dear."

"Look at that pig!" said Jean, aiming a path across the ceiling, with her finger: "Look At That Pig! JUST LOOK AT THAT PIG!"

Eventually, with great fanfare and ceremony, the main event was announced, and the celebrity caller wheeled out in front of his fans. The polished performer promptly warmed everyone's heart towards him, by forsaking the dais and walking among the populace for a few minutes. He asked groups where they were from, and how they were related. There were several WI groups.

His treatment of the Amble five was courteous, and, although he didn't speak specifically to her, the professional smile softened, and went all the way up to his eyes, when his glance fell on Jean.

There were several subordinate prizes in the build-up to the main one, four corners, a line. A number of pay-outs were claimed and confirmed, and silence descended as the big one was called.

"Mark your card, my dear."

"I will when he calls my numbers," Jean replied with a rueful smile and sighed as he missed, yet again.

The following twenty numbers all hit her third card,

"House!" She croaked weakly; she wouldn't be worrying about the price of kid's shoes for a year or two.

Part of the prize was dinner for two, with their celebrity caller.

"But I'm with my friends. I would love to, but -- Sorry."

"Jean! No! You've won it; you deserve it, and you're going, you know?"

"Let's all go, ladies, my treat." He said.

Les Girls looked at each other stunned: "It's not often I get to eat with real people, I would enjoy it, and it wouldn't cost me the Earth, you're tax deductible." The mischievous glint in his eye had them all corpsed with laughter. "We'll go back to Bournemouth together, on your bus, I'm staying there too. We'll go to Louigi's, he's got two Michelin stars, and he's worthy of them, and we'll make a night of it. Come on; it's decided."

"Thanks, that's very kind of you but it's Jean's prize, we don't want to but in, spoil it, you know."

"That's okay; I'm in Newcastle next month, I'll take Jean out on her dinner for two then, if I may."

The younger girl jerked as several elbows dug into her ribs simultaneously.

"Er, yes thank you that would be nice."

They were able to take over the back of the bus on the return journey too.

"It's a good job you're here," said Agnes to their distinguished host: "If you weren't, yon would have launched into her Hockey songs long since." She was nodding at Betty.

"Don't let me stop you," he replied.

Jean stood up and ushered him into the centre place of the back seat,

"I think you'd better know in advance what you're taking on," she said, laid her bag down in the aisle and knelt on it, facing him. "I learned this in the Girl Guides.

'We are the red men,

'Feathers in our headmen,

'Down among the deadmen,

'Pow-wow." She chanted while performing graceful, exaggerated-gesticulations, to match the words.

He smiled politely but then guffawed with laughter as she continued, and it became apparent that Jean's Girl Guide Troop probably played hockey too.

Her substitution of 'Aunty Mary' for all the foul words, and some of the not foul ones creating double entendres, even where they didn't exist in the rude version of the original, made the performance even funnier.

The journey back to Bournemouth passed quickly in laughter, and it was almost with regret that the group spilled out into the bus park, and collected themselves together for the short walk to Louigi's.

Another excursion bus, with Mine on its destination board, swept around in a tight arc in front of them, the door opened and a crowd of coughing passengers, with handkerchiefs to their faces, emerged within a cloud of sulphurous gas. Last off, and the target of several verbal javelins, the mildest of which would be termed abusive by most people, was Brenda.

Les Girls and their man stared at her horrified; from the waist down she was wearing a clinging stench of black slime.

The driver, bandana around his own nose, was analysing the day,

"You barged in first onto the wrong excursion bus; you got the stale chips because you barged in first to lunch, you barged in first to the toilet without bothering to read whose toilet, and you barged in first through the wrong door into the flooded bit of the mine. I'm sorry, but I agree with everyone else, it's all been nobody's fault but your own."

Not Poverty

{Write a story about a picture of a ragged, bare foot
family who looks destitute, and are standing in a
deserted, rain-thrashed street, at night,
but it must not be about Poverty.
Okay, so how about Riches then? }

ootsteps clicked with metronome precision down the
passage towards the newly refurbished door. Bill stood
straight, nervously glancing around for shavings or dirt he'd
overlooked in his cleaning, but as with the last six times he'd
checked, there was none. Mentally he braced himself to treat
the housekeeper's dissatisfaction with some aspect of his work
with stoic understanding. Being the best joiner in the district,
and proving it with every job he did, wasn't enough for certain
people, they wanted flesh too. The door, his new door, was
opened with a quality shlick of the lock and glided back on silken
hinges. Prepared to greet the housekeeper with his professional
smile, Bill stood mute, frozen-faced in the presence of the Bishop
himself.

"Is this it finished?"

Belatedly Bill grabbed his cap off his head.

"Yes, Milord."

The Bishop examined the door, opening and closing it several times and testing how smoothly it rotated with a single crooked finger.

"An excellent job. Thank you." He produced a purse from deep folds about his person: "How much do we owe?"

"Four shillun and four-pence, Milord." He clumsily offered a scrap of paper: "It was six 'n fourpence. But I've been paid two shillun for materials."

"Good man, honest man. I haven't any change, take this crown, keep the change for good work."

"Milord, thank you." Bill fiddled with his cap, eventually pulling his forelock.

"There is work to be done in the Abbey; Mrs Figgis will be in touch about starting you."

"Yes, Milord. Thank you." Bill knew full well that any contact with Mrs Figgis would be by scullery maid, but that was a small, bearable insult if the new Bishop continued to settle his bills promptly, and in full.

* * *

Even the weight of a full crown in Bill's pocket failed to lift his spirits as he bought the days provisions for his family. He'd managed to blot out the trouble at home for the day while concentrating on his work, but now it must be faced.

The best joiner in the district made his way into the tenement block; although he constantly reached out to touch the walls in the darkness, his step was confident along the familiar way. Occasionally loungers stirred with interest at the appearance of a figure, but lapsed back into lethargy when they divined one of their own.

He pushed at his door fearful of what might greet him.

He looked for the sheet pulled over a form at rest, but it was still the face of his younger daughter, wracked red with fever that he could see.

"How is she?"

"Still fighting," replied his woman, her strained face showed even more torture in the flickering firelight. "The crisis is near, but she's still fighting."

"I've got money. More money. The Bishop paid, paid me himself, with a tip."

"The new apothecary, the good one, he'll come, for two pence, and give the medicine, for two pence."

"I'll go and get him, Dad." A pinched boy had slid out of the shadows.

"Yes, go and ask him." Bill bounced his hand; the soft chink of coins could just be heard against the constant, sinister, background growl of the tenement block: "Tell him I can pay."

"Yes, Dad."

Young Bill had gone on his errand. A second child was now clinging to Bill's leg.

"Don't fret young Betty," he stroked her hair: "We'll win through yet." The mute child drew him over to the bed, took his hand and placed it on the forehead of her fevered sibling.

"Still fighting," repeated big Betty: "She's fighting, but she's getting hotter." She sponged the child's face again and tugged more covers into place around her. "Liz lost one last week. Same thing." Bill cuddled his woman in, in silence. He was surprised that Liz had noticed one fewer but refrained from commenting.

* * *

Young Bill was quickly back,

"He'll come," he said: "But he won't come into the block, he'll only come as far as the lights. We have to bring Ada out to him."

Without a word Bill plucked the child up, and held her for Betty to wrap a coat around her. Their faces showed that both feared that the trip out would kill their youngest, but accepted that it would only be advancing matters by a few hours at the most and that they too wouldn't enter their tenement on a dark night either if they didn't live there.

* * *

The street was deserted under the lights; the slashing rain had washed it clean of traffic. Only the occasional hansom cab clopped by.

"He'll be here when the clock strikes; he promised Dad."

"Yes, he'll be here." Big Betty had eyes only for her sick child: "He'll be here."

The Parish Church began to toll the hour.

A sturdy hack trotted into the street and suddenly veered over towards them.

"You the joiner?" Said its rider.

"Yes."

The Apothecary slid off his horse's back and began to examine the child. After a couple of minutes, he produced a flask and cup. He poured a small amount of water into the cup and added two drops of brown liquid from a small bottle.

"Drink this." He murmured in the child's ear: "It tastes horrible, but if you drink it I'll give you a candy." The little one bravely took the mixture down, her face twisting with the sour taste, and the young apothecary produced a barley sugar twist and broke a small piece off. "You can give her three doses a day. Breakfast-time, teatime and suppertime, but no more. And stop as soon as the fever breaks. All of you, only drink boiled water. You can let it cool if you want, but only drink water you've boiled, don't cool it with other water."

"What is this?"

"Infusion of leafy willow wands, there's other things too Meadow Sweet and such, but mainly willow. Remember none after the fever breaks. And boiled water only, for all of you."

"Yes." Bill pressed two pence into the man's hand, and he mounted his mare and rode back out of sight.

The family hurried back to their home, frantic to get Ada safely back under cover.

* * *

Betty pulled the outdoor clothes off their child, and Bill laid her into the bed.

Her face was no longer red, her breathing steady, not laboured; she turned onto her side, slid her thumb into her mouth and began to suckle it. Un-noticed in the dark the crisis had passed successfully, aided in substantial part by the cooling rain, and a heavy slug of aspirin.

The other four quietly knelt down around her bed and together gave thanks.

The Tragedy of the Mine

{A story from your local heritage}

The ship's officers listened to the weather forecast in dismay, the bright young thing reading it had just unknowingly added six hours to their journey, and thousands of pounds to their costs.

"Could we make it if we caught the next tide?"

The First Officer sketched the front line of the advancing storm on his charts and reached for his slide rule, while the rest approximated the solution of some simultaneous equations in their heads.

"Yes sir, with an hour, ninety minutes or so to spare." The ring of heads nodded in agreement.

"I'll get on to it," said the young Third Officer, without waiting to be told.

On deck, a squad of men were loading coal into the hold. Although three could be seen guiding the chute that carried it aboard, there were ten more out of sight in the hold stowing it away into corners, making sure there were no air pockets, and ensuring the stability of the ship, as well as a full hold.

This vital job, going by the mundane title of Trimming, was dirty, hard, and very dangerous.

Half a dozen unsuspected air pockets deep down could suddenly coalesce into one, collapse, and bury a man alive. A state he wouldn't be in, by the time his mates reached him.

The Officer called the ganger to him,

"How long Mr Umbel?"

"Five hours, Third. Mebees four and a half." The young man in his sharp uniform produced a wad of crinkly white notes with elegant, black writing on them,

"We need it done in four."

"I'll ask."

Jim Umbel dropped down into the hold, and two minutes later the endless belt carrying the coal to the chute speeded up. The Ship's officer winced, he'd been down earlier to see the trimming process for himself; even at the slower rate, the trimmers had been working themselves to death.

* * *

Deep underground Stan Umbel lay on his side hacking coal out from a seam too narrow to take his shoulders. He was already too far in, but too far down on his daily quota to take any time out to insert props. He hacked, and hoped. There was an ominous creak from behind him. He scurried backwards, and out, just in time, as the roof fell in.

It wasn't a big fall, not even bad enough to merit reporting. Sam cleaned it out and propped the remaining roof, but that was his quota bonus gone.

He loaded his coal and collected his tools. At first, he couldn't find his pick, and lost even more time searching. When he found it, his shoulders sank in dejection. It was only later that the dejection turned to anger.

Jim walked home, meeting Sam on the way. The broken pickaxe handle that Sam was carrying was seriously bad news. The brothers greeted each other with their eyes, and Sam held the handle up to be examined. The pale snapped end had wide pale growth rings, under the coal-smudged skin.

"I thought that was supposed to be hickory?" Said the astonished ganger.

"It was, but it was just dyed to look like it. I had my suspicions from the start; it wasn't heavy enough."

"So you worked all day for a couple of shillings?"

"One and fourpence. I didn't get my quota."

"Can I help? Please? I had another good day. Stingy's have some good ash handles in. You'd be doing me a favour; I've got a big note to break."

Being in possession of large currency, when most of the populace were jobless and starving, was not always safe.

"Oh. Oh well, in that case, thank you."

The ganger waited patiently to be served by Simon Stingy himself. The store-owner had similar reasons for not flaunting his wealth. Together they sorted through the available handles and selected the best one.

"We'd best talk terms in the back."

"Ah. Right."

The large white note was stored away in the safe, and replaced by a substantial bag of crowns, half-crowns and other coins.

On his way home, Jim called into his brother's house and laid the handle on the table.

"This one should last a bit longer, and your change is in the pack."

"Thank you." Said his wife, wet-eyed: "Thank you so much."

"Again." Added Sam.

At home, Jim gave his wife more money for his day's work than his brother's wife received in a good month.

"I take it that another ship needed to catch the tide."

"Bad weather coming up The Channel, we got them away early. It will make many hours difference at the other end. What's a hundred quid spread among my lads, if missing a tide will cost you thousands?"

"I saw you at Sam's --"

"New handle, the last one was white wood, just painted to look like hickory."

"That's a day's pay gone!"

"I left him some coins too."

"It'll change some day."

"It won't you know, not until the only people to benefit from the miner's toil, are the miners themselves. While we've still got mine owners, unions, politicians, advisers, specialists, quotas, targets and league tables, it won't change."

"We'll always have those!"

"So nothing will ever change. Mining is just an extra-ordinary case of the Tragedy of the Commons."

Now What?

{Story inspired by a picture of a couple in a sports car, driving down a winding road, with mountains in the background.}

George and Mary were arguing again; they always did, afterwards.

"So what are we going to do about my sister?"

"Not again. I came for a loving afternoon with you, not her." He opened the car door for her, "You've done nothing but talk about her since you got dressed."

"You've had me; you've had what you came for, now I want what I came for." She tracked him all the way around the car. "Your wife, the one you have to get rid of before you marry me."

He drove off, back along the little-used mountain road.

"I can't just divorce her. No money, I signed a prenuptial agreement."

"Got rid of, I'm not talking divorce, I'm talking you getting rid of her." The car swerved dangerously close to the valley edge as George realised what she was saying.

"Don't talk stupid."

"You could do it. Policeman. Inside track, turn the evidence towards somebody else."

"She's your sister!"

"I get my hands on my money if Margaret's dead." Insanity burned in her eyes."

"You're mad--"

It was the wrong thing to say.
The scream of a cacodemon,
"Stop the car," she yelled, spraying him with spittle.
"No!"
"Get out. You'll walk home."
"It's my car."
A moment later he was fighting for his life.
She dived across him scratching and biting.
The car leaped for the edge.
He fought it back on line, already bleeding.
She ripped the keys from the ignition.
No powered steering,
no assistance on the brakes,
and another hairpin,
with only air between them and death.
He yanked the car around.
His stamping foot bent the brake pedal.
The car turned,
shot across the road,
onto loose chippings,
and skidded sideways to a halt,
in a broad lay-by, near a grotto.
She was out,
and around to the driver's side screaming,
"Get out! Get out you pervert! You're walking home."
She heaved at his hair.
He slammed the door open,
sideswiping her to the ground.
The keys bounced across the lay-by.
He leaped from the car.
She scrambled up.
They dived for them.
He punched her out of the way, to stop her from winning.
She twisted and landed awkwardly; there was a single loud pop, like a carrot snapping.

Police Sergeant George Bolt drove home thinking furiously. The grotto would only do for a short time as a temporary grave for

Mary; he'd have to go back and get her body when he'd worked out how to dispose of it.

At home a young policeman was stretching tape across his drive; others were carrying items into and out of his front door. As he got out of the car, his partner came running over,

"George, listen, that bloody Inspector Know-it-all has the husband in the frame as prime suspect already. I know you didn't do it! You were with Mary; you'll have to get her to confirm your alibi."

"Alibi? What for?"

"Oh, I thought you knew. Margaret's dead."

George stood, still and silent.

"I'm sorry George, she was strangled, it's murder."

Amy's Elephant

{A radio play for children}

Author's Comment:

Amy's Elephant first appears in Writes En Passion.

Some people don't understand how a momentary incident can become a 100,000-word novel. There was a time when we didn't. The birth of Amy's Elephant describes exactly how most of our stories grow and evolve.

Mr Hughes describes it as undisciplined.

He may well be right -- but!

Ever since they appeared on our computer screen, {totally unexpectedly, generated spontaneously out of no-thing/no-where/no-when} we've wondered how Amy and her Elephant got on.

Here's how it started:

Lisa and I were talking about personal relationships, with boys of course!

"Take it from me it's great," said Lisa "I had it off three boys at that party last week. It was so good I was going to ask Jake if he wanted his go with me, for real like, get rid of this virgin millstone, and then his parents came home, and the chance had gone. Just as well I suppose, we would have been caught."

I smiled ruefully,

"I heard that you were being persuaded to cooperate."

"I didn't need much persuading."

"Tell me. You obviously had a good time, tell me about it."

"Is this research?"

"If you like --" I owned up: "Yes, of course it is, everything is. What you tell me will appear as a girl taking pity on her brother, or comforting a broken hearted friend, or saying goodnight to the widower she has just babysat for."

"Her brother?"

"That got you didn't it, brother, broken hearted, widower, in each case you are latched in straight away, 'Where do we go from

206

here?' 'How is this to be resolved?' 'Are they going to --?' A bit more interesting than, 'Number sixteen did it to me in postman's knock.'"

"I've never thought about my brother. Why specifically widower?"

"There's enough real betrayal in the world without me inventing more in my fiction. One day one of my characters will do it, and then I'll pick the ball up and run with it, until then -- Tell me."

"What do you mean, one of your characters? They do what you say surely?"

"No, they do what they want, I'm rarely in control. I sit down to write about eight-year-old Amy visiting a supermarket to buy a tin of beans. At the checkout, she discovers that by mistake she's bought an elephant. There are two choices, drop the elephant and buy the tin of beans, or pick the elephant up and run with it. I pick up and run with it."

"You're mad!"

Well, she could be correct.

So when Himself was asked to write a radio play for children, Amy went ahead and bought her Elephant.

Petra.

Amy's Elephant

{Himself gave his two elder granddaughters this to read, and they read it out loud. Rachael and Hannah shared the parts between them, Rachael read the part of Rajah in an Indian accent, all the other parts, in variations of their native Derbyshire. Until then he did not realise it was funny, and neither did I!}

F/X	RADIO IN BACKGROUND
MUM:	I know.
AMY:	(ANNOYED) You always know!
MUM:	I know.
AMY:	Are you psychic?
DAD:	Or physic? It even gets to me at times, that you always know.
MUM:	I know.
DAD:	Go and get your magazine, Amy. Here's a fifty pence, don't forget the lucky dip card. It'll probably be blank as usual, but somebody has to win, one day it might be you.
F/X	RADIO IN BACKGROUND FADES AWAY
F/X	BEEPS OF BARCODE READERS IN THE BACKGROUND
SHOPGIRL:	Any cash-back?
VOICE:	No thank you.

SHOPGIRL:	Sign please, thank you, your receipt and your card -- Hello Amy, is it just your magazine?
AMY:	And my lucky dip card. I got lines this time.
SHOPGIRL:	Oh! A bar code! Let's see what you've won.
F/X	TWO BEEPS NEARBY
SHOPGIRL:	That's 30p for the magazine, and you've won an elephant.
AMY:	A whole elephant?
SHOPGIRL:	Yes, take this Chitty to the big door over there, and get your elephant.
F/X	BEEPS OF BARCODE READERS FADING. FEET APPROACHING
MAN	Yes, little girl, what can I do for you.
AMY:	I'm not little. I'm eight!
MAN	Sorry Miss, my bad eyesight. Yes, you're obviously eight. May I help you?
AMY:	I've come for my elephant.
MAN	(CALLING) Joe! Bring the elephant. I'll have to open the big door Miss.
F/X	SOUND OF SLIDING DOOR
MAN:	But he'll still need to duck his head.
AMY:	Elephants can't duck.
MAN:	Well he got in, so he can get out. Here he is. He's called Rajah, and you lead him with this stick.
AMY:	Hello Rajah. I won you in my magazine. I'm Amy.
RAJAH:	How do you do, Amy. Hello, Amy. Good morning, Amy, and welcome to my world. Was that right?
AMY:	Hello Amy would do. Can you duck under that door?
RAJAH:	Elephants can't duck, but I can be smaller. You have to tap me behind my knees, to make me bend my legs.
AMY:	Like this.
RAJAH:	Use the stick. Yes, that's right.
AMY:	Don't straighten up yet, another two steps. Yes, you're out.
RAJAH:	Do you want to ride me?
AMY:	Up there? I can't get up there.

RAJAH: I make like stairs with my knee and trunk, and you climb up.
AMY: No it's okay.
RAJAH: Look like this. You can climb up easily.
AMY: (ON RISING PANIC) No Rajah! No! No Rajah! I don't like heights!
RAJAH: Oh, you should have said. I'll put you back down.
AMY: And now I'm all dusty.
RAJAH: I'm sorry about that. I bumped into a shelf with flour spilt on it. Well, it had flour spilt on it, after I bumped into it the first time.
AMY: How many times did you bump into it?
RAJAH: I'm not sure, but the flour spilt on me. I'll blow it off you. You'll have to hold on to the railings. I don't want to blow you away.
AMY: Be careful.
RAJAH: I will. Phuph! Turn around. Phuph!
AMY: Rajah! Stop! You're not supposed to blow my dress up.
RAJAH: Well that's where you were dustiest, but you're fine now, clean and new.
AMY: Humph, come on you.
RAJAH: Where are we going?
AMY: I'm taking you home.
F/X   SOUNDS OF TRAFFIC, BICYCLE BELL, AND SIGH OF BUS BRAKES CLOSE BY
AMY: Stop here, we're crossing here.
RAJAH: Do I cross now.
AMY: No, we wait for the beeps, and the little red man to turn green.
F/X   BEEPS
RAJAH: He's green,
AMY: Wait! Around here, they don't drive too well.
F/X   SOUND OF A CAR RACING PAST
AMY: See. The rest are stopping, that stupid Wally just went straight through. We can cross now.
RAJAH: Those silly little pimples hurt my feet.

AMY:	Those silly little pimples are to stop you slipping. Oh no! It's Sakes! Quick, you walk along behind this hoarding. I'll see you at the far end.
RAJAH:	Behind this? It's all nettles and prickles and wet!
AMY:	It's nothing compared to the jungle. Go.
RAJAH:	My kind of elephant does not live in the jungle. Wet, sweaty place, full of mosquitoes. Don't push I'm going. Ugh! I've trodden in something. It's all -- (VOICE FADES)
SAKES:	Aymee what are you hiding under your coat?
AMY:	(SOFTLY, TO HERSELF) Sakes is a nasty little bully, if you ignore him he goes away.
SAKES:	Aymee! Aymee! Aymee! Painy Aymee!
AMY:	(SOFTLY, TO HERSELF) Sakes is a nasty little bully, if you ignore him he goes away.
Sakes:	Little girls shouldn't have elephants.
AMY:	(SOFTLY, TO HERSELF) I'm not little, I'm eight! Sakes is a nasty little bully, and one step nearer, and I'll clatter him for that snowball last winter. Please just one more and he'll be in range. No, he's backing off, the nasty little bully.
SAKES:	(GETTING FAINTER) Aymee. Aymee. Aymee.
AMY:	(SOFTLY, TO HERSELF) I win. I win. I win.
RAJAH:	(VOICE GETS LOUDER) ... and sharp stony bits, and there's an old bedstead! An elephant of the Royal Line should not have to pick his way past old discarded furniture.
AMY:	You are a moan.
RAJAH:	I'm not usually, but look it's chipped my nail-varnish.
AMY:	Elephants don't wear nail-varnish.
RAJAH:	Well I do. I'm special. Oh, look, pineapples.
AMY:	Come on you're lagging behind.
RAJAH:	Behind what? Not another hoarding, please. Mmm, I love pineapples.
AMY:	They give you colic; I read it in Elephant Bill. The boss elephant ate pineapples and had severe colic.

RAJAH:	But that was several hundred. I was thinking more like one -- hundred -- Or maybe two.
AMY:	You're not getting any. I'll smuggle you biscuits and milk later.
RAJAH:	What biscuits?
AMY:	You'll have to breathe in here. It's narrow up this alley.
RAJAH:	Narrow! Alley! (VOICE GETS SHRILL) This is just a crack. I'll get stuck!
AMY:	Stop fussing; just push your way through. There you made it easily.
RAJAH:	My sides are scuffed! And all the primping and polishing I did to look good for you.
AMY:	You look great, come on. Not long now.
BOY	Amy what's that you've got?
AMY:	It's a double decker bus, but it's in disguise. (SOFTLY) Come on. Hurry, we have to get you hidden, before he tells Mum.
F/X	SOUND OF TRAFFIC FADES
RAJAH:	I can't get in there.
AMY:	Yes, you can. Mum's hanging the washing out. We'll slip down the side path and up into my bedroom. Breathe right in and bend your knees.
F/X	DOOR OPENS FAINT SOUND OF RADIO
AMY:	More! Go on! Push and wriggle. Now turn here. Wriggle.
RAJAH:	Can I breathe yet?
AMY:	No! Not yet! Up the stairs quick. She's coming! No that's the bathroom, squash through here.
RAJAH:	(SHRILLY) Eek
AMY:	Push! Nearly there. Right, made it. You can breathe now.
RAJAH:	Eee, Huff, Eee, Huff, Eee, Huff.
AMY:	Don't be silly. It wasn't that bad.
RAJAH:	It was dreadful. Elephants aren't supposed to climb stairs, it's in the rules, and you promised me biscuits, and you never said what kind.

AMY:	Custard creams.
RAJAH:	Oh! Oh, well in that case. It just might turn out to be worth it. (SLYLY) Can I have two?
AMY:	Yes. If you're good.
RAJAH:	And a whole glass of milk, all to myself?
AMY:	Yes. I'll go and get them, stay here. Don't go anywhere.
F/X	SOUND OF THE DOOR OPENING, RADIO, DOOR CLOSING
RAJAH:	Don't go anywhere, she says, how can I go anywhere? I'm stuck in here forever. In years to come, they'll find me all squashed and
F/X	SOUND OF THE DOOR OPENING, RADIO, DOOR CLOSING
RAJAH	Cramped. Squashed into a room that's smaller than I am.
AMY:	Stop moaning, or you'll get no biscuits.
RAJAH:	I've stopped -- These are nice (SLURP), and the milk is lovely, cold and so refreshing.
AMY:	You'll have to be quiet. I have to go down for lunch if anyone comes in pretend you're not here. I'll put my Easter bonnet on you -- There! You can make like a hat-stand.
F/X	SOUND OF THE DOOR OPENING, RADIO, DOOR CLOSING RADIO GETS SLIGHTLY LOUDER
F/X	TIME PASSES, SOUND OF RADIO
AMY:	Dad, I won an elephant in my magazine. The lucky dip card. He's in my bedroom. I put my bonnet on him as a disguise. But it's not very convincing -- Just when Mum finds him she-
F/X	SHRIEK AND BRATTLE OF FEET ON THE STAIRS
DAD:	She's found him.
MUM:	John there's an elephant in Amy's bedroom, and it's wearing her hat!
DAD:	(SUPERIOR SNEER) I know.

The Sudden Occurrence

{Written with Ann, Kathleen and Derek.}

" "Squash a noble snack, yesterday. (10)," murmured the man on the park bench. He always found it easier if he read the clues out loud to himself, but irate vibes from competitors for the speed title had taught him to do it quietly. Even now alone in the lunchtime sunshine, he maintained his quiet demeanour.

The girl jogged by as she always did, and as usual, stopped at the fountain for her breather, and to watch the ducks.

The man on the bench resolutely thrust from his mind any speculation that the young man loitering nearby, on the pretext of eating his lunch, would finally pluck up the courage to speak to her.

Finish the crossword, check the time, and then watch him tie himself in knots finding the bottle, he thought, A star-nosed mole could see she was aching for the invite. Impatiently he thrashed the paper concentrating again.

The young man paused after only one bite of the bun,

"Cooking cheese again!" The young man murmured. "And mayonnaise!" He stopped himself from spitting out the half-masticated mess in front of his dream-girl, swallowed it down, took a deep breath and addressed her,

"These buns are disgusting for humans. Do you think the

ducks might like them?"

"You could try."

He walked around to join her and laid the lunch-box on the wall.

Together they discovered that buns disgusting for human consumption, when broken up small, were gourmet food as far as ducks were concerned.

"I've seen you jogging through occasionally, do you work near here?"

"You've seen me every weekday for three months, I hope," she said depreciatingly. "I wear a scarlet jumpsuit because I'm not trying to hide. It's much safer crossing the roads if the taxi drivers can see you. I've seen you every day, in your smart suit. I like that one, but the one you wear on alternate weeks is really nice."

Her gently encouraging praise allowed him to relax and talk to her properly. They quickly discovered that they had lots in common and enjoyed talking to each other.

They fed the ducks and circled around each other, laughing occasionally. She sat back down on the wall, and jumped up immediately in alarm,

"I've sat on your lunchbox! I'm so sorry!"

"No problem, the ducks won't mind I'm sure." He gently turned her around. The last bun had sprayed its mayonnaise up her back in a pale fan shape. "But I'm afraid your scarlet jumpsuit, now has a white mayonnaise tail all the way up your back."

They looked at each other stunned for a moment; then she burst out laughing,

"I've been sandwiched."

"Sandwiched, that's it!" The man on the park bench checked his watch: "Eight minutes three seconds! That's the record, thank you!"

The Girl In Blue

{A Love Story in 250 Words}

Peterson screwed the newly fitted two-gang socket into place. "That's done." He hefted the multi-way adaptor: "I'll get this crushed, don't use one again."

"I won't," replied Aunt Liza fondly, and pointed to the leather tool case: "Serious bit of electrician's gear."

"Not bad for the money. Not Swedish of course. But it'll do for the Sixth Form."

"Time for your girl in blue, she's been to every Evensong since your last visit. Checking out our pew. No, don't do that PeeTee." She hauled his hand away from covering his mouth. "Your broken teeth are part of you."

The youngster mouthed, but nothing came out.

"Just like your speech impediment, they don't bother you in the family; they won't matter to any girl that's worth pursuing either. The problem's inside your head, you just had to think of her, and you covered your mouth. Don't!"

She was there again, surreptitiously checking out their pew, but unexpectedly vanished when they went looking for her after the service.

Suddenly,

"There you are! I've been looking all over for you."

He froze, hand to mouth; the girl in blue was heading straight for them.

"I can't stay tonight, but I inherited these, they need a good home." She was pressing a parcel into his hand. "E-mail me; tell me if you want them. See you soon."

The parcel contained her e-mail address and a pair of Lindstrom side cutters.

"She's been doing her homework on you. Are you serious? Because **she** means business!"

Out Of The Frying Pan

{Just that}

The job interview was going well, but Naomi knew not well enough to lift herself out of the ruck. She needed something else; as the thought crystallised, the opportunity was presented.

he job interview was going well, but Naomi knew not well enough to lift herself out of the ruck. She needed something else; as the thought crystallised, the opportunity was presented.

"You're office skills obviously make you well suited for the job Miss Wright. But that is true for several other interviewees. Why should we choose you?"

"My degree is in Electronics."

The panel sat up, leaned forward and consulted notes, made notes.

"You have a BA in History," interrupted The Chair consulting her file. "History and Development."

"History and Development of Electronics from the Transistor to the Controller. My University only offers BA, but my degree is a scientific one."

The secretary consulted her Master Copies.

"I'm sorry Ma'am. The briefing form is only set up to accept a maximum of twenty-five characters. Miss Wright's degree is in Electronics; her Office Management qualification is a Post Graduation Diploma."

"Can the form be revised so that this sort of misunderstanding never occurs again?"

"I've noted it as a priority."

Quickly, before the meeting got side-tracked further, Naomi enlarged on her original answer,

"When clients ring in with queries, I will understand the basics of their problem, and I will be able to direct them to the correct area of expertise, from day one."

She got the job.

Despite her appointment beginning the following Monday Naomi spent the rest of that week at work, easing herself into place.

At only four months pregnant, the girl emerging from behind her desk and offering her hand could easily have hidden behind well-designed clothes. She chose instead to wear her skirt low and her top high, revealing in all its glory her level of pride in her condition.

"Hello, I'm Melanie."

"Naomi, congratulations." She nodded significantly: "The reason for leaving?"

"Yes but doctor's orders to leave so early." She indicated the Cancer Charity donations box, prominently positioned at the front of her desk as if she was introducing a friend: "Would you be so kind?"

Naomi obliged.

"I'm in remission. Cancer treatment takes many patients through the menopause. I'm a miracle mum, so they're taking no chances. Come on; I'll show you where everything is. Call him James when you're alone with him, Mr Wright at all other times." She picked up a stout leather-bound book with gold corner protectors. "Your PA's Panic List, goes with you everywhere, to the toilet, to your bed. If you're in someone else's bed, even if you shouldn't be, it should be."

The twinkle in the PA's eye made Naomi laugh.

"This filing cabinet has all the Company's Product's Specif--"

Item by item Melanie led her through the hand-over, Naomi all the while making copious notes in a Black n' Red A6 hardback notebook.

"Erm -- Herself. Mrs Wright, I mean. She can be a bit difficult, just be professional, she'll come around eventually."

"How do you mean?"

"She's a bit insecure, thinks every girl he meets is after James. It's not true, and even on the odd occasion when it is, he behaves impeccably. She has nothing to fear."

"Oh."

"Except from herself, she could drive him away herself with her paranoia. It's just that with you being so --"

"With me being so what?"

"Never mind. Wear a Wedding Ring, be unavailable, that'll help. Be professional, and everything will be okay!"

A few days later she had the first meeting with Herself.

"So you're the new PA."

Naomi looked up. Recovering quickly from the shock of meeting her twin, she replied normally,

"Yes Ma'am, can I help you?"

"I'm Mrs Wright."

Naomi now understood what Melanie had been going to say, 'with you being so similar to look at!'

"Oh how do yo--"

"Where is he?"

"He's in the Works, doing his ro--"

"Tell him I called in. I won't be home tonight; I'm staying in town. I'll see him at the Wallace's tomorrow."

"Where will I say you're staying?"

After gurning a look that could curdle milk, Mary Wright turned and left.

It was less than a month later that Naomi realised that she had fallen for her boss. She coped by only working late when he wasn't around, and being ultra professional in everything they did together. Nevertheless, there were opportunities where only drastic action could ensure no problems.

James put his head around the door,

"Naomi, this trip to Leeds next week."

"You have two appointments, Tuesday and Thursday."

"It was the Wednesday that I was thinking about --"

Naomi too had been thinking about the Wednesday,

"I'll come home on Tuesday night, go back on Thursday morning. I think that would be best."

He looked relieved but sombre. That was a mood that was more than matched in her own breast by the prospect of forty hours away from him.

"It would remove a potential source of problems, yes."

"Fine, I'll see to it."

Despite Naomi's care and pedantically professional approach, Mary Wright's attitude towards her went from bad to dreadful.

Then the fateful day, outside the works, Mary's big red car braked hard to a halt in front of her, and the window dropped,

"Get in!"

"Oh, I--"

"Get in!"

Obediently Naomi climbed in alongside Mrs Wright. Her sense of disquiet was immediately heightened by the speed at which her employer's wife took off, and the aggressive way she forced the car through the traffic onto the bypass.

When the button on her door thudded down, Naomi really began to get worried.

"Mrs Wright, where are we going?"

"You'll never get him."

"Who?"

"I've sorted you, right at this minute you're goose is being burnt behind you!"

Naomi registered the metaphor mix, but only in passing,

"Please stop the car and let me out, Mrs Wright."

"You're selling the new chip to the Tigers in the lounge of the Falcon's Rest right now. And when you say you weren't there, you were with me in my car, guess what I'll say. My husband's safe from your clutches forever!"

"He always was! I don't steal other girl's men, please stop the car, and let me out."

"You'll never get him after you've sold the company's best advance for decades."

"Mrs Wright, I'm not stealing your man. And even if I was, what you're doing is--" Naomi killed 'silly,' and changed it to: "Not going to get me sacked. We haven't got a new chip; it doesn't work."

"Yes it does, I've tested it on my breadboard at home myself, and it works perfectly."

Mrs Wright swerved into the clear inside lane, and put her foot down, overtaking several cars motoring fast in the outside lane.

She accelerated into Points On Her Licence Territory down the long hill towards the river. The speed built rapidly towards danger level for the awkward turn at the bottom of the hill.

"It doesn't work. We scrapped it and wrote the R&D costs off at this morning's board meeting -- Mrs Wright! Slow down!" Naomi's explanation was accompanied by her eyes widening as the bend approached. Mary Wright screamed like a cacodemon, took her hands from the wheel, and attacked Naomi's face with her vicious claws.

A loud bang announced the bursting of a front tyre.

The car swerved off the road, smashed its nearside front wing into a tree, and careered on through the roadside obstacles into the field beyond. The last thing Naomi remembered as the car began to tumble and spin was the other girl taking a header through the windscreen, between the airbags.

* * *

From the safety of her coma, and hospital bed, Naomi repeatedly reviewed her performance over the weeks leading up to the car crash as if watching an interesting film. Although unaware of the fact, she had been doing it for a long time.

Every so often, disembodied voices intruded.

A gentle, quiet voice speaking reassuringly,

"We need to operate on you Mary, you're going to be fine, but we have to do it now."

The bright, loud, jolly-hockey-sticks voice always got through

"Mary it's Julie and Anne. We're going to get you ready --"

Julie and Anne constantly talked to Mary while somebody

washed and cleansed Naomi, moving her about and making her comfortable.

"Right Mary, that's you done we'll come back and see you before we go off shift."

The gentle quiet voice got through because he said the important word,

"Don't get a shock James, her face is very swollen and the stitches very obvious, but in three months or so, there will be barely a mark."

She felt warm and relaxed at the mention of her Boss's name. If only he weren't married. He was a lovely man, just not her lovely man. Then his voice, she wallowed in the sound.

"Oh!"

"I promise you, barely a mark."

"Will she look very different?"

"She's a natural blonde, so her hair will be the same, her nose will be a little smaller, and her lips may possibly pout a bit more, so there will be some differences from the photographs Melanie gave - us -- to --- work ---- from "

The disembodied voices intruded again.

"We need you formally to identify the other girl. If you can, she was severely disfigured. We have her passport and other personal effects, but she doesn't seem to have any family."

"No, she hasn't"

She relaxed, warm and safe in the sound of his voice.

"Husband? She was wearing a ring."

"Camouflage, I think."

James's voice always got through,

"What about the coma?"

"Question her constantly, even if she doesn't answer she'll be trying to formulate answers, you will be making her brain work. Bring in her favourite CDs to play to her, read her letters to her, she'll -- come ---- back -----"

And,

"I'm going to raid your personal possessions, bring things in to aggravate you. Torment -- you --- into coming ----- back ------"

A new voice, formal, official, vaguely sinister,

"Why was your PA driving your wife's car Mr Wright?"

"I don't know. Was she?"

"Oh yes. Although your wife was found tying to get out through the driver's door, she had been in the passenger seat. Her door was jammed. The branches that caused the injuries to her face came in the passenger side and the injuries to her left leg were caused by the incursion of the tree into the passenger foot-well. Besides she has the characteristic left-shoulder to right-hip chest-bruising of a passenger seatbelt. Your PA has no pre-mortem bruising at all; she wasn't wearing her seatbelt."

"I've got no idea."

The disembodied voices faded.

A face nuzzled up close, lover close,

"Naomi listen to me. I'm going to call you Mary from now on. I know you can hear me, even though you can't reply yet. I know you can hear me because you react, you're tense, and then I speak, and you relax. So when you hear anyone say 'Mary,' it's you we're talking to. Don't challenge it, just answer. It's for your safety; there are some ruthless people who are rather cross with my PA. So you are my wife, not my PA."

The pressure eased on her then increased again to comfortable, intimate level.

"Now Mary, pay attention, I'm going to read some of your e-mails off your computer. From Roger and Beverley. Do you know these people personally? Have you met them? Will they know you if you meet them again? This one's from Roger, about your new job. He begins, Hi Jiggletits. Is that your tag? I wouldn't dare say this if I knew for certain you were listening, but it is most appropriate! Mind I'd probably put Pretty in front of it. I'm going to! They all begin Hi Pretty Jiggletits, even -- the --- ones ---- from ------ girls ------"

Even his voice slipped to disembodied eventually; presently she slept.

* * *

"Mary --- Mary -- There - is a Mr Lee here to see you. He has insisted on seeing you, even though I have told him you are in a

224

coma."

"Your wife may well be in a coma Mr Wright, but she can almost certainly hear me." There was a short pause when he resumed speaking Mr Lee was noticeably closer. "Mrs Wright, I have come to return something your husband's PA stole from your company and tried to sell to my company. Item is rubbish; it does not work. The whole exercise was an attempt to make us lose face. We did not lose face because we are returning the useless item."

A package plumped onto the bed,

"You may ponder on why your husband's PA did this. I think there is much loss of face in that."

"Did you crash the car to avoid losing face, Mr Lee?" James's voice was cold.

"At time I did not know item was useless. As things turned out, any further action became un-necessary."

"I'll take that as 'No, but I would have done!'"

With a struggle, Naomi opened her eyes. She was lying on top of the bed with her left leg encased in scaffolding, which explained the pain. Several bolts seemed to enter her shin through the skin. The shock at the obvious level of damage only hit several hours later, for the moment she concentrated on the immediate problem. The useless blueprints, negatives and a dozen or so prototype chips lay on her bed. She jerked her hand vaguely in the general direction of the little black beetles,

"Keep--" the hoarse whisper died in a racking cough. "Keep--" she coughed: "Keep a chip." She coughed again. "You paid for't," she whispered with an effort, her voice harsh with lack of use.

"Yes, you are correct." He picked one up. "We should have something to remind us." He strode to the door and then turned back. "We are not barbarians Mrs Wright; we did not crash your car; there would never be any intention to hurt you gratuitously. Had we needed to kill you to achieve other objectives, you would just be collateral damage, nothing personal. As it is, I have assisted your return to your husband. If anything I deserve thanks."

"Thank you." Naomi stopped, her body convulsed with angry

grating coughs.

James held her, comforting her.

"Sorry, you were offered things for sale." She murmured finally.

Mr Lee gave a deep bow.

"You're back!" James hadn't taken his eyes off her throughout the whole exchange.

"Yes."

Mr Lee nodded and left. Through the windows, the pair watched their visitor's progress outside and into his car, in silence. Only when he had driven away did James speak,

"How long? I mean how long have you been aware?"

Again the angry grating coughs hindered her, eventually, perseverance enabled her to get the speech out.

"Dunno, it's like a dream -- I try to grasp it, and it disappears. But I remember being told I was -- Mary from now on. And now I have been told graphically why -- why I have taken your wife's identity. I just don't understand how the mix-up occurred in the first place."

"I was still in the airport when it happened; they got to Melanie first. Mary never wore jeans and top; she'd most likely done it to impersonate you. Melanie was told that Mary's car had crashed and there were two blondes aboard who were so badly injured that they could not be identified. As soon as Melanie heard that one girl was wearing jeans, the other a business suit, she jumped to the wrong conclusion."

"Oh."

"Mary telephoned me, just before she picked you up, and accused you of selling out. Something stank in the closet because you knew the chip didn't work. By the time I got home, I'd discovered the truth about the attempted sale to Mr Lee. I knew that my innocent PA was in trouble with people who deal in only one kind of solution, except that she was already dead. It was only when I saw you that I realised there had been a mistake of identification. Mary was beyond help; you weren't."

"Oh. Thank you -- Erm -- Yes it is my tag -- and no I don't mind you putting Pretty in front of it -- James, when can I get out of here?"

"You will need building up, physiotherapy. You've been away a long time. Even with the excellent care you've had, it will be a while before you can walk again for example. But I can hire in the expertise; I've already done it. So how about this afternoon? I've had the necessary modifications done downstairs. Hospital bed, hot and cold running-nurses called Briggs, the odd hoist or two. You know, nothing unusual for a drawing room."

Naomi giggled.

"We can certainly manage it before the weekend. But it will have to be after you learn the layout of the house, and after talking to the Police. They want to know how come the two of you were in the car. Why my PA was driving. Can you handle that?"

"I've got no choice now -- I'll have to handle it."

Although the silly cough still caught her by surprise occasionally, Naomi managed to talk reasonably normally by taking slow breaths and speaking softly.

* * *

"-- so can you tell us what she was doing?" Asked the Sergeant. "Why she picked you up? And generally what happened?"

"I can tell you what happened, but not why. Because I have no idea. She had no reason to do any of it. I was going shopping, and suddenly she scrunched to a halt in front of me and ordered me into the car. When I queried she insisted. I just got in; I didn't want a scene, then she roared off. She was driving very fast, and I was getting worried and said so. I asked her where we were going. She ignored me and began talking about the new chip. I told her we'd written it off at the Board meeting and she went berserk in the car. She went for me, with both hands off the wheel, and we crashed. That's all I know."

The policemen stood up, preparing to leave,

"Why would a duff chip make her so mad? It's a common occurrence in R&D, I believe."

"Sadly yes," said James.

"What kind of chip was it?"

"Controller, like a whole computer on a chip. For washing

227

machines, TVs and such. Depending on the instruction set. Watches, central heating."

"Did you know a controller has been offered for sale on the Web?"

"Our controller?"

The policeman shrugged with open palms.

"We cannot raise a response. Which would be perfectly reasonable if the seller had died.

"I didn't know there was one for sale on the web."

"Have you lost one?"

"Not at yesterday's audit. A chip itself would be of little value, and nothing at all without its datasheet, it's the print negatives that are worth money. But it doesn't work, so even they are useless."

"Not if somebody didn't know that the chip didn't work," said the younger policeman. He looked at his superior who nodded, and they bade their farewells.

"I think that will be all Mrs Wright, Mr Wright, thank you for your help."

* * *

Less than three hours later Naomi was being unloaded from an ambulance into the Wright house, and the care of a pair of nurses. These turned out to be a middle-aged, childless married couple, Briggs and Mrs, who fussed over her like clocker hens.

The drawing room had been converted temporarily into a one-bed intensive-care ward. The original furniture was still there but neatly stored away to one side under covers which gave an immediate indication of the size of the room.

"I've added disabled bars to the downstairs bathroom; I'll take you along, you can try them out."

"You'll do no such thing, that's our job," said Mrs.

James only just managed to get in front of them in time to lead the way to the bathroom by moving very quickly. He wasn't to know it was un-necessary, Naomi had learned her part well and already knew the way.

* * *

Several weeks of care and physiotherapy later, James came in to see Naomi one evening; he was dressed for a formal dinner. He grinned at her, sitting in her wheelchair, and said,

"You get your metalwork out tomorrow."

"Something I'm not looking forward to, but afterwards, when the pain settles down, yes."

"Afterwards, I've got something special lined up for you. A nice surprise--"

"I don't like surprises."

"You'll like this one I promise. Are you sure you want me to go to this client's do?"

"Yes, it's business, we need all we can get without the chip."

"I'll be very late back, don't wait up, I'll peep in on you when I get home."

She beckoned him close and whispered,

"Where did Mary keep her breadboard?"

"On her bench in her study, it's all there, just as she left it. Why?"

"She said the chip worked. She'd tested it herself."

"It sometimes does work on a breadboard; it's when you connect it up with other components that it fries itself."

"She would have thought of that, surely? But she wasn't lying; she believed it worked. I thought I'd take a look."

"Feel free; the key is the little gold one on your household set." He stood up, speaking normally: "Don't strain for anything, ring for Briggs. He'll give me gyp if you strain to reach something and hurt yourself."

* * *

Briggs caught Naomi propelling herself along the hall,

"It's okay, I'm not sloping off somewhere," she said as she saw the look in his eye. "I'm just going to do some research in my study."

"It's not that Madam. Mrs will give me grief if you come to any harm. I need to know where you are, so I can come running if necessary."

"I'm fine."

"Let me open the door for you."

She proffered the keys, with the little gold coloured one standing proud.

"This one?"

"Yes."

"Cocoa? In about half an hour?"

"Yes please." She surveyed the room and the large workbench that took up one entire wall. "Make it an hour."

Whatever else Mary was, she had been a punctilious worker.

She believed in having everything to hand. The workbench was comprehensively stocked with everything Naomi needed from the simplest resistor, right up to and including a digital camera to photograph any new circuit she designed. When she fired up the computer, the market leader Circuit Design and PCB Creation program opened, inviting her to review recent work. Mary's notebook, still open at the last entry, detailed her research in meticulous detail. Within minutes, reading her notes had Naomi up to speed on the project, and able to examine closely the circuit Mary had been working on.

She saw an anomaly that could explain what she was looking for immediately.

The stores even included, still sealed in their antistatic wrappers, several of the dodgy chips. Naomi had fried quite a few of them by the time Briggs reappeared bearing cocoa. Her writing was totally unlike Mary's, so she carefully recorded her results in a new notebook, one of several in the well-stocked stores, and locked Mary's work safely away from casual, or even suspiciously prying eyes.

* * *

"I did peep in on you as usual last night," said James over breakfast, with Briggs and Mrs still fussing over them like new chicks. "You seemed dead out."

"I was dead out."

"Dick Jepson was at the do last night. I danced with his wife, Elaine; she is a Detective Chief Inspector. She told me off the record that your evidence has virtually closed the case. We'll be told formally in due course when they do it officially. Apparently, there were witnesses to my PA picking you up and the car crash. They already knew everything you told them, you merely confirmed it."

Later when they were alone, he filled in the vital details,

"Nothing else was mentioned, the odd loose end like, why she picked you up, is being ignored apparently. I think she knows considerably more than she's told us, so if ever the skeleton starts rattling, zip up tight and ring for the solicitor. Say nowt until you have Bernard Lock or Dave Possett, right there beside you. But it's still case closed."

"Well, that's one less thing to worry about. What's this surprise that someone who hates surprises is going to like?"

"Later, after metalwork."

* * *

Naomi pushed herself down the corridor towards the waiting room, for the first time without a leg sticking out like a bowsprit. James welcomed her with a grin,

"How do you feel, you look great."

"Great! Tender, itchy, prickly, but that'll all pass. Surprise?"

He took over the propulsion and whisked her out to the car, and privacy,

"How would you like to go on honeymoon this afternoon?"

"Provisionally that sounds nice, with whom?"

"I meant married too."

"Mandated, to whom?"

James produced a piece of paper,

"This Special Licence entitles Naomi Mary Wright, spinster, to marry, anywhere and anywhen, James Wright, bachelor."

"I fell for you completely at our first meeting; consequently I would not even have dared kiss you before Mary died, for fear of where it might lead. Now that you are available, my answer is yes. Yes please!"

"Oh -- Good! Erm, that's perfect."

They smiled at each other in silence for several minutes.

231

Presently James went to stow the important document back in his pocket.

"I know strictly speaking it should read widower, but I wanted to leave as faint a trail as possible."

"Hence the wrong name."

"You will answer to your legal given name. Naomi. You can have as many others in there alongside it as you like."

"This afternoon would be fine, but have I got time to buy a white outfit?"

"Couple of hours, it's not necessary you know."

"I know that even with a scarred face--"

"The scars are temporary, they're already fading, and they'll be gone by Christmas. Before!"

Naomi began again,

"I know that even with." She waved across her face. "A twenty-four-year old virgin is a rare beast, but until you take me to bed tonight, I am one. I'm entitled to white, and I would like to."

"Oh, sorry, I never gave it a thought, just assumed -- Are you quite happy that you and virginity are to part company tonight?"

"Oh yes! I expect it will hurt my leg as well as -- Which will make my first time a little bit different, and simultaneously a little bit the same. Yes, no question!"

"Well, in that case, my darling, certainly. Where to, Bride, Wedding?"

"The Great Day please, they've got an elegant white cocktail dress that I really like."

* * *

"Congratulations Mrs Wright. Mr Wright, you may kiss the bride."

* * *

"Where are you taking me on honeymoon? And what about Briggs and Mrs?"

"Briggs and Mrs are looking after the livestock and the garden. I told them the truth, the bit about going on honeymoon, except I fudged it a bit, I said second honeymoon, which is only a half lie--"

"For you it's true."

He nodded,

"Mrs practically pushed me out of the door. We are going to spend a week leisurely touring the Two Star hotels of the West Country, looking for your Wedding Present."

"Lovely. What are we looking for?"

"Whatever takes your fancy."

"Ah, right. What do you want?"

"I've got what I want," he replied, waving generally at her.

"How about a new World Beating Chip?"

"That would be a nice cherry on top."

"The useless chip works."

"What?"

"It's perfectly good. It works, but at three Volts, not five. Mary's circuit was still set up on her breadboard. She'd put diodes in the supply to prevent back-EMF when she switched off. So she'd never run it at the full five Volts, always a couple of diode-drops short. I set it up with outside components. At five Volts it fries." She graphically demonstrated with unfolding hands. "It's slow, unstable and hot enough to burn your finger at four Volts, but it works. At three Volts it's stable and fast. It works, and it stays cool. Happy Wedding Day, husband."

Nobody Loves a Traffic Warden

Bill Boles was horrified.

"How long?"

"Until the painters get out to paint the sign in the space."

"How long has Joe Public to think he has a parking space, only to be slapped with a thirty pound fine because he's in an unmarked disabled bay?"

"Until a week on Tuesday, but the bay is marked, the metal plate is up."

"Those metal plates are smaller than a stamp. And the reason for that is to make sure that nobody sees them. To extract money from motorists, who basically haven't done anything wrong. Just been caught out in a simple error. It's despicable, and you can tell that poisoned troll in head office I said so!" His boss waited until the irate traffic warden had stormed off out of earshot, as imperiously as a full limp would allow, before replying,

"No Bill, I don't want you fired, I need you."

The following morning Bill clocked on early and patrolled the source of his anger. A slender little white van slid into the parking place as it did every working day morning. He strode over and peered in under the peak of his cap, at the gorgeous little russet-haired dolly, behind the wheel.

"I'm sorry miss, but they've changed the usage of this space, it's a disabled bay as from today." He could see the panic in her eyes. "Do you have a blue badge?"

"No. Where am I going to park, I always park here."

"Yes miss I know, I'm sorry -- Do you ever leave before six?"

"Hardly ever."

"Go around the corner and down the cut to the coffee shop; I'll meet you there."

When she arrived, Bill showed her the small oddly angled space at the end.

"If there's nobody else in the next space you can reverse in here; it's an all-day space." He waved at the next space. "That's only a two hour one."

"Thank you."

"Of course you can't get out until the next space is empty again."

"After six!"

"Yes."

Bill spent all day ensuring that nobody got caught out by the change of use. Most motorists were ruefully grateful for having been saved thirty pounds, some were disgruntled or abusive, and Councillor Sheepson, viciously offensive.

"I park here every day, and I will continue to do so."

"You have not parked there during the working day for six months at least that I know of, and it is now a disabled bay." He pointed at the lamp-post, and the tiny notice secured to it, high above their heads: "Please park your car somewhere else."

"You monkey, upstart monkey, do you know who I am? Go away and leave important people to get on with their business."

"I know exactly who you are Councillor, and if you leave your car there, I will write you out a ticket now."

"You insolent peasant, I'll have your badge!"

Bill produced his dictation recorder and showed her it was working,

"I don't think so. I have just shown Councillor Sheepson that I am recording this conversation. Move the car Councillor." He slid the recorder back into his pocket, turned away and limped off to check the other cars in the row. When he returned, the disabled bay was vacant.

Jane Mitton locked her little van up, thanked her traffic

warden, and left him at a run. On arriving in the front shop, she made a fuss of her favourite, before passing through into the surgery behind, and plunging into her day.

From time to time, as necessary, she reminded herself not to get involved, not to let things become personal.

On her way home, she felt sick as she surveyed the now empty stall, which only that morning had housed her favourite.

She had singularly failed not to get involved, yet again.

It's no use, she thought, I couldn't have. It wouldn't have been fair. But that didn't dull the pain, not for a single wag.

At home, her little bed-sit room was warm, welcoming, but as always, lonely. There was little prospect of that changing either. She was usually so shattered after her nominally eight-hour shift, which was seldom that short, that she rarely ventured out. She preferred to curl up in bed, with a good book, rather than try to watch television, and wake up in the small hours in her chair. That, or go out to the pub, and fall asleep across a table full of glasses. When she did allow herself to dream of Mr Right changing things, more often than not, much more, he was an older man with kind eyes, who walked with a limp and wore a traffic warden's uniform.

Bill carefully weighed out the puppy's food,

"You will wolf this off in seconds and be looking for more, but you are not getting it. I want a sleek, healthy Labrador, not a pumpkin that can barely lift its belly off the floor." The dog's name tag read Goldie on one side, and Bill's address, added that day while he waited, on the other. He wasn't entirely happy about 'Goldie,' but the dog already responded to it when he bought him, so Goldie it was.

"Nobody loves a traffic warden, do they? Well wrong, because you love me don't you? Even if it's just because I provide food." The thought that, perhaps, after this morning, someone else might have similar feelings, he stifled before it could do any harm. Taking solace in the already muscular tail, thumping furniture, as the dog replied.

Every morning, when she parked in her new regular place, Jane looked for her traffic warden, to thank him, she lied to herself, as she scurried off to work. Every night, he wasn't there either, but that was to be expected, she never arrived back before six.

On his way into work every morning, Bill checked Jane's empty space. Several times during the day, and every night on his way home, he checked her slender little van. For weeks they watched for each other, yet failed to see each other, despite walking straight past each other, on several occasions.

In the supermarket, while heaving her loaded trolley about on her monthly visit to stock up straight from work, Jane hardly noticed a man in a tweed jacket with a thinly stocked basket, waiting patiently for his bacon to be especially thick sliced.

In the library, with Goldie secured outside, Bill paid scant attention to the young nurse he gave way to, to let her carry research volumes to her already loaded place.

The evening walk through the park became a ritual, with Goldie clocking up the many miles he needed daily, by quartering the grass and shrubberies and re-asserting his dominance at every corner. Occasionally near home, with Goldie's enthusiastic permission, Bill took a detour; his gorgeous redhead's slender van was invariably in its place, but there was never a sign of its owner.

Then a tanker flushed illegally at sea; Jane had barely arrived home when the telephone rang.

"Hello."

"Jane, it's Morag."

"Hi, Boss."

"You know that oil spill off Souter Point?"

"Oh, we've got oiled-up sea-birds have we?"

"Dozens of them, with more on their way, every veterinary practice in the area is inundated, can you come?"

Jane grabbed her coat and checked that her car keys were in the pocket.

"On my way. Bye."

"Thanks, bye."

She locked up behind her; her handbag, still on the tiny trolley-table table and totally uncharacteristically forgotten in the crisis, slowly keeled over onto its side.

When she arrived at work, the vet greeted her nurse with relief,

"Oh, you're here Jane. Great. Basically just grab one and start scrubbing, they've sent us loads of detergent with the birds, thank goodness, so we're in with a chance."

Jane surveyed the dark glooping lumpy mess,

"Oh my, what's birds and what's not?"

"Yeah. We'll lose some, save the healthiest first, that way we'll be most successful."

Suited up, Jane thrust her hand into the filthy cauldron, plucked out a wriggling lump and set to work, scrubbing. Sporadically, as they managed to get on site, the other nurse, the receptionist, and the Saturday Girl joined Jane and her Boss.

Presently someone switched on the lights, and shortly after, another load of birds arrived.

Yet another arrived with the dawn,

"That's your quota. We've only brought what we think you can save; the dead are piling up on Marsden Beach. When you've done them you can stand down, and thanks."

* * *

Morag loaded the last cage into her van and peeled off her coverall,

"Thanks, everyone, go home. I'll drop these off on my way. I'm closing until Monday. Thank you, that was a gargantuan effort, well done."

It wasn't until Jane was preparing to leave, and went to pick it up, that she remembered where her handbag was.

While approaching her van, her remorse at how many birds they hadn't saved, was given an even more jagged edge by the certain knowledge that she'd have a parking ticket, and be blocked in. There was no way the space next to her would be free, mid-morning, on a Saturday.

No handbag, just keys! How do I get home? She pushed the thought aside; she might not be blocked in.

She was.

"And how much on the ticket, I wonder?" she said out loud. A big, shaggy, blonde head with a shiny, black nose and bright, alert eyes popped around from the far side of her van and looked at her. A moment later her favourite came bounding up to her, barking, whining, and wagging his tail,

"Goldie!" She crouched down and hugged him: "What are you doing here? It's lovely to see you. I've been up all night losing seabirds, fighting to save them, but losing too many of them, and I'm blocked in, and by now I'll have a ticket."

"No Miss." A man limped from behind her van: "Goldie Sit! I knew there must be something up; I bought you a day permit, there's no ticket."

"You're my traffic warden! In a tweed jacket."

"And you're my gorgeous redhead." He touched her hat: "But it's hidden under a nurse's cap." He surveyed the rest of the uniform. "A veterinary nurse's cap."

The sobs racked her body.

"What's the matter?" When she didn't answer immediately, he enveloped her into his embrace and laid his cheek tenderly on the top of her head. Her face came up, little by little and slowly, and he kissed her forehead, her eyes, and, as she flowed against him, finally her mouth. She clung to him fiercely, kissing him back, as the story about the birds poured out, and losing Goldie, and fearing she had a ticket, and --

"Thank you, for everything. I need to get home, but I haven't any money, I just dashed out. You couldn't possibly--"

"Not even remotely possibly, but I live five minutes walk away. In a few hours when you're rested, we'll come back for your van. We'll get a takeaway in, and discuss where we go from here."

"I need a bath."

"And some TLC, with flowers. That florist has a large bouquet waiting for you; it just needs making up. At my home, there's a bath, and breakfast and a bed. It's my bed, but as that's where I want you to sleep from now on, you could road test it by yourself today, see how well the prospect of sharing it with me pleases you.”

"Oh -- Oh -- Oh, all right then, Mr Caring Traffic Warden. Bouquet. Bath. Breakfast. Bed. Recover van. Takeaway and some serious talk about where I'm sleeping from now on. Yes. Please take me home."

Green

Buy stones in bags; they call them seeds,
And bury them in soil.
Water and warmth, that's all it needs,
And up the green shoots toil.

How can this be, from dead to quick?
Trick of life? Don't kid me!
The truth's much darker, t'is no trick,
It's ma-gic ak-chal-ly.

Before 21 June 1999, I Was Immortal
{Now I know different, and I am considering the options}

Paradise and hell are regarded as opposites, obverse and reverse, seeing face to face or through a glass darkly, one to be striven for, the other avoided, depending on the circumstances.

Whether one can be experienced without knowledge of the other is debatable; their state of total separation, as distinct, disjoint entities, is in serious doubt.

Inside the mind, at least, we can have occasions where they meet and shake hands.

Consider the case of being able to prove a truth that you don't believe.

The set of integers and the set of multiples of {say} ten are in one to one correspondence. This is because, and means, each member of one can be paired off with precisely one from the other using a global relationship. In layman's terms, one to one correspondence means that they contain the same number of members.

Proof:

Set of Integers	Set of Tens	Pairing Relationship (x 10)
1	10	1 x 10 = 10
2	20	2 x 10 = 20
3	30	3 x 10 = 30
and so on until	and so on until	and so on until
∞	∞	∞ x 10 = ∞

This proof is totally valid. Face to face Paradise has been achieved.

Unfortunately, however, every member of the tens is also in the integers, but the integers contains {merely for example, there are infinite more}, the number 2, and the tens does not, so how come they have the same number of members?

Hell has come around to bite your leg, darkly!

Escalate the thoughts to the other end of the scale.

The Universe, according to Hoyle, is more of the same forever, expanding and spontaneously re-generating as it goes.

Hawking, however, says it started with a Big Bang, and will either stop expanding and collapse back in on itself, or swell up indefinitely, cool down, and eventually become cold and dead. The outcome depending on whether the Universe contains more or less than the critical mass required for gravity, eventually, to stop the expansion.

A third theory has discrete, complete Universes, bumbling around in time and space, each the result of its own individual Big Bang, and the next could happen anywhen, and anywhere!

So what happens when I die?

Is that it?

Do I live on only in the memories of those who knew me, for a brief, bright flicker, while they live? I reject this on the frail premise that I refuse to believe in something so pointless.

The alternatives, however, are, if anything, even more frightening.

Another Big Bang, which just happens to begin up my left nostril!

A steady state Universe that regenerates forever!

That collapses in upon itself or expands to dark, cold, empty

I specifically choose to grace the last description with neither noun nor full stop, as neither is suitable.

And with my Immortal Soul witnessing it all, as hell bites my leg off, face to face!

Out of all this, I find Utopia in ignorance. There can be only one hell worse than not knowing anything, and that is knowing everything.

So my Utopia is that, despite my brain, compared to Knowledge-Infinite, I know next to nothing, not quite darkly, and strive as I may, I will always reach not quite face to face, and thus having avoided my two worst hells, I sleep at night.

The Visit to Penshaw

My boy was running up the stairs calling to me. He was excited.

"Come on Ted. Get ready. We're going out."

"Oh no!" I replied: "Not another trip to town to get my forehead bashed by shopping bags."

"You won't get bashed by shopping bags. Not today." He picked me up and sat me straight so that he could push the stuffing back in through the tear in my belly button. "We're not going to town." He straightened up my loose eye, suddenly I could see properly again. "We're going to Penshaw. To walk up to the monument."

"Oh no. I'm going to be lost again."

"You always say that. And it was only once. I only left you on the Metro once."

"Once? You left me on the Metro, and on the big train."

"That was a new once. I've only lost you once."

"Once on the bus to town, once on the bus from town. Once in a taxi, once in Granddad's car. Once--"

"Oh shut up, stop moaning and get ready."

I toured carefully around my paws murmuring to myself,

"Once at the supermarket. Once at the Museum, once at the Fair, once --" I'd been around my paws four times. How many new onces is four times around a Teddy Bears paws?

I was grabbed up and taken downstairs. Bumping down the stairs like Christopher Robin and Pooh. My loose eye wriggled out, and I could see where I was going and where I'd been at the same time. Again. It makes me feel very strange going upstairs to get down. I was glad when my boy noticed and popped it back in, and made everything look normal again.

Our Mam drove us to Penshaw. She said you could see for miles from the top, and you can. Right inland to the motorway, right out to sea the other way.

My boy sat me down on a tuft of grass, at the foot of one of the pillars and I watched my family playing with a ball. Then a sheep came by and knocked me off my tuft of grass so that it could eat it. Of course, my loose eye slipped again. I could see the sea behind and the road in front, at the same time. It looked as if the ships were sailing across the road and the cars were driving along the sea.

Very silly.

My boy picked up his ball, and our Mam loaded him into the car and drove off through the waves.

It got dark, and a sheep lay down to munch its dinner again. Unfortunately, I was underneath it. Sheep don't wash as often as they should, and this one was long overdue for a bath.

"Do you mind getting up please, you're squashing me," I said.

"Sorry," she replied: "I'm a sheep; I don't understand what you're saying. I don't speak Baa."

"I speak Bear not Baa, and anyway how can I understand you, if you can't understand me?"

"Sorry," she repeated: "I'm a sheep; I don't understand what you're saying. I don't speak Baa."

"You've said that, can't you say something new?"

"Sorry," she repeated again: "I'm a sheep, I--

"Don't speak Baa, yes I know. When did you last have a bath?"

"Sorry, I'm a sheep, I--"

"Yes I know the rest--"

My interruption was itself interrupted, as the sheep got up and went away. A torch shone on me, and my boy said,

"Come on Ted, don't just lie there, you should have come home with us."

"It--"

"You do smell. What have you been rolling in?"

"It--"

"We've had to come all the way back for you."

"It--"

"Come on our Mam's waiting in the car for us."

I was bumped down the hill like Pooh, again, while my boy kept talking about how badly I smelled, and the trip home, and how badly I smelled, and how much he had enjoyed the visit to Penshaw, and how badly I smelled. At last, I managed to get some words in,

"It's once at Penshaw Monument as well now!"

Carole

{Mystery. Rather than Whodunit, this is a Howdunit. You have met Jim before Dear True Reader, in The Creation Of Chicago Lynes.}

"**B**oss! We've been hit."

Jim's door had burst open, and his deputy's agitated face was thrusting around it.

"Over the weekend we lost three litres of Tritium Oxide. It's not a clerical error, we've done a Sellafield."

"You're quite sure Simon?"

"Yes, Boss. It's the third time it's happened, so we made double check records, notes, photographs even. We hoped there was a clerical error that we could nail with the tighter checks. But there's no mistake. They were stolen over the weekend. Between six o'clock Friday night and six o'clock Monday morning. The checks have proved the theft, not the error. We even know which jar it went from. It's not a clerical error Boss, honest!"

Company Accountant, Jim Teale, nodded,

"It's okay, I know."

"What!"

"You'd better come in and si' down Simon. Shu' the door please."

The younger man did so.

"I found the first thef' las' Tuesday, in the accounts. I' took me until today to find the second. It's being covered up by a very sophisticated little snooper program massaging the figures by converting them back and forth between hex and decimal until the figures match on the computer."

"Using the decimal place throw-away?"

"As you say."

"Well how on Earth did you find them?"

"I check the paper records as well. Jus' because a clerk writes tha' they carried forward so much money or stock from one page to another, doesn' say they did, I check. The computer records balance perfectly courtesy of our little snooper, bu' the paper records don'. I think tha' the clerks are taking the computer printou' as true and either ignoring the mismatch, or they may be unaware of i'."

"Or the clerks are stea--"

"Tha' too is a possibility, each page balances, bu' the carry forwards have neatly los' nearly six litres of heavy water."

"And another three over the weekend."

"So you tell me."

"The Security Staff think they know who."

"So throw the book!"

"At the chairman's daughter? Who walked out of here carrying nothing more sinister than a case of Boule? Three litres is a small bucket."

* * *

The Security guard was nervous, but she was also brave, and adamant,

"The Leger entries show this is t'third time, Mr Teale-Sir. Eight weeks between t'first two, then a six-week gap, and t'photographs show exactly which bottle was emptied. I'm sorry Sir. There's no mistake."

"Okay. You've convinced me. We've los' i'. How much?"

"We can prove t'three, but we suspect nine, Sir."

"Okay, all nine litres. I'll go along with tha'."

"Sometime in t'six weeks beginning four weeks from now another bottle will go, Sir, my guess, how do we mark it?"

"It's already marked, it's radioactive," murmured Simon.

"Sir, what if she's drinking it?" Asked the guard.

They both looked at her astonished.

"Three litres! And anyway no-one would be daf' enough to drink carcinogenic water, surely?"

"They would if they didn't know Boss," argued Simon: "You can't tell. It looks like water, tastes like it, well it is water! It's heavy, but heavy is relative; a cupful of tritium oxide would only weigh a bit more than normal water, not like." He shrugged: "Twice as much, you wouldn't notice it."

"I' has been decided tha' she's guilty then has i'?"

"No Mr Teale-Sir. T'evidence says she is, but I don't believe it. Miss Carole's a strong personality, but she treats people right. I know her from t'First Aid Competition Team, she's nice, and she's straight! I'd been competing alongside her for weeks, but I didn't know who she was, other people did, but I didn't. She was just Carole who works in the office. Then she invited us all over to her little flat for tea on her birthday, and I found out who 'Carole who works in the office' really was."

"Why is she in the frame then?"

"It's just that on all three occasions she was in t'building shortly before t'loss was discovered, Sir, and on all three occasions she carried out her Dad's case of Boule. We haven't discovered another common factor, not yet."

"She'll have to be told." There was an ominous silence while the others considered the implications of Jim's statement. "We'll go public, tell everyone, bu' let's concoc' a feasible story, no' mentioning tritium."

"A company that doesn't know aspirin from bicarb is making sophisticated anti-cancer drugs; that's a public domain fact, Boss. It's vague enough if we just leave it at that, maybe just a hint at industrial espionage, but it's where our tritium's going, we're pretty sure."

"That'll have to do." Jim turned to the guard: "Thanks, Barnaby, you did a good job. Keep thinking on, jus' because you've found this much, let's no' assume tha' everything's known. Also, see if you can come up with any other angles tha' migh' give us clues. Clues either way, eliminating the innocen' often helps focus on a suspec'."

"Yes Mr Teale-Sir, I will."

Alone with Simon, Jim began outlining his response,

"Okay, tonigh' we comb administration with a Geiger counter, see if she lef' any traces."

"A case of Boule wouldn't hold water, and I doubt it would hold three litres even if there weren't any boules in it."

"I know, bu' we check anyway."

"Yes Boss, the lesson has been learned, from now on I always will -- You didn't tell Barnaby that you'd found the other six litres in the books."

"Need to know Simon, besides which, she did a good job finding i' herself, she deserves her thunder."

"Ah."

* * *

The broad spectrum Geiger counter exploded into furious noisy activity, as soon as Jim switched it on. The Chairman's office should have been a relatively radiation-free zone, but apparently not!

"Ge' Jessica in here! Now!"

The senior technician took one look at the reading and had everyone into protective clothes immediately. Then with a nod of agreement from Jim, she took over the search,

"Right! Turn the sensitivity down until we only hear something when we bump into it." Even on low sensitivity, a sporadic background clicking was in evidence. "Now quarter the room." As they approached the book benches at the side of the room, the counter once again went berserk. Turning the sensitivity down and down, allowed them to home in on the floor in front of the bench.

"Righ'," said Jim. "Every speck of ash, grain of pollen, and dus' mite vacuumed up off tha' floor, and the room sealed for decontamination. The story is tha' somewhere the chairman mus' have picked up contamination when he visited another factory. It's easily done anyway. No' a breath tha' we suspec' i' came from ours."

* * *

"The first rush-results are back from the lab Boss; they've isolated the radioactive source. It's probably tritium, and if so possibly our missing 3H. Or --" Simon was still reading the sheet, looking astonished.

"You think I'm no' going to like this. It's okay spi' i' ou'; nothing could be worse than Miss Beaumon' being a traitorous thief."

"Yes. It could bring the Company down."

"I wasn'' thinking of the Company, I was thinking of me!"

"Oh -- Sorry, I didn't know."

"Nobody does, and say now'! Please. Jus' -- It's essential tha' you know, in case I --"

"In case your heart gets in the way of your head, I know, and I won't say anything. It's not whether you'll like it or not, it's believe it or not. The alternative is radioactive wood."

"Go on."

"The radioactivity was concentrated in sawdust grains."

"Le' me guess, finely sawn, quality, fine-grained wood."

"Yes. Possibly some kind of hardwood, but fine-grained."

"Well, a' leas' we now know how our three litres of tritium oxide vanished into a little box tha' would have difficulty holding i'."

"Do we?"

"How do you crush a quar' into a pin' po'?"

"You can't, water's incompressible; that's the whole idea behind hydraulic systems."

"Bu' you can jus' pour i' in, perhaps no' the full quar', bu' -- like making an egg stand on its end, easy when you know how."

"Boss, are you feeling all right?"

"Well, a' leas' we now know she's no' drinking i'. Bu' is i' a purloined letter, or does she know she's carrying i'?"

A few minutes later,

"How long have you and Miss Beaumont been an item?"

"We're no'. I've go' i' bad Simon, never fel' this way abou' anyone before, well, no' since my teens anyway, bu' she's only half my age."

"I'd never have guessed, emotionally, outlook, you're young at heart. I had you down as middle-twenties."

"Add a decade. You should see the portrai' in the attic."

"It's probably the ballet."

"I didn' know you knew abou' the ballet."

"Everybody knows. That and the porn films; how does a shy person like you do them?"

"The shyness grew a tough skin behind the scenes a' Ballet School. I jus' forge' the camera is there and enjoy the experience."

"That comes across, the female half of the works have pictures of your butt on their bedroom wall, only a very few of 'em encased in ballet tights."

"Hmm! I'm quite chuffed -- Never mind as far as Miss Beaumont's concerned; I'll ge' over i' -- maybe."

"Why don't you give it a try, the age difference doesn't matter, sixteen or seventeen years is nothing and will get smaller with time."

"Wha' is this -- Are you playing Cupid?"

"I like her a lot. I don't believe for one second that she's a traitor. If I wasn't fixed up already I'd -- So I'd like to see her with somebody I respect, rather than that slimy git Harold."

"I think all the running comes from him, no' her."

"Dripping water Boss!"

"Hmm."

"And Barnaby informs me that in Miss Beaumont's picture, you're not wearing the tights."

* * *

Carole Beaumont tapped on his door and put her head around it.

"Mr Teale, I got a message that you wanted to see me."

"Yes please, Miss Beaumon'. Please come in, may I offer you coffee."

"Yes please."

The Company Trouble Shooter aggressively filed away his personal feelings for his young guest and over coffee outlined the problems that cutting-edge business had in keeping their R&D out of the hands of their competitors.

"Yes I know; Daddy worries about it all the time."

"Recently, a factory in some tropical Fiefdom tha' hasn' ye'

253

discovered the wheel began producing anti-cancer drugs tha' took us ten years to develop. They are selling them a' half the price i' costs us to make them, and that's before we recoup our research costs."

"Someone stole the formula?"

"Possibly, certainly the manufacturing technique, everything they needed. We are investigating, naturally."

"Of course."

"I wanted to tell you personally."

He stopped and waited, Carole Beaumont eyes narrowed as realisation dawned.

"You're investigating me?"

"Everyone, everyone on the payroll, and clients, visitors and family, and tha' includes you; I wanted to tell you personally. If it's any consolation, i' also includes me."

"Historically, the best spies were those most trusted; the wife is always the last to know; parents only think they know what their kids are up to and all that. Thank you for telling me first."

"I' means your movements will be checked, activities watched. You may sometimes be followed. If you think you're being stalked, ask, I will tell you if it's us." He looked at her over the top of his glasses with tipped head: "Jus' in case i' isn'."

"Yeah, right! Thank you."

"One other thing please Miss Beaumon'. Differen' people are being investigated to differen' depths; you and I are being watched much more closely than the boy tha' delivers the papers through your letter-box. When this comes up in conversation, listen more than you talk please, and I'd be grateful if anything interesting was subsequently relayed my way."

"Be a Management spy?" The beautiful eyes were narrowed with anger.

"I' is your company!"

Slowly the anger drained away, to be replaced by reluctant acquiescence.

* * *

Jim sat down beside the Chairman, and pedantically stirred a teaspoonful of brown sugar into his black coffee,

"Mr Beaumon', you're into Boule, aren' you. There's a se' in the Broadmoose Sale, I saw them yesterday. Liked them, jus' they seemed a bi' small."

"Did you buy them?"

"No, I waited to check with you firs'."

"I saw them too, they're small executive toys, not real boules, and call the game Pétanque, please Jim. Pétanque is played with boules. There are three or three and a spare in a set. Or multiples of course, and a cochonnet, which should not be painted, only stained, so the set in Broadmoose is wrong on at least three counts."

"Oh."

"I'll lend you a real set then if you decide you like it, you can buy your own later." Seeing the expression on his accountant's face Paul Beaumont continued, "It's okay I've got lots of sets, I'm always forgetting them, Carole's sick of being despatched to fetch them from the office. If I'm abroad, I have to buy a new set. I know I've packed them, know it, and when I go for them, I haven't. So I have to buy a new set. Crazy."

"Yes, Miss Beaumon' would be really sick if you sen' her home from abroad, jus' for your boules."

"She never comes with me on Pétanque trips. She nearly had to last time, she came to get them from the office and took them straight to the airport and gave them to me at check-in, another minute and she'd have been too late. And you know what, I lost that set, completely, had to buy another."

"How did you lose i'?"

"How do you lose anything travelling? One second it's there, the next it's gone."

"Do you lose many completely?"

"No just that one. The others I know I've packed, then discover I haven't, I always find them at home later, that's why I've got so many. I'll bring one in for you. I might even have one in my office now."

"Why do you keep them in the office?"

"I don't, I keep them in the car, Alice empties the car and brings them in, and I haven't the heart to tell her."

Jim understood immediately, his Boss' conscientious-to-a-fault PA would be devastated to discover that she had been doing something wrong.

    * * *

Jim and Simon were analysing their progress.

"Miss Beaumon' is definitely carrying the goods ou' of the factory. That's virtually proven."

"Yes, I'm sorry about that Boss."

"S-okay, we already knew. What's less clear is, does she know? There's a Pétanque club outing soon. Aler' Barnaby specifically for tha' weekend, bu' tell her to allow the thef', jus' if possible record who. My guess is Miss Beaumon' will be dispatched to ge' the boules from the office, possibly even take them straigh' to the airpor'. Let's arrange for them to be stolen, by a bag snatcher."

"Sneak thief boss. This is Carole Beaumont we are robbing, we want him to succeed, and live through it."

"Good point."

* * *

Carole saw her Dad drive into the airport car park, and walked over to greet him,

"Well, do I get dispatched to your office for your boules?"

"You don't, I put them in the boot of my car yesterday, specifically!"

His daughter opened the boot and regarded him laconically,

"Well, they're not here now!"

"What!"

An hour later, back at the airport, Miss Beaumont's attention was diverted by a faulty wheelchair spilling its elderly occupant onto the concourse right in front of her. Dozens of people saw it, but only a few went to help. When The Chairman's daughter had finished giving first aid and reassurance to the shaken lady, she discovered to her intense annoyance that the case of Boule had gone.

"I don't --" She killed the expletives in time: "I don't believe it."

"You don' believe wha', Miss Beaumon'?"

"Someone's stolen Daddy's Pétanque set -- Erm -- What are you doing here?"

Jim waved some papers towards her while looking about for thieves,

"Delivering some las' minute figures to your Father. I've go' one of his spare sets in my boo' if you're desperate." He offered the papers: "Hang onto these, I'll run and ge' them."

The pair waved the Chairman off. Jim was aware that the attitude of the daughter had changed from gratefully friendly, to professional, which was a shame,

"How are you getting home?"

"I came by taxi."

"Can I offer you a lif' then?"

"That would be -- Nice. Thank You."

They hadn't motored far when Carole spoke,

"If I'd been carrying a handbag instead of a bum-bag, would that have gone too?"

Ah right! He regrouped instantly, his secret love, far from being cleared, was immediately back in the frame.

"I'm afraid so."

"So what's in the case?

"In the one I gave you, boules. In the other, I don" know for sure, bu' no' boules."

"No, sorry Mr Teale, it's only got boules in it, I checked. I've been doing a lot of thinking and checking since our last conversation."

"So the lif' home wasn' -- Nice?"

Carole's reply was hard-edged,

"I said nice, but 'the least you could do,' were the words in my mind!"

"Well seeing you're on to us, would you like to see the res'?"

"Of course."

Jim slowed and repositioned the car to take a different exit from that he had originally planned at the approaching roundabout.

"You do realise tha' this morning's little escapade was also a tes', which by rumbling us--"

"I've now failed."

"Yes."

"That's a pig's bum. Never mind, better a suspect under your scrutiny, than a nonentity you never see."

"What?"

"Never mind!"

"There are several ways to hear wha' you have jus' said."

Carole turned away and looked out of the car window with a scowl on her pretty face,

"Are you always this infuriating?"

"Only when I'm no' sure of my ground." This effectively killed any further conversation to the laboratory car-park at Beaumont Pharmaceuticals.

"Would you ge' the case please? I' should be in the boo'."

The beautiful eyes flashed fire,

"You are always this infuriating!"

"Jus' teasing, sorry."

She retrieved the case of Boule from the boot and carried it into the building.

The senior technician, in protective clothing, halted their progress at the door of the laboratory. An assistant, also heavily suited up, took the case away while Jessica waved a Geiger counter around them,

"I'm sorry, Miss Beaumont, but you are mildly radioactive, can you come this way please?"

Carole's eyes opened wide in shock; her cry was from the heart,

"Jim!"

"We didn" know for sure, that's why I asked you to carry the case; you'd already had i' for a while. Go with the technicians; they'll take you through Decontamination, it's no' pleasan', bu' i' is effective."

Jim had barely sat down to wait for Carole, when Simon appeared, shepherding Barnaby, who was carrying a video camera.

"Come into Jessica's office Boss; you'll want to see this."

Together, the three clustered around the camera's tiny monitor; they watched as an anti-radiation-suited figure came into view, transferred some colourless liquid from a storage jar to another container, and left carrying the swag. As with all Beaumont specialist gear, to facilitate quick recognition in an emergency, the suit was personalised with the owner's name. It was in clear view most of the time.

Jim's heart sank under the pain.

The name was Carole Beaumont.

He stood up and sighed deeply.

Barnaby and Simon watched him struggle for control.

"She's in the building; she's in Decom. You can pick her up on her way ou'."

"Security won't be taking Miss Beaumont anywhere Boss. Tell him, Barnaby."

"It's Miss Carole's suit Mr Teale-Sir, but she's not wearing it. When that was happening, Miss Carole was helping my brother at a party for disabled children. Two weeks ago I found out she did charity work, on t'quiet. Traitors don't do that, but t'Miss Carole's of this world do!"

Hope began to flicker in Jim's breast.

"So I set it up especially for last night, ready to block her, or cause her timetable trouble, or, as I hoped if we'd guessed t'right weekend, to give her an alibi."

Suddenly Jim could breathe again.

"Watch, our thief comes back to tidy and check, Barnaby used her chance here."

The view zoomed in on the figure's feet.

"Our thief is wearing the brand of trainers that Miss Beaumont prefers, Boss, but --"

The suit legs were too short revealing a narrow strip of very masculine, dark leg-hair above the socks, and for a couple of seconds, a table leg gave an accurate measure of scale.

"T'thief is a man, an average sized man with big feet, Miss Carole takes a four, they are nine or ten. He could wear her suit, just, but not t'shoes."

"It gets better," said Simon.

"We were interested in who might be working late, so we checked that too, Sir. We've listed everyone."

"Besides Security and Cleaners who should have been on site, there are two that had no business here. An Accounts Clerk, and her Section Head."

"Harold?"

"Mr Harold, Sir, average height, but with big feet. Now that we know where to look, and what to look for, I should think that Miss Carole's suit will provide most of t'forensic required. Hair; skin; not to mention that foul deodorant he wears. And Mr Harold's locker will give us t'rest." She raised an eyebrow: "I'll need authorisation, Mr Teale-Sir."

When Carole returned, her head and hands were the only parts visible projecting from the coverall. She was unnaturally pink from the scrubbing she had received, not to mention her anger.

"Have you been through there?"

"Once, tends to discourage you from needing to go again."

"I can't decide whether you're a sadist or just a heartless bastard!"

"Try lovesick fool who doesn' wan' to make a mistake tha' will break his hear'. This way."

The girl followed him in silence, through into a room where Jessica was waiting. On their arrival, the technician called them over to a glass-fronted radiation cupboard and thrust her arms into the gloves,

"We waited until you were here," she said: "The outside is only mildly active, less than you were Miss Beaumont, Jim tells me you opened the case, did you touch anything inside?"

"No, no I don't think so."

Jessica opened the case. The boules lay in their nests, with the cochonnet. The resident Geiger counter screamed, and the technician hurriedly turned its sensitivity down. She pulled the TV camera into place, turned up the magnification and traced all the way around the edge of the case,

"Yes," she murmured with satisfaction and then quartered the boules, examining their pattern lines closely.

"Ah! Here we are." She flicked a switch, and the screen above them lit up. A highly magnified boule with a pair of pattern lines was in centre view. "Notice anything?" she asked.

Jim didn't and said so; Carole was squinting hard,

"They're different. One's a groove; the other's a cut." Again Jim examined the screen; he must need new glasses, he could see no difference, even though it was what he had been expecting.

"A join Miss." The magnification went right up. "And that's a screw thread peeping through." A gigantic pointer appeared, blocking out almost the entire view and painted the landscape black. Jim looked back into the cupboard in shock, Jessica was merely drawing with a fine felt tip, to mark exactly which line it was. She transferred the boule to a dish, grasped it firmly and twisted; the smaller segment smoothly unscrewed like the top of a jar. As the sections parted, the Geiger counter went crazy.

Neatly sealing the larger space was a thin plastic membrane. Through the seal a brown deposit was visible.

"Alf will be glad to recover this; just don't ask me to get it back out of that lot."

"What is it?"

"Sawdust Miss, that's the packaging, but it's carrying our magic bullet, the vital ingredient of our groundbreaking anti-cancer drug. Tritium. You might know it better as Heavy Hydrogen, very heavy Hydrogen, Hydrogen three."

"I know what it is. But it causes cancer! Are you saying it cures it too?"

"Yes Miss, when we've processed it, it sure does. Only certain cancers, sadly, not all. It's not easy to get hold of, so our competitor has been stealing ours. And you, Miss Beaumont, were the courier, you and your Dad."

"Did you know?"

Carole turned to Jim; the beautiful eyes were clouded with fear now, not flashing with anger.

"No, I had no idea."

"Your willingness to carry the case never mind look inside it does suggest you didn't, Miss. You've carried stolen heavy water out of this factory on a number of occasions. There are another three litres here."

"Where's the rest? Even if they're all full, there's barely two litres here."

"Nearer five Miss, counting the sawdust too. And the velvet lined support is not that good a fit, not for a quality product like this. I suspect that when we remove it, we will find more sawdust under it, in sachets or plastic tubes. If you treat it right, very fine sawdust will soak up its own volume of water, and still be sucking.

In the world of the very something-or-other, the normal rules you're used to working inside go out of the window. Miracles get done at once; the impossible takes only a little longer. Very cold, you get super-conductivity. Very fast, time slows down. Very whatever strange things can happen. The holes in sawdust are in the world of the very small."

* * *

Carole Beaumont surveyed her company cover-all and bootees, the only clothes she was wearing over her company disposable knickers.

"Could you possibly give me a lift home Mr Teale, I'd rather not be out in public dressed like this."

"There's been developments. I've only jus' become aware of them. So yes, I'd like to give you a lif' home, bring you up to date. Bu' would you call me Jim, please Miss Beaumont, if you can use the familiar under stress, i' shows you wan' to. I also wan' you to, and tha' being the case, please use i' always."

"In that case, it's Carole -- Jim, please take me home." Her manner changed quite markedly. She tossed her hair back, breathed in and spoke in a low controlled voice. "But developments can wait! You can begin by explaining, 'Lovesick Fool'!"

"And from your tone. I' had better be good!"

The beautiful eyes were flashing fire again,

"Oh yes! You are going to pay dearly for today, with either The Sack or The Rest Of Your Life, depending on your explanation!"

In Sunderland, On Christmas Day

{Given a verse, add two more to make a short poem,
or in my case pome.}

In Sunderland, on Christmas day,
I heard an old man sighing.
I stopped and asked the reason why,
My dog, Sir, lies a dying.

Sigh not; your dog was loved 'til death,
Life is for the living.
There's canine presents on the moor,
E'en now outlived their giving.

On Redcar Beach, on New Years day
The man danc'd wild with glee,
I did what you said, c'lected strays,
Now I've got seventy-three.

Talking to the Artist

{Michelle Bomey is a major character
in the Novochester Chronicles Novels}

Shelley sat quietly to one side, while her teacher praised her progress over the year. Her parents listened with joyous amazement; eventually, Anton just had to comment,

"We never thought she'd learn to write, never mind reach phrase level."

"The English is 'See Spot run,' the computation lasts only as long as the fingers, but the writing is beautiful, probably because she considers it to be Art. There's just one more thing," Anton and Gillian Bomey who had been preparing to go, settled down again. "I know she's only a youngster." He glanced at the autistic child-woman sitting nearby, who, as usual when her name had not been mentioned, seemed unaware that she was the subject of the conversation: "But has she got a boyfriend?"

"She met a boy on holiday." Said Anton: "We tried to watch her, but not cosset her too much, not stifle her. She was very happy, she's a good swimmer, and they swam together a lot."

"We let them swim out to the island." Gillian added: "In the afternoons. And kept our fingers crossed, like all parents. They got on very well; we had wondered just how well."

"You could be about to find out. She communicates through her Art. I want to show you some drawings; I've called them her Triangle Series. I've kept them hidden until now. I think you'd better take them home, and store them away carefully. She always gives her work a title; I got her to sign them and date them as well because I think they're good, very good; someday they may be valuable." Reggie retrieved Shelley's file and slid out the five drawings in the Triangle Series. He selected one and placed it face down in front of Shelley's parents. "Prepare yourself. Turn it over when you're ready."

With a glance at his wife, Anton reached out and turned it over. The picture was coloured pencil on heavyweight cartridge paper. There was a neat white border, but the rest of the paper was covered in coloured, curved-sided triangles, tessellating and overlapping, an almost aggressive, accretion of colour. In the bottom left-hand corner was neatly written,

Happy Toes

Michelle

1982

"Her friends think that she draws volcanoes or fireworks, but I think we know different."

The drawing shimmered, and changed, and moved, and if you looked hard she disappeared, but gaze with slightly unfocused eyes, or blink rapidly, and there she was, as clear as clear, a self-portrait, Shelley, wriggling in orgasm. The teacher spread the rest out in front of them. Voluptuous sex, gloriously consummated, leaped off the paper at the three of them.

"Goodness!" Said Gillian, gawping at the wanton display before her.

"I think her talent should be encouraged, take her to some galleries, and show her some of the Great Masters. If she can draw 'Achievement,' or 'Anticipation,' like she can draw 'Sex,' she could have a future as a card designer or commercial artist. A visit to a sympathetic, understanding doctor might be in order too."

* * *

To their relief, whereas the tests performed by the family

doctor confirmed that Shelley's holiday fling had most probably been very friendly indeed, it hadn't left her with any unwelcome consequences that they could find.

Gillian took her daughter on tours of the local Galleries and Museums. Every so often the girl would stop in front of a painting and examine it closely, presently her Mum realised that she could forecast which paintings would command Shelley's interest.

Enigmatic portraits, those where there seemed to be something going on, a family group with two younger children sharing an ill-concealed joke; or a picture of a girl in white, chaste and virginal, until you noticed that the look in her eyes was neither. Abstracts that made you feel good to look at them; Landscapes full of hurry and bustle and matchstick figures; and anything, absolutely anything, by Max Escher.

When Gillian went in to check on Shelley before retiring, she discovered a pencil sketch of herself in the Gate Gallery, fondly watching her daughter appraise a picture. Shelley had bent the wall around so that both mum and daughter were about three quarters face on to the viewer.

A photograph, it wasn't, a moment snatched from the eternal river, it definitely was. She picked it up to take to show her husband, only to find underneath it several sheets of preparatory sketching, she took those too.

Anton agreed with her, not only were the pictures stunning, but a serious attempt should be made to encourage Shelley to blossom artistically.

"And we won't worry if it fails, even if it's an expensive failure, which if it fails it will be?"

"I won't worry, you're the one obsessed with waste," he replied.

"OK, I promise that I won't worry."

* * *

"Shelley, you have a lot of drawings."
"Yes."
"And a lot of pencils and crayons."
"Yes."

"You need a new cupboard for them."

"Oh."

"To put them in -- to keep them safe."

"My hands are happy."

Gillian sliced up the pamphlets she had acquired. She ended up with pictures of several 'Cupboards' which she wouldn't mind her daughter having in her room.

"Choose your new cupboard."

"Oh." One by one the cut-outs were discarded, {'Sad!' -- 'Loud!' -- 'Salty!'} Suddenly one was handed back to her,

"We like that one," said a strange voice. Gillian flashed it back in front of her daughter,

"This one?"

"Yes, happy cupboard," said Shelley.

The cupboard that Shelley had chosen was a huge tallboy type, with drawers under, combination unit.

Anton had to measure up carefully; it only just fitted into her room after a serious reorganisation. Shelley however, knew exactly where it and the existing furniture were going, and to her parent's surprise, when they followed her instructions, it all fitted and looked right.

* * *

Gillian steered Shelley around the display areas, in the large Art and Craft Suppliers in downtown Novochester. Shelley looked and looked.

"The paintings in the gallery?"

"Yes," The youngster replied.

"These are the kind of paints that the artists use."

"Oh!"

"Would you like some?"

"My hands are happy."

Gillian began making up a mental shopping list, the heavy brass bound cases, in various sizes seemed a good starting point.

"These are happy books!"

"Can you read them?"

"Yes, this one is a clever book." Gillian spun around; her

daughter even looked different; she had heard that voice once before, selecting the store cupboard.

"Can you read it?"

"Yes."

"Even the long words?"

"Yes, of course."

"And you understand them?"

"Yes. Shelley doesn't, but I do."

"May I see them?"

The strange person in her daughter's eyes handed the books over, the one she had been reading was a beginner's guide to painting in oils, canvas preparation, base pigments, mixing, application methods, finishing off, all covered from beginner up to Under Graduate level. The book contained no Composition, no Style, no Art as such, only mechanics. She turned to the assistant,

"Have you got a kit with everything listed in this book in it, it is vital that nothing is missing."

"All of these kits contain everything in that book, Madam," he said, indicating the larger range of brass bound, wooden cases.

"And referred to by the same name?"

"Name and Number, Madam, and I can put together a selection of canvases to match as well."

"I don't think that you have quite got it, I meant nothing missing! A brush would have been a rather large omission; canvases would have been the end of the World, my daughter is autistic, she wouldn't understand."

"Ah, canvases, Easel,-"

"Apron, racks, stands, protective floor-covering, nothing missing, how long to put a kit together?"

"About an hour, Madam." The slightly chastened but now clued up assistant replied.

"Will I need a truck or will a car do?"

"I could get everything into an estate car." Gillian had been doing her arithmetic in her head and wrote down an astronomical sum on the desk pad in front of them.

"Don't exceed that figure, and I expect an offer of discount for your preferred method of payment. I'll take the books now, and see you in about an hour." She hadn't needed to decide whether to buy the second book too. While touring the galleries, Shelley never walked past an Escher; she always studied them closely. The second book was a volume devoted to several of his more brain-challenging works. The assistant looked from the books to Shelley,

"Is this young lady your daughter?"

"Yes."

"I don't want to seem impertinent, but this kit that you want, it's not really a young person's selection. Only a seriously professional artist would need all this."

Gillian slid *'Happy Toes'* out from its carrier and unrolled it,

"This is what she creates with crayons on paper. So what do you think?"

There was a short silence; slowly the assistant stood up to his full height, his demeanour radically changed.

"The kit will be ready for you in about an hour Madam."

Gillian paid for the books and turned; it was Shelley, not the stranger, who looked at her from out of her daughter's face. "We have to go shopping."

"Oh."

"We will come back later -- for the paints." Shelley smiled, relaxing,

"My arms are happy."

Gillian carefully arranged the walk so that the car was almost directly between her last shopping stop and the Art Shop. She told Shelley that the Art Shop was there, on the other side of the car, pointing carefully and graphically, and they would put everything in the car, and drive it down to the shop. When Shelley got into the car without demur she relaxed, her daughter had understood.

Anton helped unload the car and store everything in the middle of the floor in Shelley's room.

"Put it all where you want it kept."

"Right."

Gillian pulled her husband away,

"Leave her; this may take some time."

* * *

"Go and get your sister for tea, will you Bobby, tell her that-"
"She's here Mum."
"Oh, right."
"Shelley, have you put your paints away?"
"My thoughts are happy." Shelley's parents looked at each other and Anton slipped away to check. Her room was spotless. The thick dust sheet was spread over most of the open floor, like a huge denim rug. Her easel, rising from the sheet like a tower, stood centre stage, with a canvas resting on it, landscape. He peered into the paints cupboard. Inside, her stores and tools were neatly arranged in racks and containers. She had done a several person-hour clean-up job in a little over forty minutes, alone, and tidied too.

* * *

At the next School Parents Evening, Reggie congratulated Shelley's parents on her progress,
"The Artist's given some lessons on painting; the whole class have improved our technique under her guidance, including me."
"Oh." Exclaimed Gillian: "I'm so jealous, I'd not want to lose you know who, but I wish the Artist would hang about longer so that I could talk to her more."
"Well ask. Ask if you can speak to her, whenever we do, you know who always lets us."
"What do I say?" Reggie turned to Shelley.
"Shelley, can I speak to the Artist?"
"Yes."
"When you gave your first lesson, the one on how to draw leaves, did you feel nervous?"
"A little," said the deep voice: "But nearly everybody wanted to know how to draw them, it was okay."
"Who do you think will make a good artist?"
"Jennifer, but she will do better at sculpture, or building

bespoke belongings to order, she makes wood sing.”

"Shelley are you okay?"

"My arms are happy."

"Good -- You know who is back now, but to speak to the artist again, all you do is ask."

The Girl in the Café

*{Write a piece inspired by a picture of a girl in a café.
The girl looked vaguely like 'Michelle' in 'Allo 'Allo,
hence the setting}*

Miriam sat gazing out of the plastic café window at the cardboard bus shelter outside. Technicians climbed all over her, measuring light intensities, checking just how far she could lower her left arm, before the powerful key light reflected off the face of her wrist watch, and burned out any take, no matter how good.

"Can you say the louse line please Miriam?" called the soundman. "Low, intense, for level."

"You're a louse, but you'll never be a louse to anyone else."

The soundman fiddled with his controls,

"Again,"

Miriam obeyed him.

"That's great." He looked up at the cameraman: "I'm ready for the walkthrough."

"Okay, let's have Ben in. Standing by the table first."

"It's Ken," muttered the young man as he stepped forward and carefully hit his mark by the table.

Again sensors were thrust offensively into someone's living space; Ken managed neither to flinch nor blink. The technicians withdrew comparing readings, the sound man opened his mouth to speak, but Miriam launched into the scene without the prompt.

"So where were you really last night?"

"Don't start that again," replied Ken, sitting down: "With John, I told you."

More technicians thrust other instruments at the couple.

"John was with Rosie, all night, he was still there when I called half an hour ago. So where were you really?"

The intense, bitter argument rumbled on. The sound man tweaked his controls, while the cameraman checked his angles.

"Can you see the gun?" Asked the director.

"These kids are good, better than the real actors if you ask me," murmured the sound man to his assistant.

"Gun?" Said Props to Continuity. "The gun's on the props table." The pair looked at each other and Props hurried over to the table to double check.

"No it's tucked in nicely behind the saucer," replied the cameraman.

"Loads of passion. They should get them to learn the real lines," replied the girl adjusting her headphones.

"Right let's get the actors in," called the director: "Out guys! Now."

Props held up the gun for Continuity to see.

"Why bother?" The sound man studied his dials closely: "The ones they're making up are much better."

The couple stood up, glaring at each other across the table.

"You're a louse, but you'll never be a louse to anyone else," said Miriam; her hand came up clutching the gun, and she shot her colleague three times in the chest.

The sound engineers screamed and whipped their headphones off, swearing profusely.

Ken fell face down.

"You're stand-ins, you're not supposed to do that!" shrieked the director frothing at the mouth.

Miriam stowed the gun in her overcoat pocket and strode off the set.

"Get up you. Whatever your name is, thingy--"

"Ben."

"Ben! Get up! You're messing up the set."

But Ken didn't get up; he began to go cold and stiff instead, as a red pool spread out from under him.

On a canoeist catching a surfing wave

{For the first time}

C'noe stands forward on its nose.
Racing down green hill ahead.
Gasping, frightened, can't stop now!
Leaping speed, fills me with dread.
Lean in to the steep green glow,
Rushing past my right elbow.
Panic not, be brave my heart,
World is being torn apart.

Boat a-roar, wave a- thund'ring.
Paddle in the growling jaw,
Angry she bear, shielding whelps,
Hidden deep, within the pour.
Seeking, from my grasp to tear.
World is noise, frantic, warfare.
She bites again, I cannot see,
Hang on in there, doggedly.

Spray begins to fall in front,
Wave is breaking over me.
C'rect to run more down the hill,
Run on out to open sea.
Turn more back along the wave,
Back inside the tumble cave.
Run in and out, Shout with glee,
'All just for to pleasure me!'

Looking after your Ms
- Novochester Style

{While Himself was on Work Experience at George Angus, the Machine Shop Foreman told him, "Always look after your Ms." (Men; Machines; Materials; Markets, and Money.) Himself's Employers would have done well to take heed. Breaking with my usual stance I will tell you Dear True-Reader, while the characters are fictitious, this story is true, in every important detail, nearly SEVEN DECADES after Queen Victoria's Death!}

Stewart Baques addressed his friend across the otherwise empty staff room,

"Ash, you're in the Open University aren't you?"

Ashley Deeps looked up from the book he was marking,

"Yes, were you thinking of applying?"

"Research, is it any good, I've heard conflicting reports."

"It's brilliant. The only people saying differently are those academics who are scared for their jobs. The ones that are any good at teaching are already working in it, part-time. I even know some that are using the units in their day job."

Such an unconditional endorsement from the usually hard

to please Ash was amazing and made up Stewart's mind for him.

"Sounds like I should go for it then."

His friend double-checked that they were alone before,

"Yes do! I've got long-term plans in place for this school. But those plans can only include you if you have a degree. You can do the job I have in mind for you now. But the degree is necessary to get you on the shortlist for interview."

"Wha--"

Brusquely interrupting, Ash went on,

"The first thing you need is a letterbox this big." He mimed a shipping container in the air. "And you will have to dedicate that little box you call your second bedroom as a laboratory."

"A lab! Will The Old Man, fund it, or let me borrow stuff do you think?"

"It all comes in with the cost of the course, and you only have to send certain things back. Anything else you need -- He'd be accommodating."

That night Stewart went home and re-read the prospectus. Impulsively he completed the half filled in application form and made a special trip out to post it before he changed his mind yet again.

Although he was too late to be included on the roll for the following year, he was accepted for the January after that. After much heart searching and realistic assessment, he enrolled for a pre-University admissions course while he was waiting. The course had twelve students on it in September, by December there were only two.

* * *

The Science Foundation course, S100, was a whole credit, and he was advised to make one credit a year do. Advice he was only too anxious to take.

"What's your problem?" Asked Ash. "I'm not suggesting you go for more than one credit a year, but you're making a big deal about not doing so. Enrolling for extra preparation tuition and that."

"It's confidence. I've always known I would fail. Teaching's the only thing I've ever succeeded at."

"That's because you discovered Canoeing, began to teach it out of school, in your own time, found the sport at which you excel, and in doing so, found yourself."

"Is that what I did?"

"You work hard and expect your kids to do the same. Those that don't do it for love do it because they respect you."

"I always worked hard but for naff results. That's why I enrolled in the preparation course. It helped a lot, but mainly because since I've become a teacher the kids I taught have taught me how to work effectively."

"Really?" Replied Ash. "That explains a lot. I've always wondered why you were just Certificate Trained, with your brain." He walked off, leaving Stewart goldfishing in his wake.

The following day his laboratory was delivered. It came in two egg-box sized crates lashed together, with a thin sandwich-filling crate between them. The lab was exhaustive, Biology, Physics, Chemistry and the newly re-named Earth Sciences, the filling turned out to be an expanded polystyrene rack full of bottles of Chemicals.

He didn't need to borrow a thing.

* * *

At his first Tutorial for S100 Stewart met up with several hard-working housewives and Certificate Trained teachers like himself but from neighbouring Education Authorities. The housewives checked with the teachers exactly which books were really necessary, and which could be safely disregarded on cost grounds,

"You'll be okay, being a teacher; the Authority will pay everything for you."

"Will I? Will it?"

"Yeah," interjected a lad from Northumberland. "Just ring them up and ask for a claim form."

* * *

The switchboard at the Civic patched Stewart through to the

relevant department,

"Hello."

"Oh hello, I'm in the Open University, and I'd like a claim form for my fees please."

"So what's your employment?"

"I'm a teacher at West Novochester."

"Sorry, we don't fund teacher's fees for courses, just the Summer School, on the Teacher's Short Course Scheme, but you'll have to come in to get it nearer the time."

"Oh -- Oh -- Alright then."

Later that day he bumped into Ash.

"I've just been brusquely turned down from claiming my course fees."

"You will have been, Novochester doesn't fund them."

"I'm sure the Ashington lads said they got their fees."

"Oh yeah! If you lived one mile north of where you do they'd be paid, everything, including your bus fare."

"You mean I work for the wrong Authority."

"No! You **live** in the wrong Authority. All my expenses are paid by Northumberland, even though it's Novochester that benefits."

Stewart scrupulously checked up, only to find that what his friend said was true. If a teacher wanted to increase his fount of knowledge, although Northumberland would fund it for nil return, his own employing Education Department specifically refused any financial help. The Orwellian Double-Think required to get his head around such an anachronism defeated him.

* * *

In the Spring Stewart visited the Civic Centre for his Teacher's Short Course Grant claim form and was directed to Room C6.

A thin, elderly man made his way across the office to the little reception counter to see to him. Stewart had to wait while several junior staff kept intercepting him, needing the older man's attention and his ruling on matters of protocol. Stewart got the distinct impression that he was dealing with the boss and that the man's genial, friendly attitude was due to his imminent retirement.

"May I have a Teacher's Short Course Claim Form, please? It's for my OU Summer School."

"Ah sorry, you've come to the wrong room, you need Room C8, across the corridor."

"Oh I'm sorry, I must have misheard."

"You probably didn't. This is the room to claim the OU Course Fees."

For once in his life, Stewart was awake, aware, and on the ball,

"Well can I have a claim form for them then, please?"

"Certainly."

Across the corridor, Room C8 was just as accommodating.

At home, Stewart filled in both forms and sent them off. In due course, two cheques arrived, which he banked and spent with indecent haste.

* * *

Ashley pulled him in the School corridor,

"You know you told me you'd got your fees?"

"Yes!"

"Are you sure? Just, my brother tried, but Novochester wasn't having any. Are you sure it wasn't just the Short Course Grant?"

"I got that as well. And the fees were ten times as much! I got them alright, I've spent them."

"Hmm! Well done!"

Musing on his good fortune later Stewart suddenly remembered that the first time he asked, before being refused he had been asked what his job was.

I wonder what the reply would have been had I said City Councillor? He thought.

* * *

The following Spring he presented himself at Room C6.

"May I have a Claim Form please, for my Open University Fees?"

The young man behind the counter checked Stewart's employment before, as expected, refusing.

"Sorry, we don't pay Course Fees for teachers."

"You paid them last year."

"No we can't have done, we don't pay Course Fees."

"You paid mine last year!"

The younger man visibly recoiled from the polite but assertive stance, and asked,

"What's your name?" Before he retreated through the office into the back. When he reappeared, he was studying a file, walking slowly, and constantly turning a page back and forth.

"This is a mistake."

Stewart said nothing, too busy girding up his loins for the coming scrap.

"But as we've paid it once we will have to pay it until you graduate."

Again Stewart blanked the clerk. That was a freely volunteered admission that he'd have paid handsomely to hear.

When the two cheques arrived the second year, Stewart banked them quickly but spent them with deliberation.

* * *

The Spring after that he presented himself at Room C6 yet again,

"May I have a Claim Form please, for my Open University Fees?"

Again the bright young thing behind the counter checked Stewart's employment before, as expected, refusing.

"Sorry, we don't pay Course Fees for teachers."

The teacher put on his braadest Geordie to reply,

"Ya pays miyne! Check mee fiyle!"

When the clerk returned, he was carrying only a claim form.

Novochester does not look after its Ms, the first one in particular.

Letters From Petra To Amelia Harris.

{On Amelia being understandably not thrilled at having 'Hannah' returned, rejected by a publisher.}

Dear Amelia,
Rejection.

In any relationship, there are at least two viewpoints, usually many more than two.

Himself spent most of his career trying to change the 'Us and Them' dichotomy between teachers and pupils. {Then had to watch in fury as Anne Robinson earned many times his salary gratuitously ruining his life's work. Cough -- Spit -- Vomit, sorry even typing her name causes the bile to rise.} One of the best tips he learned as a teacher was if he wanted to change someone's attitude to him, change his attitude to them. So how about this as a variation on that theme?

If a publisher doesn't like Hannah, that's not fundamentally Hannah's fault but shows something lacking in the publisher. History is littered with rejections that with hindsight seem extraordinary.

J. K. Rowling. Now every other new book on the shelves is Harry Potter and water.

Frederick Forsyth. I shudder to think how much The Day Of The Jackal made for everyone involved in it eventually.

The Beatles. Was it Decca turned them down?

James Bond was described as 'Fleming's nasty little hero,' Fred Astaire as 'Can't act, can't sing, can dance a little,' and Beethoven's Fifth as 'Promising.'

I could go on --

The only rider I would add as a caution is if several criticisms say the same thing.

Then and only then go back and ask yourself 'Should I do something about this?' And seriously consider a 'Yes!' answer.

It happened to Himself once.

Having written his reports on a Fourth Year Top Set, only the second Fourth Year Top Set he'd ever had; he asked them to write a report each, on him.

At first most of the kids were looking sideways at him, but they accepted his assurance that he was serious, and wrote one for him.

He read them at home that night and was a very quiet sober person for a while afterwards.

If somebody had written, 'You are an egotistical, power crazed buffoon and I hate you.' you laugh it off.

After all, that's an improvement on your own opinion of yourself.

But when twenty-five of the thirty-two write 'Sometimes what you say is confusing.' And five of the rest write variations on that theme, then you sit up and take notice.

And do something about it!

It's just a thought.

Meanwhile---------

Who did you write Hannah for?

Most of our writing Petra wrote for US!

We can't really remember why we first tried to write, just that Himself was sitting at his computer plinky-plonking away, and I stepped in and tried to write an erotic, sexy, love-scene. My emphasis was on tenderness, joy, mutual sharing and the like, all spiced up with more than a little naughtiness.

Until then he hadn't even suspected my existence, but we thought it would be easy, and that we would enjoy re-reading it afterwards, so he gave me my head and let me get on with it.

And realised that we'd got just about every preconception wrong. Everything except that we would get pleasure out of it afterwards.

Anyone can write grotty anything, writing decent stuff is hard, {especially when you went to a Grammar School that didn't teach you the basics of Grammar,} and that applies to erotica too.

It is not easy to write.

And in addition:

Even though I usually tone my output down from what I really want to write, I frequently shock Himself, and nearly always embarrass him, because I wallow in activities that he could hardly ever see himself doing in real life. But, of course, always from a loving, friendly-fun viewpoint.

Having done Mr Hughes Courses, we can now file off and fettle the worst of the casting rags of writer's ignorance, and enjoy our books for what they are.

And Himself can be gently shocked and embarrassed in private.

Stories written by his wild-child, feminine side, for US!

If somebody decides that they think they could make money out of publishing them, excuse us if we don't get in the way.

Holding Petra's novels bound up as books in our hand, was/is/and always will be a thrill.

It would be staggering to see them on a shelf for sale in a bookshop.

We'd not believe it!

But fundamentally they were written for US.

Who did you write Hannah for?

Sorry I do go on a bit sometimes,

Love,

Petra.

{On the finer points of the English Language.}

Dear Amelia,

Don't worry about the stumble or hiccough in your Grammar.

Yes keep researching to make it as near correct as you can, but you'll often find that the experts disagree. Anything you miss, your editor will find, once someone realises that Hannah is an undiscovered best seller.

I still haven't got my head around:-

"Don't worry," he said, "but do run."

or

"Don't worry," he said, "But do run."

Neither of which stands close scrutiny, or dissection.

So to be safe, I have resorted to:

"Don't worry," he said. "But do run."

Which may be crude, but is correct!

-- I think!

or

"Don't worry," he said: "But do run."

Which is acceptable,

-- I think!

The only trouble is there are a lot, an awful lot, of the first two still embedded in my early books.

You accused me of being busy.

How did you guess?
But busy doing what?
Writing?
I wish!
Fencing?
Nearly finished -- yes nearly!
Relaxing?
That's writing and carries the same answer.
Gardening?
I cut the lawn, sans grass-box, because it was so long and got played war with, for making a mess. That apart no.

This week I am replacing the radiator in the dining room.

Replacing an old radiator with a new one poses certain interesting aspects of problem-solving.

New radiators come in only two sizes, too big, and too small.

I chose too small, as it was actually marginally nearer the correct size.

So I now have to replace the feed pipes.

Have you heard about the guy who had a wobbly dining table?

One of my radiator feed pipes was routed up through a joist -- actually THROUGH the joist! At an angle!

While his wife was out, he decided that he would saw a bit off the longest leg to stop it wobbling.

I wasn't going to replace through a joist, so I had to rethink that pipe run.

Faced with a slightly less tall but still wobbly table, he decided to cut a bit off the new longest leg.

The pipe run on the other side was on the wrong side of the joist, with the radiator being shorter.

Now with an even less tall wobbly table, the man began to panic and sawed bits off both the two new longest legs.

So now I had TWO rethinks of pipe runs to contend with.

By now the man had only a wobbly coffee table, and in his panic sawed a bit off the shortest leg, by mistake.

Lateral thinking, instead of going under the joists, how about thinking out of the box, {or out of my skull?} and go over them?

And this was only yesterday, planning the job.

I haven't started telling you about today yet, where I switched the heating electrics off, drained the system, cut into the pipe, and was faced with Niagara Falls!

What about the man? I hear you ask.

His wife came home to find that he had laid himself out on a large wobbly stool.

I also want to replace all the Thermostatic Radiator Valves in the house.

New TRVs come in only one size, too small.

But I can't get the picture of that poor deranged man out of my mind.

Love,

Petra.

{A few days later, reflecting on progress.}
Dear Amelia,
I'm losing it.
I mean I never was much in control, but now I'm losing it.

I finished replacing the radiator yesterday, closed up the holes in the floor and sealed them with decorators caulk like the carpet fitters had done when they laid the carpet fifteen years ago. I cleaned up and replaced my tools in their cases and boxes.

I was a big screwdriver missing.

Even after tidying away completely and vacuuming through, I was still a big screwdriver missing.

My bike picked up a puncture on Friday.

I've just repaired it.

As I had the bike out to see to it, I went to put my large Curver box, full of plumbing tools and consumables, back properly where it stays, behind the bike.

I'd staggered out with it yesterday and stored it temporarily out of the way until today, knowing I was going to have my bike out.

I have several large Curver boxes for special purposes, Plumbing, Electrics, Wood off-cuts, Cramps, Heavy tools like hammers, etc. etc. There are four red ones and four blue ones which live down the right-hand side of my hut behind my bike, and several more, blue, bottle green, yellow, grey which are scattered about, full of other stuff.

I spent a quarter of an hour commuting from hut to dining-room, like a headless chicken, looking for my blue plumbing box.

Here!

There!

Everywhere!

No Blue Plumbing Box!

I ended up standing in the middle of my garage shouting out loud,

"This is ridiculous!"

And realised that I was shouting directly AT my DARK BOTTLE GREEN plumbing box.

I put it away and replaced my bike!

Although I'd found a thorn and a piece of glass in the tyre I'd been unable to find corresponding holes in the inner-tube, and had re-inflated the tyre in the hope that it only leaked when the intruder was pushed into the inner-tube.

The tyre was not as iron hard as it had been when I finished inflating it --

I'll not be cycling tomorrow.

Then I remembered where my big screwdriver is.

Yes! You've guessed.

Oh -- and the new radiator leaks.

I'm going to dig a hole, get in it and pull the earth back over on top --

Love

,

Petra.

In recognition of the contribution of --

{Mrs Patterson, (Edgefield Primary School --1947-1948--), to my teaching style. Don't feel sad for me over this one Dear True Reader, Mrs Patterson got hers in 'Delia.'[6]}

Brief: Tell a story entirely in conversation.

"Your son's a little treasure."
"Yes. He cleans and tidies; he's a great help."
"How old is he now?"
"Adam will be five in August."
"Does he want a brother or a sister?"
"Shh, we haven't told him."
"Do you think that's wise?"

"I see her at number fourteen's carrying a bump. And her man fighting his way across Germany."
"Aye, but he was home for a weekend before Christmas."
"How convenient."
"Don't be like that; she's going to find it hard on her own. Good job she's got that little one, right little treasure he is."
"But for how long? Been man of the house for five years, the

war can't last much longer they say, and then there'll be two in front of him. Her man and new baby, get his nose pushed out, you mark my words."

"Tonight we're having a big party; it's for VE day, the war's over, Daddy will be home soon."

"Oh, will he get here in time for the party?"

"Not quite that soon, but in a few weeks."

* * *

"Welcome home darling, just in time; I don't think it will be long before baby arrives."

"Is Adam excited about it?"

"Er -- I haven't told him."

"Oh. Well, I hope it gets here soon, I'm only home for a week."

"What?"

"Got to go to college. There's an emergency training scheme for teachers. They give bonus years for the war service. I've signed up, that's why I'm home now. It's all right, I'll be home at weekends, and it's only for fourteen months."

"But still, oh feel that kick, still, I hoped you'd be home for more than a week."

"Fourteen months, then I'll be here all the time."

"What's that?"

"That's Roger, he's your baby brother, do you like him?"

"He's very small."

"He's big for a baby."

"Where did he come from?"

"A stork brought him."

"A grass stalk?"

* * *

"Mummy can--"

"Pass me that towel will you -- Thanks."

"What are you doing?"

"I'm going to feed the baby."

"Where's his dinner?"

"Never mind, I have it. Go and play in the garden."

"It's sleeting--"

"Well go and play in your bedroom."

"Can't I--"

"Go and play in your bedroom. Shut the door on your way out."

* * *

"I don't understand it, doctor, he seems fine, but every nappy is full of these little black bits."

"They're--"

"Quiet Adam. Go and play in your bedroom."

* * *

"Is that it? Are you home for good now? You're not going to tell me you've got a teaching job in Liverpool or something are you?"

"No. It's in Ryker, it's two buses, but my home city."

"What's for tea Mum?"

"A walk around the table and a kick at the pantry door. Go and play in your bedroom."

"The place is a bit of a mess."

"That's Adam's toys; he never puts anything away."

"Adam -- There you are, get this mess cleaned up! I scrimped for those cars, and you leave them all over the floor."

"I di--"

"Don't argue, get them cleaned up -- Just a minute, where are the tyres?"

"Roger eats them!"

"And the axels are bent!"

"It's Roger; he bends the axels as wel--"

"How can a two-year-old eat tyres, and bend axels?"

"He does, it's all him, they were fine before he came. And I put them away this morning; it's Roger, he scatters them about."

"Clear them up now."

"Do you realise you are teaching that child the way to get attention is to be naughty."

"Rubbish mother, of course, I'm not."

* * *

"I love these roasties; I hope there are seconds."

"You're a mouth on wheels, Adam. Who else likes School Dinners but you?"

"Seconds!"

"Yes please, Miss."

"All right Adam."

"Where are we going after lunch?"

"Let's go in the factory."

"Find some tops."

"There are loads of roasties left still."

"Yuk."

"We're going to look for tops after, are you coming?"

"We're not allowed in the factory."

"Ooh, scaredey-pie Adam, not allowed."

"I'm not scaredey-pie either!"

"Well come in the factory then."

"The watchman's looking."

"Ooh, scaredey-pie Adam, the watchman's looking."

"I'm not scaredey-pie either!"

"You boys! Back you go, you're not allowed in here!"

"Scaredey-pie! Running away!"

"I'm not scaredey-pie either!"

"Well shout something back at him, tell him to bugger off."

"No."

"Ooh, scaredey-pie Adam, scared to shout."

"I'm not either!"

"Well shout it then, shout bugger off."

"Bugger off!"

"Do you know what Adam did, he shouted bugger off at the factory watchman."

"You said to do it!"

"I'm telling."

"What's he doing in our class? Boys don't belong in a sewing class."

"Who?"

"That Adam, Mrs Patterson's just dragged him in."

"Oh no, he swore at the factory watchman."

"He's always doing something silly."

"To get attention, she'll kill him."

"He was set up, Terry 'n them called him scaredey-pie until he did it."

"Tell the girls what you said. Tell them. Tell them!"

"I said bugger off."

"She'll kill him."

"I can't look. Is that him screaming?"

"Yes. I don't care what he's done that's too much. Oh no."

"She's pulled his socks down, going for the backs of his legs now."

"Why are you dropping all your stuff, Adam?"

"My hands don't work. They won't hold anything."

"Mrs Patterson broke three rulers across his knuckles, and then slashed the back of his legs with her belt."

"Let me see?"

"There's no white left; you're black and blue from ankle to bum."

"I don't know; it hurts to try to look."

"Report her. Tell your Mam."

"No."

"Why not?"

"I'd just get another hiding at home, for swearing."

* * *

"Now that you are retiring from teaching Adam, can you sum up the secret of your successful teaching career?"

"Oh yes, that's easy. Half a century ago, more, I was taught by a middle-aged battle-axe called Mrs Patterson. So whenever I had a teaching problem to deal with--"

"You just thought, what would Mrs Patterson do?"

"Precisely! Then I did the exact opposite; it was never wrong!"

Love At Sea

The first night aboard the cruise liner, several members of the Sixth Form had a communal Eighteenth Birthday Party in an alcove off the trendy bar.

Philip, resplendent in his officer's uniform, wandered over attracted by the genial crowd; an immature boy was boasting about his down in one prowess,

"I'll take anyone on, never been beaten yet."

"Ever taken a girl on, Trevor?" Maggie asked innocently.

Trevor looked around; Kate was watching the exchange.

"Nobody can beat me," He said straight into the tall girl's eyes. She shook her head sadly at him mouthing,

"Don't -- Don't" Trevor grinned,

"Nobody."

Maggie grabbed Beth and thrust her forward deaf to her protests.

"I don't want to."

Maggie continued to ignore her,

"Let's make it interesting, a fiver each in a kitty, winner takes all?"

"I told you I don't--"

"Let's make it ten," interrupted Trevor imperiously while flicking away in Beth's general direction with his fingers.

Her eyes narrowed; her chin took on an annoyed tilt.

"Okay." She rummaged in her purse and plonked the note

down: "Ten it is."

"Tenner to play. Down in one, winner takes all," called Maggie. "Is there anyone else wants in?"

For just a moment Philip thought about amusing himself by joining in, but a couple of boys looked into the circle then withdrew.

"Not with Beth's eyes aflame," murmured one to the other.

"No way, if I'm going to drop a tenner, St Oswald's can have it." Came the soft reply.

Philip's interest soared but as a spectator. Despite her urging, Maggie couldn't get anyone else to join the competition, and so it was Trevor and Beth who squared up across a table, a brimming pint in front of each.

"You start on my say so, no spills, no stops, nothing left or you lose. Right?" The contestants neither moved nor spoke. "Take your pints." Trevor took hold of his glass. " -- Go." Trevor upped his pint and noisily gulped it down. Beth leisurely reached out for hers, lifted it up, disposed of it down her throat in one, swallow-less pour, and set the drained glass back down. Trevor, saucer-eyed, missed a swallow in his shock, and sputtered to a stop, a gill or so short, and with beer fanning down his front like an unkempt beard. Beth picked up the stakes,

"Don't like it that way, you can't savour it properly. Come on 12MC Girls," She waved the notes aloft, heading for the bar: "The drinks are on Trevor."

"Impressive," said Philip as she passed: "I was thinking of joining in, now I'm glad I didn't."

"And who might you be?"

"Philip Smith. Ship's Gymnasium Senior Instructor. There's a ladies only Keep Fit class every afternoon, why don't you come along? It's Beth isn't it?"

"Beatrice Eithne Thoro'goodfellow." She offered her hand. He took it, smiling,

"Nice name."

"Spheroids! Those that hear it misspell it; those that see it mispronounce it unless they're Irish. My friends call me Beth, what time?"

With the appointment completed Beth went off to join Kate, and pay for the round of free drinks. She gushed at length to her friend about how they would join Keep Fit and develop their bodies. Philip caught parts of the exchange as he drifted past.

"-- seems like fun, nobody else does it in our form, they're all football and hockey, and we won't have to put up with Trevor and Maggie fighting. We'll go tomorrow. Start Keep Fit, start a whole new phase in our lives --" There was quite a bit more. When Kate managed to get some words in,

"Have you considered Deck Tennis? Rather than Keep Fit--"

Beth thrust the error of her ways forcibly back down her throat.

"Don't be silly, we've never considered anything like this before, and now we've got a Heaven-sent opportunity to do something new and different, and straight away you want to try something off the wall. We'll go and join Philip Smith's Keep Fit class, nobody will know us, we'll be the only people we know who do Keep Fit and --"

* * *

During their first session, despite repeated advice to the contrary, Beth threw herself too hard into the Keep Fit routines, performing squat thrusts and step ups, and running until her legs buckled.

The following day she could hardly get out of bed.

At three-o-clock, Philip came looking for the girls in time to see Kate help Beth limp away up the aft stairs towards the sun deck.

"Where's your gear?" he heard her ask.

Beth prevaricated for a minute waiting until the wall panels became scenes from classic literature depicting Greek Athletes, heralding the proximity of the Gym, before dropping her grenade. It produced the justified explosion,

"What d'y'mean? You're not going?"

"I don't like it."

"Beth! I started because you wanted to go. I've got all my stuff. I've bought stuff."

“See ya.”

Kate disconsolately watched her exasperating friend disappear on deck.

Philip decided he was too likely to be discovered to pretend he hadn't heard,

“Kate, could you open up?” He gave the tall girl his keys.

“Beth's not coming.”

“She's probably hurting; she tried too hard yesterday. I'll be back in a minute.”

Even though he ran quickly to catch her, Beth had vanished. He couldn't even try to persuade her to return. He felt a totally novel thump of loss in his guts.

This is stupid! You don't even like her that much! He thought. Like, No! Love?

Philip returned to Kate in a thoughtful mood. While waiting for him, she had changed into a brand new, and very fetching, sports bikini.

“Today we will concentrate on your arms and upper-body, your legs and stamina need another day to consolidate, and recover. We'll give those another go tomorrow.”

“I'm glad of that; I'm hurting too.”

The session went well, and at the end, Kate asked.

“Would you wash my hair for me?”

“Sure.”

Once in his private shower, Kate turned her back to him and snuggled up as he lathered her hair. Slightly embarrassed, Philip retreated. Deftly she followed him. Presently with his back hard up against the wall, there was nowhere else to go. She still pressed her thinly-clothed, sensuously-wriggling bottom gently into his groin, with the inevitable result. He rinsed her hair off, by which time his arousal was so obvious it could no longer be ignored.

“Somebody's getting very interested in my bottom.” Kate turned and viewed his shorts, rampantly bulging: “Can we see if you're as interested in my lips?”

“Erm--”

She had closed up and was kissing him enthusiastically.

Philip tried, he really tried, but the vision in his mind was of a shorter, plumper, much less-nice girl altogether. Kate came up for air, released him, and glanced down at the wilting flower between them.

"When I was ten my big brother smuggled me into a teenage Postman's Knock game and called my number to make sure I got at least one go. Got snogged by at least one boy. So I snogged him as a thank you. He snogged me with more commitment than you just did."

"I'm sorry; I didn't mean it to be that obvious. I wasn't -- I didn't --"

"I thought that's what you wanted, but obviously not."

"It was, up until a couple of days ago. I've only just realised myself how much things have changed. I'm sorry I misled you."

She shook her head,

"Not really, I misread the situation as much as anything. Can I still come to Keep Fit?"

"I'd feel an even bigger louse if you didn't."

After dinner, Philip joined the youngsters in the bar and went over to speak to Kate when she gave him an obviously genuine smile of welcome. He leaned in and gave her a gentle smoochy kiss on the lips,

"Thanks for being for being so forgiving earlier," he whispered. She smiled ruefully, and they chatted for a minute or two on general topics. Finally, he decided to reveal all.

"Where's Beth?"

"She was over by the bar a minute ago, Trevor was trying to get her to down the half yard of ale."

Philip strained to see; Beth had the long glass raised and was pouring fast.

"Does she know about the airlock?"

"What airlock?"

The airlock broke, with the acknowledged down in one champ un-warned and unprepared for the resultant tidal wave.

Soaked, one down to Trevor, and her reputation as a sink not quite in tatters, but badly dented, Beth stormed off to change her clothes while aggressively refusing all offers of help. On deck, having successfully discarded her peers, she began to repulse Philip's offer,

"Come on; I'll come with you."

"No I can manage by--"

"Please? An olive branch?"

"Oh, sorry, didn't see it was you. Okay, an olive branch,"

He guided her out onto the deck.

When they were alone,

"I'm surprised that the Queen of the dunk didn't know about the half yard of ale."

It was meant kindly as he pointed out later, but at the time it was the flaring match into her powder keg.

Beth went skywards, a jagged lightning flash, fizzing as she went. Before he was able to form any sort of defensive reply, she had covered several topics of sexist behaviour, sports where you were hot, embarrassed, and sore simultaneously, and his inability to make the correct choice when faced with only two options. She stopped, eyes blazing.

"So what did you do?" he replied, equally angry. "Did you fight, or did you quit? You crawled away beaten by someone who didn't even know she was competing with you. Didn't even mean to compete with you." The justice of the accusation did nothing to cool the exchange, rather the reverse,

"Why her? Not me?"

"No reason," he was now shouting as loudly as she was.

"What's wrong with me?"

"You weren't there!"

"I hate you."

"I hate you back."

They stopped, the silence after their shouting, strange, eerie, punctuating a cusp moment.

"No I don't," he continued softly: "I think you're lovely."

She leaped upon him, the fire in her eyes even more intense. The still wet dress plastered tightly against his front soaked his clothes instantly.

Beth didn't make it back to her cabin that she shared with Kate that night; in fact, she never slept there again.

"I'll have to ring, she'll be worried if I don't, report me missing I shouldn't wonder."

Philip paused in his suckling only long enough to reply,

"We can't have that. Ring."

"Kate? -- I'm fine, couldn't be finer -- Listen; mess up my bed for me, as if I'd been in it -- Just do it, I'll see you tomorrow -- You're a doll." Beth hung up. "Right, where were we?"

"Discussing our future. I don't just want a Cruise Ship Romance; I want more. I've been offered a big promotion ashore. Manager of a big leisure complex in Leeds."

"When?"

"September. If I accept, it starts in September. We could see each other, I could come up, or you could come down, it's only a couple of hours. By train, it's even less."

"I go to University in Leeds in October. D'y'want a lodger?"

Story in 100 words

{Write a story about a picture, in just 100 words. The picture is a living room, a pin-stripe suit, wide-boy-type is holding the telephone, and yelling excitedly. A woman carrying a tray of crockery, a man in a chair, and a dog are reacting to pin-stripe's news with astonishment.}

Mavis went through to brew the tea, leaving Fred alone with the dog.

"What we need is a Three Wish Genie. I'd wish for a huge inheritance," said Fred.

"I'd wish that I could still sniff my bum," growled the portly pooch, sorrowfully.

Mavis returned with the tea,

"I'd wish you two far away," she said: "So that I'd get the inheritance." She accidentally rubbed the telephone as she brushed past it.

The sharp pinstripe exploded out of it.

"I'm De'Odgydealer, the Genie of the telephone, here to grant three wishes!"

"Oh good," growled the dog peering over his shoulder.

Acknowledgements: -
Himself took the picture that was the source stimulus for this work to Chesterfield because we were having trouble with it.
Our thanks to:
Eldest Granddaughter and second Grandson for likening

the central character to a dodgy car dealer, and realising that he could have come out of the telephone, like a Genie.

To middle granddaughter for the dog's wish.

I joined the ideas up.

Petra.

Letters from and to Victoria

{English Grammar is not our strong point, unusual for lifelong word-smiths, so Himself attended a suite of Creative Writing courses and Advanced ECDL Word Processing.

After the final one he received an unexpected letter.}

Dear Mervyn,

      Re: Learning opportunities

Have you considered further study from your Clait or ECDL course? Learning opportunities exist with N------ City Learning to study for an NVQ level 2 IT User.

This qualification is designed to be suitable for staff who work with IT skills in their everyday work.

This NVQ is designed to reflect the work of everyone who uses IT skills for different purposes in their day to day work roles, and recognise skills and knowledge already acquired either through other qualifications or previous experience and learning. Individuals need IT skills to maximise efficiency in their occupation. Using IT can range from routine word/transaction processing to constructive use of the powerful application packages that are available.

If you are employed in the role mentioned above, have your employers permission and if you are interested in studying for an NVQ level 2 It User, please contact Victoria Toomey at N------ City Learning telephone: ------

Yours sincerely

Employability Coordinator.

On the face of it, a polite, if tortuous letter, drawing the recipient's attention to educational opportunities in the workplace. It was also nice to see the correct sign off after addressing the recipient by name, although Lynne Truss would probably have something to say about 'employers permission', and with justification! A typo worthy of **Me!**

The problems arise when you consider for whom the letter was intended, and to whom it was sent. The main paragraph has a readability SMOG Grade of over 17, which is about ten more than NVQ Level 2, and about twice that of most of our books. When Mervyn had stopped laughing and picked himself up off the floor, I wrote back, concentrating on to whom the letter was sent.

* * *

Dear Victoria,

Mervyn thanks you for your kind letter inviting him to broaden his qualifications by studying NVQ Level 2 at his job.

He is considering framing it.

His memory these days isn't ace, but he seems to remember, before he retired, studying for and gaining a GNVQ qualification that entitled him to tutor and assess Level 3.

Although his degree is merely a BA, hinting at no Science qualifications, it is only because that is all his University offered.

The degree is mainly in Science and Technology, including Electronics.

Although you personally might, only just, but might be excused for not knowing these facts, because a tiny smidgen of research would have unearthed them, the ignorance of them on behalf of the department you represent is inexcusable. Mervyn worked for N------ Education Committee from 1/9/1963 to 27/2/2000. Consequently, their sending out a letter demonstrating gross ignorance of the circumstances of the recipient, despite the ready availability of same, sadly is no surprise. The only way to cope with such draconian disregard of decades of selfless service by your employees that Mervyn knows is to be generous, regard your ex-employer as a particularly crassly-inept Pantomime Dame, and see the funny side of it.

He hadn't intended his employment to terminate when it did, but in 1999 all but one of his options were removed by, and at, a stroke.

So he will not be taking up your kind offer to study further from his Advanced ECDL course via NVQ Level 2 with or without his employer's permission, because: -

One:

He is Sixty-Six Years old.

Two:

He is retired, and although informally self-employed, in the respect that he does not vegetate all day but keeps busy, he has no paid employment.

Three:

His GNVQ qualification is higher than NVQ Level 2.
Four:
His academic qualifications are considerably higher than NVQ Level 2.

All this information is, of course, in his records held by the Education Department.

HOWEVER - - - -

If you have a course on: -

'The Vagaries Of Microsoft Word and How To Stop It Behaving Like A Pillock,' or similar, at a Level far above ECDL Advanced Word Processing, we would be interested.

But be warned, as a budding author, who really pushes the specifically Word Processing boundaries, the problems we need solving are acutely difficult, far off limits difficult.

This is not a flippant sign off Victoria; it is a serious enquiry. Word's stupid quirks are driving us nuts, which no amount of book or www research can assuage, we need genuinely advanced help.

We look forward to your reply,
Yours sincerely,
Petra Ceason,
on behalf of Mervyn.

Sadly the reply did not include an invitation to sort out our problems with Microsoft Word but did include a subtle moving of the buck towards the computer, and a belly laugh.

* * *

Dear Petra,

Re learning Opportunity for Mervyn.

Thank you for your letter dated ------. The opportunity was given to all learners who've studied an ECDL/Clait course within the last academic year if they met the criteria to study for an NVQ for IT Users. I'm sorry if this was deemed inappropriate to Melvyn and was not intended to cause any affront.

Unfortunately we do not have a course on Word Processing which is more advanced than the ECDL advanced course already studied. However if a course does become available in the future I will keep your details on file and notify you accordingly.

I've returned your self addressed envelope.

Yours sincerely,

Victoria Toomey,

Employability Coordinator.

Prompting my reply:

* * *

Dear Victoria,

Mervyn thanks you once again for improving his day.

Your first letter created no affront, as explained in my reply; he thought it hilarious.

Your second one caused him to laugh out loud when, in the middle of the actual sentence apologising for the non-existent affront, your typist got his name wrong.

The upside of this correspondence is that it has become the short story, 'Letters From And To Victoria' and is amusing enough to be included in our short story collection:

Collected Short Stories And Pomes
{And No It's Not A Typo}
by
Petra Ceason

which hopefully will be published sometime next year.

We are sorry you cannot help us in our quest to overcome the vagaries of the World's most bloated word processor.

We will always be interested if that changes.

Please let me know if you would prefer your name greyed out of 'Letters From And To Victoria' before it goes for publication.[7]

Yours sincerely,

Petra.

---

[7]   I met Victoria personally to give her a pre-production copy of Collected Short Stories And Pomes. She is a very nice and helpful lady, and seems not to have been bothered that her name is in print.

i before e except after c

{If you are intelligent but, like me, word blind, and consequently have had to put up with the sneers of your lesser contemporaries, this one is for you.}

Mrs Cumpbell instructed her Media Studies Sixth Form Class to video her lessons for a day.

"But Miss, it's PE, the inter-form Basketball competi-"

"It's all arranged, permission obtained, you're with me all day." She spun on her toes and set off after some imagined miscreant.

"It wasn't arranged with us; you didn't get our permission." But the irate boy pragmatically had waited until the detested and vindictive, sawn-off-teacher was out of hearing.

Period two was the Fourth Year, Tim, Rosalind, Jennifer, Colin et al, and it was three days after Tim's rite of passage night with Jennifer, and the day after he and Ros had got each other sorted out. Consequently, he was emotionally ten years older than when the poison troll had last seen him, four days previously.[8]

The populace guessed that the reason that she picked on Tim so often was possibly because he was the best Chemist in the year. His English was excellent, and his spelling always acceptable, usually good, but he had a few favourite words that

8   See my novel, Rosalind And Timothy, An Exercise In deflated Self Worth; *Petra Ceason.*

he occasionally got wrong. In his essay that morning he had a character 'recieving a justified reward'.

He sat patiently through her parade of his ignorance finishing up with,

"-- only an illiterate scientist like yourself would be unaware of the rule i before e except after c!"

With the baleful red eye of the video camera on him, Tim nodded gravely at her, and enunciating clearly for the microphone, said,

"I'm sorry Miss, we had some emergencies in the height measurements of our experimental species societies yesterday and, until then, I had fancied that my ancient tendencies to being inaccurate had been sufficiently curbed, but I'm either a conscientious, efficient Scientist or I get granted heinous credit for being so, but I acquiesce to you that I am an illiterate, and cannot spell consistently well."

The troll preened herself on her victory and moved on.

Nobody twitched, shuffled, or moved. Everyone sat frozen-faced, and the lesson rolled smoothly on to its end.

The only comment was made by Colin, in the corridor immediately afterwards,

"How many?"

"Depends how you interpret 'after', either way, it's double figures."

"Did you learn it off by heart?"

"Yeah, somebody who can't live with her lack of height, referred to illiterate Scientists once too often in my hearing."

"I know lots of unscientific Artists who wash their hands after using the toilet, yet think nothing of sitting on a table intended for food."

"Exactly!"

Not that it mattered, but it was nice to know that the most mature and universally respected boy in the whole School had understood.

There were a couple of training days that the kids had off a few weeks later, after the Christmas Break, and when they came back, Tim was referred to vitriolically as Mr, Ebsenter by the troll, until February Half Term. The sixth form Media Studies told everyone why.

On the first Training Day, the English department had been co-opted to be the group leaders for some in-house training on Staff Literacy. The troll had used The Fourth Year's lesson as a visual aid in her group, which, by pure chance, was the Maths, Technology and Science Faculty Staff, fans to a man of neither the teacher nor her bullying style.

"She got us in to run her lecture for her."

"Not content with screwing up the Basketball competition, she took away our day off too."

"But it was almost worth it--"

"No almost about it, it was definitely worth it. Her theme was illiterate scientists, probably because of whom she had as her Tutorial Group."

"And she showed the tape of your lesson--"

"You know i before e except after c?"

"Yes." Accompanied by nods and smiles.

"We couldn't believe it; she showed that clip, Timmy's broadside."

Everyone had fallen about, the sixth formers hiding grins behind their hands but the staff openly chuckling, when Tim stuck fourteen examples of her 'rule' being broken legitimately, {seventeen if you count acquiesce, two for societies, and both beings} into his one sentence reply to her bullying.

"It was about halfway through his speech when suddenly all the teachers realised by her reaction--"

"That until then, she hadn't twigged herself that Timmy Ebsenter had hung her out to dry."

"The chuckles became belly laughs!"

"We nearly wet ourselves."

"What d'y'mean nearly. I did!"

Or in Verse, if you prefer:

i before e except after c!
She'd ordered Media-Studies
to video teaching,
to keep a personal record
of Tim's beating.
i before e except after c!

i before e except after c!
His pen wrote recieve,
learner slow.
"Only an illiterate,
doesn't know,
i before e except after c!"

i before e except after c!
Tim checks red eye of
the camera on,
Enunciates clear
for the microphone.
i before e except after c!

i before e except after c!
"I'm sorry Miss,
but truth to tell:
--------------------->

Emergencies arose in the
height measurements of our
species
societies yesterday. I had
fancied that my
ancient
tendencies to
being inaccurate had been
sufficiently curbed, but I'm
either a
conscientious,

efficient
scientist or I get
heinous credit for
being so, but I
acquiesce to you that

<--------------------
I am an illiterate,
and cannot spell."
i before e except after c!

i before e except after c!
Troll preened in vict'ry,
Pleased with her ploy.
Kids frozen faced,
Hiding their joy.
i before e except after c!

i before e except after c!
Outside a bit later,
"How many? The score?"
"'Pends how you read 'after',
a dozen or more."
i before e except when **it's not!**

A Christmas Story

Dear True-Reader you may not like this one, it depends where you stand on Political Correctness.

I am against BULLYING, in all its forms, Racism, Sexism, Fatism, Class, Moneyism, Media A lists, etc.

Top of the heap, way out in front on its own is the worst of all, yet another worthless Media invention.

That puffed up, worthless, empty bladder, known under the title Political Correctness!

Evil is wrong because it is EVIL.

Not because it happens to be on a list of activities that someone, with a hidden agenda, has decided are Not Politically Correct! (sic)

The first time 'Poppy' surfaced into the public domain, I was asked,

"How can a fourteen-year-old working girl stay out of the clutches of the Authorities? The Social Services will have something to say about it!" [9]

The answer is that, provided that he or she avoids committing an offence involving injury to pride, or finances and restricts their activities so that they stay under the media RADAR a determined teenager can serially outwit the Authorities without raising a sweat, we've seen it done!

Himself's job was trying to keep youngsters on the straight and narrow. For many it was easy. There were others who could see no point whatsoever in obeying the standards and norms of people who had no comprehension or understanding of, nor relevance in, their lifestyle; they were already out of reach. He kept trying, spurred on by a few who, later, sought him out and told him they now wished they had listened to him earlier. To those, He says, 'Thank you!' Your feedback kept me going.

9   Rita Who? *Petra Ceason.*

For the purposes of this story, it is necessary for Samantha, who started her working girl career well before the age of fourteen, to evade Social Services, and also buy on credit.

But a minor cannot get credit.

Or can she?

Samantha Hutt is a sufficiently major character in the Novochester Chronicles to have her own book.

This short story concerns her Christmas 1985.

Petra.

A Christmas Story

{Precisely that}

Several people sat around the curved end of a huge boardroom table trying to negotiate the conditions of a credit sale.

Money, both deposit and income, was not the problem. Under any ordinary circumstances, there was enough of both; the problem was that neither the prospective purchaser, nor her Company Director Guarantor, chairing the meeting, were old enough to enter into any sort of credit agreement, and in addition --

The Banker was being patient, but adamant,

"The problem is--"

The purchaser interrupted,

"I know what the problem is; I have no fixed abode, so I don't exist--"

The Banker bridled a little at being blamed for vagaries of law,

"Miss Hutt, besides being only fourteen and--"

"Look this is getting us nowhere," interrupted the Company Director: "I've had an idea. If we're too young for credit agreements, I'll buy them." She produced a huge chequebook from her briefcase. "Right now, at the agreed price less discount for cash, shall we say twelve point five per cent for instant settlement?"

The vendor, predictably, became animated,

"What? You can't just change the price like that."

The youngster ignored him while she wrote. Then she tore the cheque off and brandished it,

"Look!" She said, thrusting it under his nose. The numbers filled the entire space allotted to them behind the £ sign, all that was missing was the signature. "Agree, and you get this in exchange for all four. All four! It's less than you hoped for, but it's a fair price, a fair profit, an immediate fair profit, on all four but with only one set of fees."

The huge company cheque, printed on a pastel shade miniature copy of one of Turner's masterpieces was very obviously a tempting target.

The vendor conferred with his legal representative.

"Will that be honoured?" Asked the solicitor. "She's only fourteen too."

"Oh yes," said the Banker: "If she signs it, we will honour it. We could not sanction any credit deal for Miss Shirley, but a straight purchase for that amount, no problem."

"Deal?" Asked the tall brunette, her pen hovering over the signature space.

"Deal."

"Contracts completed and exchanged tomorrow!"

Again legal minds were consulted.

"They're written, they just need the final figures and signing," urged Shirley, her pen still hovering.

"Contracts exchanged at noon. Agreed."

With a flourish, the Director signed the cheque.

The working girl let the others go before she raised her objections.

"We still have the same problem. I live in a squat, so I cannot get credit. I cannot buy it from you."

"You cannot buy on credit Sam, but I can sell it to you, on my personal credit at a price to be agreed, and a rate to be negotiated."

Instantly the small girl threw the switch from personal mode to businesswoman,

"What price?"
And was rewarded with an identical change,
"The price I bought them for, divided by four."
"What rate?"
"One per cent below Underlying Inflation Rate."
Samantha reared up, claws out,
"Like hell you will Shirley! That's even worse than charity because it's covert. You've already cut me a huge discount!"
"I cut myself a huge discount. Make me an offer then."
"Variable Mortgage rate."
"No way! Inflation less nought point eight per cent."
"Inflation plus one point three percent."
"Inflation less nought point six per cent."
The argument rumbled on with the protagonists getting closer and closer, but Samantha, with a stubborn tilt of her chin, stuck at inflation plus half of one per cent and refused to go any lower.
"I'll deal on that if you agree to being insured fully comprehensive by me."
"That's--"
"Deal Sam, please! I need to feel good about this, and it will simplify the paperwork enormously."

* * *

Samantha approached her house through the upper storey of the derelict terrace opposite, lowered her burden silently to the ground in a dark corner, and then peered through a narrow gap at the frontage of her home. The squat looked even more forlorn, with the extra aura of desperation it had acquired since Chris left. The expected watcher was there, hiding in one of the less obvious observation points. Presently he checked his watch, shrugged and departed. Samantha moved over to a hole in the floor and, for a moment stared hard at a dark corner beneath her in the next house. Satisfied, she slipped back to another vantage point in an adjacent street, right next to a nondescript blue van. As the expected watcher approached an older man got out of the van, and they talked.

Patiently Samantha waited.

After a delay of several minutes, a shadow passed by, close enough for her to have reached out and touched.

"I think they've moved," said the shadow.

"Oh my! You gave me a shock!" Said the younger man as he came down from his jump, holding his heart.

"No, they're just better at hiding than you are, they've got more at stake," said the older colleague. "Samantha could walk past you in broad daylight on a deserted street, and you'd never have known; she's probably listening right now."

"Where?"

"My guess is she could reach out and touch you. Don't bother looking; you won't find her. Enjoy your Christmas Sam; we'll catch up with you after New Year, come on." He gently ushered his staff towards the van, and the three of them climbed into it and left.

The tiny working girl tracked the van right down onto the bypass before returning home and retrieving her load. Even then she crossed the road like a wraith and entered the dilapidated terrace by a door several removed from her final destination.

She usually would paste on a clear-eyed smile for her kids, but tonight the smile arose spontaneously. She picked her way carefully through the broken building, easing the huge new holdall past the dead spikes that tore at everything that passed, to the snug and dry room at the back. A single battered hurricane lamp provided a warm yellow glow inside. Thankfully, she dropped her bulging load down.

The twins were waiting for her. Sid rose straight away, carrying a table centrepiece over to her while Jean continued to tend the meal. Samantha admired the log, their home's entire Christmas Adornment, with its decorations of berries and greenery and recycled tinsel scrounged from the locality.

"Very nice." She hugged him and kissed him: "It's lovely, we'll get some new candles for it, red ones."

Her brother glowed with pride,

"We saw the Church Warden delivering the Service Cards," he said waving one. "We helped him. We did Langley Road, all five hundred houses; we've got spares for the squatters."

"That's good. Sorry, I'm late; I had to hide outside until that new Social left. Did you spot him earlier?"

"Yeah, we came in the long way, under the floor."

"There's a new girl too, but we saw her. Dinner's ready."

"Be wary of the girl; she's quite good. I've found a new place for Christmas."

"This is okay you know," said Jean: "We'll get used to Chris not being around."

"Well as I've found the new place, can we try it for Christmas? If it doesn't suit, we can always come back."

The twins locked eyes as they always did, then Sid answered for both of them,

"Okay."

"Do you know where we're having Christmas Dinner?"

"The new place, there's a new flatmate too; I think you'll like her. She's French; she's called Monique."

"Is she a working girl too?" Asked the boy.

"No, she's a student. She was an au pair, but Mr Employer wanted her to be his own personal unpaid working girl, so she blasted out."

"What about the food?" Asked the little cook as she began to dish up, voicing a constant concern.

"You'll not need to worry about it being stolen while we're at Church; the new place is much more secure than this."

"Oh, right."

"Chris's coming on Christmas Eve. He and Frank will take all our stuff to the new place while we are at the Children's Crib Service. So I want all your valuables packed in these holdalls." She waved at her recent burden. "By tomorrow night. Everything you want to take with you."

* * *

True to his promise Chris arrived, halfway through the afternoon of the twenty-fourth, being chauffeuse driven in a black limousine.

Despite never making any attempt to disguise his sex, he was

321

just about the prettiest person Samantha knew, and one of the nicest. A thickset, middle-aged man, wearing expensive clothes, levered himself out of the rear of the car after their friend.

Chris introduced Frank to them all, positively glowing with pride at his new love. Samantha held onto Frank's hand,

"I always meant to say this on a suitable occasion; I think that's now. My friend Chris is nice. He's a good cook and a seriously good housekeeper. You'd be mad to pass him up. And he's pretty too."

"I agree with all that."

"Take care of him."

"Oh, I will! I promise."

They loaded the bags into the spacious boot, and when she could, Samantha checked on the other arrangements.

"All seen to," murmured Chris: "Monique will have tea ready when you get there."

Back inside the room for the last time,

"Right kids, last check! We are not coming back here, what have we forgotten?"

The twins locked eyes.

"Nothing!"

"Nothing!"

"And nothing from me as well!" Finished Samantha: "Right, we're off to Church for the Family Crib Service, I'll ring you on Christmas Morning, Chris. Good luck."

Chris hugged her. Then the group picked their way through the squat to the front, and minutes later the limousine sighed and rolled away. Jean and Sid stood patiently holding hands while Samantha neatly crossed out the word 'Taken' on the door-post, and replaced it with 'Vacant'.

* * *

The Church was warm and welcoming, the warden that they had helped deliver cards greeted the twins with a complicit grin.

The Sunday-School Children, many of whom were under five, performed a nativity play. There were several mistakes, which other members of the cast put right, and a few 'put rights' that were actually mistakes, but the event was gently bodged through with the eyes of the tiny ones revealing their level of joy at being in the limelight.

Carols were sung enthusiastically, and then everyone was given a candle to carry in the procession.

"I'll keep mine for later," murmured Sid, blowing it out.

"No need," said his big sister relighting it from hers, we have all the candles we need at the new place."

Presently the Vicar called for all the under-fives to join him to bless the crib.

"There's still space. We'll have the under." He paused, looking directly at the twins: "Sevens."

"No!"

"That's Shan!" Called Jean and Sid simultaneously, in mock disgust.

The Vicar grinned and called for the sevens and eights as well. The twins scuttled forward giggling happily.

At the end of the service, the family left shaking hands with the clergy on their way out.

On their way home,

"You know there isn't a donkey on that crib," said Sid.

"There's a mule, but no donkey," confirmed Jean.

Discussing the wrongness of having a crib, but no donkey, and making plans to purchase one after Christmas, and donate it to the Church, filled the walk home and provided a useful cover to distract the youngsters' attention from the fact that they were heading into a new, luxury-housing estate.

Suddenly Samantha grabbed their hands and had them away down a path to a side door in a building.

She knocked on the door, which was opened almost at once by a swarthy girl with black hair heaped up on her head.

"'Ello Sam," she said: "And 'ello Jean and Sid, I 'ave 'eard lots about you."

Sid's bags were in the green bedroom, and Jean's were in the lilac one.

"For now these are your rooms. If there's anything, you don't like we'll talk about it later."

"Can't I be in with Jean? I get cold if I can't cuddle up."

"No sorry. You're older now; you're supposed to have your own place. You'll not get cold I promise, the heating works."

"Really! Is there bathwater?"

Was ever the sacred cow of never deserting a sister's bed so quickly sacrificed?

"Hot bath water, like at the public baths?"

"'Ot bath wateur, durant toute la journée, all day, tous les jours, eveuryday."

"But for the four of us only. Nobody else walking in demanding we hurry up."

"How?"

"This isn't a squat, is it?" Said Jean: "Is it your house, Monique?"

"No, it is not mine. I am just the 'ousekeepeur."

"Well, whose is it?"

"It's ours! I've bought it. It's my Christmas Present to us. Merry Christmas darlings."

The twins locked eyes and then hurled themselves at their elder sister.

"Thank you! Thank you! Thank you!"

The Enchanting Antique Shop

{Write a story suggested by a picture of a bric-a-brac shop window. There seemed to be something not quite right about the picture; it was empty and soulless. This one is decidedly darker than most of my work.}

The twins celebrating their tenth birthday stopped outside the little antique shop. Its bright green conifers at the door looked beguiling. The open door invited entry, 'Come inside, wondrous happenings within,' it seemed to say.

"Great Uncle Ben has one of those," said John, waving into the shop window, at the penny-farthing: "I saw it last week; it's the tallest in England. I only come up to the pedals; even you wouldn't be able to ride it."

"That's it then," said Sibyl, peering at the tall object: "That's what it says on the ticket. Tallest penny farthing in England."

"Where?" John could see the bike, but no ticket; he couldn't see a ticket anywhere, not on the drum, nor the box. The helmet, lamps and pot had loads of points from which to hang a ticket and he supposed that you could always stick one on the pictures and the plant, and stand one on the chair, but there weren't any to be seen. "Where?" he said again, plaintively.

"You're blind, on the handlebars, there." she stabbed her finger at the bike. "That diver's helmet's cheap, £1, cheapest thing in the window, it must be worth ten times that as scrap.

I'm going to buy it."

She headed for the door, but John restrained her,

"No, wait. Where're the tickets, I can't see any."

"You are being stupid. I'm off to buy the helmet." He followed her to the door and grabbed her again, spinning her around.

"Don't Sibyl. Don't go in; it's not the same room. That one's got a grandfather clock and a table; this one hasn't."

"Don't you mean a long case clock?"

"It doesn't matter what it's called, there's one there," he pulled her back to the window: "But not there. And there's no penny farthing in there, no helmet."

She stepped back to the door and looked in,

"Penny-farthing, helmet, fish on the wall, no longcase clock. Satisfied?" and walked into the shop.

The door closed behind her, with a little tinkle of bells.

John strained to see in through the lights in the door, but he just couldn't, wherever he looked the view was fuzzy, out of focus. He walked around to the side window, but if anything that was even worse. The glass was clear enough, but there wasn't anything that he could see behind it, just swaying random shapes, like swirls in mist, but not like mist either, some trick of the light.

He walked back around to the front again, past the open door.

The kite leaning against the wall, in front of the penny farthing was beautiful, he'd never seen anything so striking, and only £1. It was the cheapest item in the window.

He had to have it.

He just had to have it.

He entered the shop, ahead was the chair with the helmet in front of it, to his left the penny farthing and the kite.

Behind him, the door closed with a little tinkle of bells.

Being A Good Samaritan
{Has Its Own Reward}

Brief: On the theme of Revenge

The Grammar School he was joining as a First-Year turned out to be a huge rambling box.

A century ago it had been four gloomy-Victorian classroom tower-blocks enclosing an oblong quadrangle, but the quadrangle had been glass-roofed over long since to create the school hall. Only the colonnade around three sides remained of the original space, and these now supported the gallery.

Fred, small of stature, shy, unsure, and hiding his fear behind bravado, had carelessly mislaid the only other boy from his Junior School.

Now buried in the press of boys around him, he was also lost in relation to his surroundings. While he was committed to shuffling along with the flow of bodies, the dim, almost dark, space that he'd been in for several minutes suddenly brightened and opened up with light from above. Disorientated, he stopped to appraise his position. This was a mistake that as usual, he failed to realise fast enough.

He was pushed and jostled several times, by more bodies pressing in from behind him, boys who were, in turn, being pushed by others behind them.

"Out the way!" Snarled a voice in his ear and he was shoved violently sideways. He lost his footing and fell awkwardly through other pupils, against a column. Besides being hurt, Fred earned further abuse from the other pupils who instantly blamed the pushed, not the pusher. The owner of the voice marched on, laughing.

Fortunately, the crowd was called to order almost immediately and a list of names read out,

"-- Those go with Mr Cowling."

Fred was horrified, had his name been called or not? He wasn't sure. Another list was read out.

"-- Nichol; Pate; Peters; Smith, Andrew; Smith, Frederick; Taylor; --"

The feeling of relief was short-lived; he'd missed the name of his Form Tutor due to having relaxed, and only managed not to be lost off by attaching himself to a group who were leaving, in the desperate hope that it was his class. Once again the relief at having guessed right was short lived.

Fred's registration group, and hence all his lessons, also contained the boy that had assaulted him. Having got away with it once, Nichol made a point of applying the lash whenever he could, correctly judging that if he stopped just short of outright war, he could prolong the persecution indefinitely, well for five years anyway.

* * *

"Why do you let him?" Asked Billy-Mac.

"I don't!"

"Every day he pinches your cap and throws it away. And you just let him!"

"I don't," protested Fred weakly, but he did. He daydreamed time away gently, and every day was unprepared for the attack. Nichol would then escape, while Fred had to concentrate on retrieving the cap before worse misfortunes befell it. Fred got to hate the required item of uniform solely because it was such a handy implement with which to torture him.

He would also be ridiculed in classes where the teacher was too weak to stamp on the ridicule. By the end of the lesson, Fred was only too pleased it had ended and with it the ridicule. He never gird himself up to challenge his tormentor to a fight that he was not sure he could win.

* * *

The incident that caused him most pain occurred at an Air Force Cadet Camp. Flights were awarded in an arbitrary manner, and Fred had been lucky enough to have five hours in a bomber, and also half an hour in a Chipmunk trainer, which he flew himself for ten minutes. Then he was awarded another trip in a Coastal Command flying boat, while some other cadets had not even been off the ground. He didn't need telling it was grossly unjust and went looking for Billy.

"Fred!" Called his sergeant: "Billy's not been up, would you give him your flight?"

"That's what I'm doing; I'm looking for him to ask him if he wants it, I can't find him."

"He's in the Machine Shop, come on."

The pair set off briskly for the Motor Pool. Suddenly, across a passageway crowded with younger cadets,

"Smith! Ye give your flight to Billy-Mac, or I'll do you."

"Shut up Nichol; he's giving it."

"He'd better, or I'll do him!"

Fred, as usual when unjustly attacked, was groping for words, and failed to reply before the bully made his customary escape.

"Just ignore him."

That was all very well, but the threats had been made in public, most people didn't know that he'd been willing to donate the flight on the grounds of justice alone, and would assume he'd done so because he'd been threatened. The alternative, to tell Nichol to 'Eat beans!' would go against what he wanted to do.

Justice apart, Billy was more a friend of his, than Nichol's.

Fortunately, his customary memory lapse in favour of some new stimulus intervened when a squad of guards appeared, armed with real guns, containing real bullets.

Fred was a first-class shot with a .22 target rifle, but these were close quarter machine pistols, designed to take out a roomful of terrorists in one burst. He stared in horrified fascination.

How many enemy soldiers had these men accounted for already?

* * *

When the obligatory years of Secondary School were up, Fred parted company from his tormentor. However, the mark Nichol put on the boy, showed up on the man.

Throughout Fred's career, whenever he stumbled across bullying, he fought against it. The older he got, the more sophisticated his offensives, and the more effective his actions in isolating and neutralising bullies.

He met a nice girl at University; they married when they graduated and had two daughters very quickly. As soon as she could, Amy Smith returned to work where rapid promotion followed. As her responsibilities increased, so did her time away from the family home and despite their best efforts not to, the pair grew apart. Matters came to a head when an important Asian contract began a southerly slip, and without notice, Amy had to leave for an indefinite stretch.

"So when will you be back?"

"Two weeks -- Two years -- I don't know -- Erm -- There are excellent married quarters on the site --"

"I don't want to leave, nor do I want to hamper you -- Erm --"

"This isn't going to work is it?"

"It hasn't been working for a while."

"Do we get divorced now, while we still like each other?"

"I'd much prefer that to us fighting like dogs in two year's time," he replied softly.

"Who gets the girls?"

"You do of course, so long as they can come to me, whenever they like. Or I can come to them, even unexpectedly."

"Okay. Do you want it in writing?"

"It might be better if it was, then there's no dispute if I forget the details later."

"If either of us forgets -- I still love you, you know."

"But it's not enough, is it?"

It was well over two years before Amy, and the girls returned to the UK permanently, and then they relocated down South, but the daughters visited Fred regularly, and he and Amy swapped cards and telephone calls to mark important anniversaries.

When their younger daughter chose Novochester as her University, and subsequently her home, her parents met again and became close friends.

* * *

Retirement was looming comfortably close, and Fred was about to be faced with the choice of continuing in a job he loved, or moving on into a less financially secure, but less stressful future when fate intervened and chose retirement for him when she felled him at, and with, a stroke. The younger daughter alerted the other two Smith girls who dropped everything and raced to his bedside.

The second, killer, stroke was averted by the excellent medical care he received in hospital, and, closely supervised by My Sirens, as he referred to his ex and daughters, Fred made a slow but effective recovery to walking pace with all his faculties intact.

* * *

Fred checked through his briefcase and then addressed his home help,

"Right, I'm going to town, to the Building Society, to John Lewis's and I'm coming home."

"You need to bring something in for your lunch," she replied: "There's the hot pot for your tea that your daughter brought in yesterday. It's in the fridge, but you've got nothing for lunch. I'll see you on Friday as usual."

"I'll bring something in. Can I give you a lift?"

"No I've still got things to do, now have you got your keys, and your bank book, and your cards --"

Fred parked his car and set off sedately for the Building Society. At nine-o-clock in the morning, the Shopping Mall was almost deserted. Consequently, when a thickset man, walking briskly, overtook him and only a little way ahead of him staggered and then fell, Fred was the only witness.

One look was all he needed.

He even knew which part of the brain had been hit; the man was twitching ineffectually and trying to speak with even less success. His staring eyes were alight and filled with terror. Fred moved in close and captured the attention of one them.

"Can you understand what I'm saying?"

The eyes gleamed, he understood all right. Fred reached out the mobile phone that his family had bought him and insisted that he carry at all times, and summoned help.

"-- Yes, right at the top, just outside The Pen Shop. I'm not a medical man, but it looks to me like a stroke in the brain stem. He was walking along fine, then suddenly he fell down, he can't talk, but he's fully conscious of what I'm saying, I can read it in his eyes -- Okay, I'll stay with him. Some shop staff have come out, but I'll stay."

"Are you family?" Asked the young Paramedic as she closed the ambulance doors.

"No, I just happened to be here."

"Between you and me, I don't think you're wildly wrong. Stroke."

"I had one a couple of years ago. That's how I knew. It wasn't like that one though, compared to that I got away lightly."

"He hasn't." She climbed into the cab.

"Where are you taking him?"

"Straight to the Patrick, Stroke Ward, I'm that confident. Bye, and thanks for your prompt call."

"No problem. Bye."

She fired up the sirens and accelerated away through the still largely deserted, pedestrians-only walkway.

* * *

Fred gave it a couple of days then called in to the Patrick Memorial Hospital. Face to face with gentle, courteous enquiries; he reckoned he was less likely to be fobbed off. The girl he chose to speak to, mainly because he found her attractive, just happened to be the Ward Sister,

"I'm making enquiries about the man in that sideward."

"Are you a friend?"

"No, I'm the one who found him."

"Saved his life."

"Was it that bad?"

"Oh yes, I'm afraid so. Would you visit him again -- Please -- You're his first visitor. I suspect you'll be his only visitor."

"What about his family?"

"Estranged, they wouldn't come. Flatly refused. As did his work colleagues, neighbours --"

She was much younger than he, but not young, so he decided to follow his desires,

"You're not wearing any rings. Is that because you can't because you're a nurse, or because there isn't a special person in your life at the moment?" He returned her suspicious stare, with a look that was as gently encouraging as he could: "Tell me, and I'll tell you why I'm asking."

"Yes to both. What's that got to do with visiting?"

"I will visit him. I promise, whatever you say, but can I have a date, take you out to dinner, maybe a show? If you say no, I warn you I'll ask again when I visit him; I'll keep on asking until

333

you say yes."

Her suspicion dissolved into warm pleasure,

"Well, in that case, Mr Smith. I'll say yes now and get it over with. Anyway, I think I'd like it."

Fred was astonished at being addressed by name, to the best of his knowledge he hadn't told her. She read his thoughts,

"You don't know who I am, do you?"

"Erm -- No."

"I'm your daughter's frumpy friend from Uni. Plump? Shy? Braces on my teeth? You were kind to me when my dog died."

"Oh, I remember, it's -- it's -- June isn't it?"

"Yes." An alarm sounded. "Sorry, gotta go!"

"I'll come to see you before I leave, about arrangements."

She nodded, smiling, and hurried away.

The patient seemed to be asleep when Fred walked through into the side-ward. He sat down to wait. Presently he dozed. When he awoke the patient was still asleep, nevertheless he addressed him quietly,

"You can hardly imagine how much pleasure visiting you has brought me. Seeing you alive, like this, when you could have died."

The patient's eyes opened.

"Getting a date with that lovely dolly in charge would normally have made the whole exercise worthwhile, under these circumstances, it's merely a wonderful bonus."

The head he was watching moved a fraction.

"I know you're aware; my guess is you have all your faculties."

The eyes struggling to focus on him gleamed.

"That will make it even harder for you, imprisoned inside an unresponsive body. I know how hard it was for me, and my body still worked. Slowly; unwillingly; and weakly to start with, but it still worked. And I had the support of family and friends. But eventually, if you try really hard, one day you might be able to operate one of those -- I think they call them Possum Machines, you suck and blow into them, and they feed your face and stick a potty on your bum. You'll have to be careful not to get the commands mixed up." He paused smiling gently at the possibility. "Yes -- One day -- The tea trolley is on its way. Do you want yours now?"

Again the eyes gleamed.

"Okay, I'll go and tell them you're awake. I'll tell that generously upholstered Sister, while I arrange my date with her for tonight. I'll come back tomorrow, I was asked to, but I'm enjoying it. Bye for now."

Fred found June and finalised plans for the date.

The pause after reaching agreement became too long. He leaned gently towards her, half expecting to be smoothly repulsed with the subtle professional avoidance that she probably had to execute automatically a dozen times a day. She must have been waiting for the invite, however, because to his surprise and great pleasure she met him halfway. The kiss although quick was full-blooded and very pleasant.

"I've wanted to do that for nearly twenty years," she said: "And a lot of other things! I hope you realise what you're taking on!"

"Oh -- Good -- Erm -- Erm -- That's fine -- That's nice -- Erm -- Mr Nichol is awake; he reacted positively when I asked him if he wanted his tea now. I'll be waiting out front at ten. Panting and eager." He nodded, mirroring her smile, waved and strode away with a full heart.

A slight change in retirement plans

{Write a story inspired by a street-plan
of a village/small town.}

"Is this the great secret then?" called a voice.

Bob blinked as he turned to look, narrowing his eyes against the glare. The weeks spent polishing Sword's brass trim to a silver-like sheen had been effort profitably invested.

He shaded his eyes; his friends were regarding him with amused grins from Tunnel Bridge.

"This is what I wanted to show you."

"You're celebrating your retirement with a narrow boat holiday then," said Pat. "Strenuous, I hope you're fit."

Bob beckoned them down the stone stairs which lead to the landing stage. The pair gingerly worked their way down the ancient, heavily-dished steps, adding even further polish to the iron safety rail's two centuries of caressing hands.

"What d'y'think?"

"Very nice," said Fred with meaningful stress: "How long have you hired her for?"

"Ever."

"What?"

"She's not a hire boat; she's mine. It's taken nearly ten years, since Mavis died, to find what I wanted and bring her up to five-star status, but I've done it. I've got her as I want her. Bedroom, bathroom, living room, kitchen, you name it; I've got the last word on board. Study, even a workshop."

"What would Mavis think?"

"That she is a fitting tribute to her dying wish."

"What about her other dying wish?" asked Pat.

"Ah well, I haven't met her yet."

"There's several would be only too willing," she said gently.

"To organise me, and get me sorted out. No thank you. I am organised. Sword is licensed for every waterway in Europe, and I'm going to explore most of them by the end of the decade." He drew the couple along the jetty, "Come aboard, I'll show you around."

Back out on the deck, Fred and Pat were delighted for their friend but really disappointed on their own account. Fred put his fears into words,

"So that's it. We'll never see you again after today."

"You'll see me at Christmas, and other times, but I'll be away most of the year."

"Come on Fred, don't be glum. He's doing what I'd love to do. In ten years time, we'll use your experiences as a guide to our retirement."

Her husband painted on a smile,

"Okay. What are we doing for our last day then?"

"Number one, we are going to the Library to research why this canal is called William Street, instead of Warfield Pennington Canal, like the other thirty miles of it. Two, we are going to the multiplex, for a private hearing, and finally, we are going to the White Bear for a meal."

"That's a wonderful itinerary, Bob. The Library was missed off the Council Plans for the new town centre, so it never got built, I've seen all the films I ever want to see, and I'm barred from the Bear."

"The library we are researching is in the Town Hall, and you misheard what I said about the cinema. The Bear is under new management, and you are no longer barred if you promise not to juggle with the yard of ale, and drop it like you dropped the last one."

"Oh."

"Any more reasons why today is not going to be a brilliantly memorable experience?"

The trio sauntered along the towpath to the next bridge, occasionally passing anglers, several of whom were into fish. They watched as a boy reeled in a huge bream, and stowed it away in his keep-net. He managed it without removing the great slab from the water. A few metres on, a girl was struggling with a rod bent over at ninety degrees.

"That must be a huge fish," said Pat: "It's pulling much harder than the other one."

"The other one was a bream, that'll be a carp," replied Bob. "Bream are like pulling up paving slabs, carp fight back." At that moment a barbelled mouth broke the surface, followed by the familiar long rake of a carp's dorsal fin, and disappeared again. "Yes carp, it's a fair size, and on light tackle. She'll be busy a while yet."

The steps up to the roadway were a mirror image of the ones at Tunnel Bridge, but easy to climb safely on such a warm, dry day. It was the one thing Bob was not looking forward to, on slushy-snow, or frosty mornings. They crossed at the pedestrian lights and entered the magnificent portico of the Town Hall, where an official in uniform barred their way.

He demanded passes.

"Wonderful," said Fred. "This public building, staffed by public servants, and paid for by me, is not open to me unless I have the right bit of paper."

Nothing changed in the official demeanour, not even his eyes looking straight through them.

"Passes."

Bob produced a paper and held it up to uniform's gaze then walked past him,

"Come on; we get the identity badges inside."

"Just a minute--"

Bob replied without turning around,

"No. Your rudeness has been noted and will be reported, our pass has been shown, and we are going in."

Inside, they exchanged the pass for identity badges, and a moment later a girl arrived to greet them.

"Hello, Uncle Bob." She kissed him warmly, "I've got them all out ready, the old maps and town plans, they're along here." She drew them away into a side room.

The early maps were bewildering; they bore no relation to the modern town. It was not until,

"We're looking in the wrong place," cried Pat: "Look, this crossroads here, there's West Street -- Coatbridge road, that's Eaton Avenue now. East Street is Perry Street, and the Springfield Road used to be George Street. The Old town centre is here; the Football Ground is on the old Market Place."

The researchers, now properly orientated, suddenly found that the maps made sense. Most of the Town Centre didn't exist until the early Nineteenth Century, when suddenly, William's Strait appeared, winding its gentle way east of the village. On the next map, it was William Street, and not blue any more.

"The canal's name is a clerical error!" said Bob's niece. The other three just looked at her.

"Like the Library!"

Everyone laughed.

* * *

The small room in the multiplex seated only about three score people and was deserted.

"So what am I going to see?"

"Hear. We are to sit in seats D3, D4 and D5, and you, specifically you, are in D4. All the speakers are aimed at D4.

The room darkened as the curtains drew back from the huge, steeply-dished screen. A star-scape grew upon it, and all three crouched in their seats as the Inter-Stella cruiser, carrying Princess Leah in her vain attempt to escape, thundered overhead. Despite knowing what was coming, the appearance of the pursuing Empire Starship, had them cowering even lower.

* * *

A couple of hours later,

"Thank you, Bob. That was magnificent; now I know exactly how that amazing soundtrack should sound. Thank you so much."

Dinner in the Bear was up to its usual impressive standard. They were served by a pneumatic young waitress whose striking height was outclassed only by her stunning beauty.

"Which is the tall tribe?" whispered Fred.

"The Maasai, I think," murmured Pat: "They're good looking to Western eyes, and they wear those beads too, she'll be Maasai."

Every time the girl came into the room, Bob found himself smiling at her involuntarily, and getting a dazzling smile in return.

She came over carrying a brush,

"I will clean under your table," she said in a southern African accent. She swept under the table recovering assorted rubbish, and, as they simultaneously took evasive action, comprehensively ensnared her brush in Bob's feet. The two chuckled together as they disentangled themselves.

"Sorry, but here's a present to make up," he said, balling up the debris on their table, and dropping it into her waste bag. He glanced at his watch, if the restaurant kept licensing hours it would have to close shortly, it probably closed in the afternoon anyway. Pat and Fred had to go soon, the rest of the day was either set off now or wait until tomorrow.

Wait where?

"What time do you close?"

The girl paused for a moment, then,

"The restaurant closes at three." She leaned a little closer to murmur, "But I get off at two-thirty."

Pat giggled at Bob's thunderstruck expression, as the girl carried the rubbish away.

"Well, what did you expect? You've smiled at her, played footsie with her brush, and given her a present. You can't blame her for what she's thinking."

"She's young enough to be my daughter! Damn near young enough to be my granddaughter."

"That will not have escaped her attention, but it obviously

doesn't bother her, and she's lovely."

"That had not escaped my attention."

Fred stood up,

"My advice is go for it. Time for us to leave I think Pat, thanks for a lovely day, we'll phone you at the weekend."

"And ask you how you got on, bye."

At two-thirty, the girl appeared. She had changed out of her working smock into a glittery white blouse and very short denim skirt, and she'd put her heels on. With her natural attributes and the beads, the overall effect was dazzling. It became apparent that the 'get off at two-thirty,' was permanent, she was carrying a huge rucksack, and saying goodbye to her boss,

"All the best Princess, when you're next in the area call in. We'll be delighted to see you. You can have a job any time."

As he stood up, she closed up to Bob,

"It will have to be your place; I have not got one. I'm leaving, heading out."

"It's a houseboat, a big, converted narrow-boat. I'm soloing around Europe."

"Oh. Do you want a first mate? I would love to crew around Europe for you."

"I'd love it too -- Erm -- There's only one bed. It's a double, King-size, but there's only the one."

Her sunburst of a smile lit up the locality. She sized herself up against him, there was little in it, and despite the heels, she was still looking slightly upwards.

"You would need King-size. My guess is it will be big enough for the two of us. Shall we go and road test it then?" She replied, linked him, and drew him away.

The Severed Head

{Write a story entitled The Severed Head. I already had, as a theme in Karen[10], here is some of it.}

The Birmingham Trade Fair was as bad as the Novochester delegate had feared. There had been hours of waiting around fawning to minions, with no guarantee of a sale. That this was his chief gripe was not a secret, he'd said it in so many words in the Sales Bar.

"You price are too high, for poor Country."

"I know that. But quality costs."

"Little sacrifice on quality, big save on cost, big sale, big profit."

"I sell what we produce, have made to order, branded products. Quality stuff."

"You good seller. Sell cheaper goods no problem. You become Buyer, buy from me, you sell, you make profit."

The big man turned away,

"Just another sale trying to turn a trick, I'm selling, not buying, or hadn't you noticed."

"Not you company, you Mr Man. You are Buyer, you sell, you profit. Think to it. I see you at Europe Fair. Next month. You buy from me, big profit." The portly man waved Goodbye and sauntered off through the throng, occasionally stopping to speak

10   Karen, The Girl That Would Be A Plumber. *Petra Ceason.*

to contacts, arrange meetings. At his own stand, later that night, in his own language, he spoke to the unacknowledged colleague that he'd left watching the delegate.

"Well?"

"It was easy. He is a bully; he likes to beat weak ones. He tries to beat everyone, but the weak ones, he beats without mercy. We will buy a girl for him to beat."

"Girls are cheap enough."

"That's not what we will tell him though, is it?"

* * *

In a dingy back room, less than a mile from the glittering facade of the European Trade Fair, a girl was cowering away from her punishment. Unable to see, scream or dodge she waited meekly for the next punishing blow to descend on her unprotected back. It never came; instead there was much shouting in a foreign language, which she didn't understand, but which was almost as frightening.

The plump man had plucked the stick from the big man's grasp as it was raised for the next blow. Beside himself with fury, the other was screaming for it to be given back.

"No, no, my friend, you not kill her yet, she is not paid for. Girl are expensive; you must pay before you break." He assertively drew the other through into a different room and began to negotiate their contract. "Here is portfolio, I can supply anything. At a price." He waved into the room behind him. "Even girl, at a price. Speak to you client, if you cannot make sale at company price, try my price. You Buyer! You buy from me, you sell, you make big profit, you able to buy girl."

* * *

The big man checked unobtrusively that he could not be overheard before leaning past their pints to talk to his friend.

"I've been offered some goods to trade at cut rate. I can handle the paperwork, but I need someone to take charge of the logistics. Interested?"

"Depends on what I get out of it. I need serious cash man,

serious!”

The big man smiled as he passed a note across,
“That serious enough for you?”
“Oh, yes, split how many ways?”
“That’s your share. Still interested?”
“Come to Daddy and tell all.”

* * *

The profit on the first, modest, spares-order, was astronomical. Subsequent orders began to generate income on a scale for which no plans had been made.

Not everything had gone smoothly, however,
“You need to get onto our supplier, his last load was a day late,” reported the Logistics Manager.
“I’ll do it tonight.”

* * *

“Oui.” said the familiar voice of his supplier’s secretary.
“It’s Buyer.”
The girl switched to her excellent English.
“Hold the line; I’ll put you through.”
“Hello, Seller.”
“Your man Gantel was late.”
“There are problems.”
“I don’t pay for excuses; I pay for goods delivered on time. If you can’t do that, I know some who can.”
“The matter finished, you not see him again. And I replaced bolt you lost so carelessly.”
“It was never delivered!”
“No shout at me. He is replaced. That all?”
“Make sure it’s on time.”
“Oui.” Seller put down the telephone, intentionally cutting off any further exchange. “Customers!” he snarled in his own tongue: “But I don’t need this aggro,” he addressed his partner. “When is Gantel due in?”
“Tomorrow night. The reception committee is already waiting. The story will be that he never got off the boat, we had

to retrieve his lorry ourselves."

The next shipment was processed without a hitch and was on its way within a few hours of delivery. One of the more substantial crates was marked as containing high tensile steel bolts.

* * *

A busy tropical market hadn't seen a threaded piece of metal for sale for three years. Consequently, when a consignment of spares and parts arrived, swarms of locusts descended, chose, haggled, paid, and departed with their booty.

The most prized items among the poorest people were the splintered pieces of packing case with their reinforcing wire and staples attached. With these, arrowheads, spears, fish hooks, and hence tomorrows lunch, were only time and effort away.

In due course, a shipyard, discreetly tucked away out of the mainstream of nautical business, took delivery of the crate marked as containing high tensile steel bolts.

* * *

The small World War Two frigate limped into dry dock. Her engines would have eagerly thrust her more forcibly, but her decrepit hull would have been weakened still further. She had had several lives already, smuggler, armed blockade runner and pirate were only the last three, and she was about to return to smuggling, but people this time. She was to be given a refit, the kind of refit she wouldn't get several thousand miles away at Swan Hunter. While tucked away out of the mainstream of nautical business, her cabins and holds were stripped out, and open-plan, horizontal-shelves replaced them.

The ageing, and now slightly buckled plates of her deck and hull, had enough of their missing rivets replaced, using any fixings handy, to staunch the worst of the leaks, while oakum and other rammed fibres stemmed the most enthusiastic of the rest. A coat of paint conferred upon her the new official title of Ferry, while her revised interior provided packing space for many more than was officially claimed.

* * *

The ferry entered her home harbour on the falling tide, intentionally just as darkness was setting in. Her Captain was eager to have her away before dawn, well before it was light enough for some busybody to notice her Plimsoll line, and start asking stupid questions. Although the tides meant she had a comfortable ten hours to load and leave before the falling water level trapped her again, scurrying to fulfil the other requirements ensured that they managed it in just six.

Dockside, the passengers boarded by the weak light from a few sad bulbs. The cargo meanwhile swarmed up netting lowered from the seaward side. Most of the passengers had paid for their short legal trip with a few dollars, many of the cargo for their longer, illegal one, a much higher price, and occasionally not in currency.

Among the many human interest stories crammed together, a honeymoon couple finding themselves pressed in on one side by a group of brigands, who made no attempt to hide their occupation, and on the other by a scrum of drunken salesmen, consoled themselves that it was only for a few hours. Elsewhere in the crush, shrouded in a dark cloak, the fugitive from justice kept her head down, physically and metaphorically.

As the ferry slipped her moorings, a pretty but penniless young girl, followed four seamen up onto a tarpaulin-covered bale of deck cargo, to pay the next of many instalments on her ticket out.

The passengers expressed surprise when they were herded together into a single lounge. They would have been astonished to see the cargo lying on their shelves, shushing distressed youngsters, fearful of discovery.

Hot, weary and tightly packed together, they all stoically settled down to make the best of it.

Outside the harbour, the elderly lady turned and punched her way through a quartering sea. The old, but freshly serviced engines, built the revs up steadily. As the gale built behind her, hurrying her southwards, she brushed aside a large piece of flotsam disdainfully.

An oversize bolt head that was standing up proud of her plates, and made to a design never intended to be used in a ships hull, caught the tree trunk and spun it around. The tiny sea creatures securing themselves to their new floating homes took no notice. Despite carrying High Tensile Steel markings, the force of the impact severed off the bolt head, revealing its true, base-metal identity. The hull plates it had been anchoring together sprang apart. After a moments pause, the increased strain upon it caused the next bolt to fail.

The next failed instantly.

An L shaped tear opened up in the hull, like a zip in a hurry.

The still powerful engines drove their craft on, in a shallow dive, like a scoop thrust into flour.

With no bulkheads to prevent it, she flooded in seconds.

She was still doing a respectable forward speed when the waters closed over her in an orgy of slaughter.

There were five survivors, the four seamen, and the girl at the centre of their attentions. The unsecured deck cargo had turned out to be buoyant.

The official fatalities ran several hundred short of the true figure.

A British broadsheet gave the incident three inches on page five. Of the many statistics included in the filler it managed to get the date the disaster occurred correct. Buyer glanced at it, sneered at the ineptitude that had generated the tragedy, and moved on to the weather.

The tabloids ignored it. It had happened in a hot part of the World after all, and no dogs or horses had been hurt.

A Lovely Crisp New Fiver

{Written with Kathleen}

Henry and Mavis Smith were browsing the High Street looking for a Birthday gift for her.

"Let's look in the Antique shop."

Henry bridled,

"Let's not, I was thinking more of toilet water from Boots."

"Alright, don't pull. That vase on the table looked just like a Chinese Dragon vase."

Henry stopped so abruptly that Mavis walked into him.

"What vase?"

"The one on the table, the £50 one." Mavis pointed enthusiastically through the window.

"Come on." Henry was grinning to himself, as he pushed open the shop door. "I've always wanted a Chinese dragon vase."

"What?" said Mavis looking stunned.

"You know I have," exclaimed Henry as he closed up to the proprietor. "I'll have the vase, what's your best price."

"It's £150, but to you Sir, £135."

Henry exploded but had to back down when the proprietor explained that the £50 was for the table. It took serious negotiations to get the price down to a mere £100.

Outside, clutching the securely wrapped and padded vase, he refused even to discuss the matter with Mavis. Instead, he began rehearsing her in their forthcoming visit to Aunty Mabel's.

"But we were shopping for my Birthday present--"

"Yes, but now we have more important things to do." He waved her into the car, barking constant instructions.

They drew up outside Aunty Mabel's

"Now remember the plan."

"Yes, Henry! Yes!"

"I need at least five minutes."

"I don't know why--"

"We've agreed. Go with her into the kitchen and keep her there for five minutes."

"I saw the car draw up," called Aunty Mavis from her front door. "There are hot scones in the oven they'll be ready in a few minutes."

Henry and Mavis followed Aunty Mabel into the house, and it was a natural progression for Mavis to follow her aunt into the kitchen. Meanwhile, Henry ransacked upstairs. After only a few minutes, his red and angry face appeared at the door.

"Where's that Chinese Dragon vase that you used to have? You know; the one that would be valuable if it were a pair."

"Oh, I sold it to that nice Mr Peabody, him that runs the antique shop on the High Street. He gave me five pounds for it. A lovely crisp new fiver."

Falling Forward, Jumping Back

{Fantasy}

The radio announced the snippet of non-news in hysterical terms as if it was saying something of import,

"-- President Bush has not ruled out Military Action against Iran over her Nuclear Policy."

"He'll have to find out where it is first," said Petra without a smile, which triggered a chuckle from her husband as he withdrew their pension money from his wallet.

"In addition, I doubt that he's ruled out the possibility of the moon being inhabited by mice," he replied: "But he may not know where that is during the day either."

Petra put down her arms-full of pens, notebooks and dictation recorders, and began gathering up her ironing.

"Talking of not knowing, I've made a decision," she said: "I've waited long enough. After lunch, your Dad is going to part with enough of his life story for me to make a start."

"He'll talk fishing," warned her man: "Canoeing. The bed-hopping antics of the murderous heroines in the novels you write. Anything to sidetrack you."

"I know! But today I'm ready for him. He's been everything from a talented horseman in the Royal Artillery to a leading man on stage. He's been everything! A Roundsman, a Sparks on board ship, a -- a--"

"Playwright! Not to mention thirty years in a classroom full of kids," prompted PeeTee as he laid the money on the table.

"Whatever. Today he talks, and I take notes. Can you bring the rest of that ironing up for me love?"

PeeTee took the remaining sheets, plodded slowly up the stairs after his wife, and laid his contribution beside hers on the ottoman. Petra opened wide the airing cupboard ready to store the linens and dodged back in alarm.

* * *

The Milk train was late, even by the station clock, which had been slow for nine years, ever since the squire's son climbed it on Armistice Day.

Peter revelled in the luxury of a few minutes rest on his flatbed trolley between the empty churns, hiding his thin frame from the wind and pulled his jacket tighter around him. He looked down at his toes as he continued to clench and unclench them, and occasionally wiggle them, with any luck, the feeling would be back in them by the time the train arrived. He'd heard that the wounded amputees from the war often could still feel their missing limbs. He supposed what he was feeling was the same, in reverse.

"Here it is," murmured the boy with the rags bound around the handle of his trolley. Peter had been searching for some rags of his own, ever since he realised how much easier, the trolley was to pull, with a warm, padded handle.

There was a certain amount of jostling as the train pulled in, and angry exchanges as the children pulled their trolleys into a ragged line, and the usual serial queue-jumpers tried to gain places. Despite being one of the smaller boys present, Peter did not have to fight for his space; he'd done that on his first two mornings on the job, which ensured that from then on he wasn't challenged.

"Oh good it's Roger today, we'll get served properly," said Polly-Jane.

The genial-granddad of a guard good-naturedly supervised the exchange of empty churns for full ones.

As the punishment for queue jumping in his presence was banishment to the end of the line, the exchange was carried out briskly and fairly, and the children scattered towing their trolleys to their various destinations.

"Goodbye Peter, I'll see you tomorrow," called Polly-Jane as they parted on Station road.

"So-long," he replied, turned and bent into his task, pushing his toes into the grykes between the cobbles for extra purchase up the slope.

He took note of the time as he passed the Post Office, half past five. That wasn't too bad; if he really worked hard up the hill, he'd make it to the Dairy by six.

When he drew level with the Co-op, he turned automatically to pull the trolley up the short steeper stretch backwards, trying to make the pulls as continuous as possible so that there was less chance of the disaster of the churns moving and tipping off. Consequently, he did not see that the road had collapsed. He stepped confidently backwards onto the top of a cone-shaped space and fell straight down it.

The Tee-bar handle of the trolley, being too wide, jammed across the hole and Peter's numb hands were jerked from their grip on it.

He plunged on downwards.

* * *

Petra whipped her skirts out of the way as a barefoot boy fell backwards onto the landing and his bottom. Despite its impossibility, he had apparently fallen out of the hot water storage tank.

"Ouch! That hurt!"

The couple looked down at the new arrival. He was grubby, tatty to the point of being raggedly dressed, and his hands, face and feet looked unwashed for some days. The thing they noticed most obviously was that he was half starved.

By the time he had finished speaking Petra had shelved her surprise and fast-forwarded into Caring-Grandma mode,

"Are you hungry? Would you like some soup?"

Peter, almost swamped by the prospect of soup, made an attempt on reality,

"My milk, where's my milk?"

Petra looked into the airing cupboard,

"It's not here, was it a cup, or a bottle?"

"Two churns -- on a trolley."

"Ah well, in that case, it's definitely not here love, where did you last have it?"

"On Biggs Bank, outside the Co-op, I was taking it to the dairy. I fell down a hole."

PeeTee and Petra looked sharply at each other,

"When was that?" Asked PeeTee gently.

"Half past five."

"No, I meant what year."

"This year. This morning. Now."

"Humour me; I'm not being stroppy honest. What year is it? Just tell me."

"Nineteen-Twenty-seven, it's November, a Tuesday. I don't know which day."

"What's your name?"

"Peter. Peterson, it's from the Norse, but everyone calls me Peter."

"An excellent name, I'm Peterson too, it's our family name. But call me PeeTee. This is Petra, come on, get up, we'll go downstairs and feed you soup. You need it, and it's cracking soup, more like stew. You'll love it. After food, we'll talk about where your milk could be."

"I have to find it--"

"I know. Now when we go down, things might look a little strange to you, but don't worry, after soup, we'll get everything sorted out."

They gently surrounded the boy and drew him downstairs. Ken Bruce changed records with a cheery quip.

"What's that noise? I mean who--"

"It's like a fancy gramophone," said Petra: "I'll turn it off."

A lorry changed gear outside and laboured heavily up the hill. Peter covered his ears.

"What was that?"

"A special kind of tram, noisy I'm afraid."

"Oh," Peter nodded, but then looked puzzled again. "What's that thudding?"

The couple listened. Faintly, getting louder, they could hear the rapid beat of an approaching Chinook helicopter.

"A flying machine, like an airship, only noisier."

"I don't like all this noise. Why is it so noisy?"

"It'll be fine Peter. Just sit down love; I'll get the soup and bread. You like bread?"

"Yes please."

Peter sat at the table as Petra switched the radio off; he looked about him suspiciously.

"Yes, everything will look a bit strange - don't worry - and don't panic, I'm trying to think of a way to get you back to your milk," said PeeTee gently.

"I'm not where I lost my milk!"

"Well, yes you are, nearly, just a few metr -- yards away. This is Biggs bank, the Co-op's right there." PeeTee pointed vaguely in the direction of the top of the room wall, above the fire. At least it was. Eat your soup -- scrumptious isn't it?"

"Why aren't you having some?"

"We are love, very soon."

PeeTee waited until more soup had been enjoyed, then re-emphasised the dropping brick,

"Biggs bank was built on rubble, left by a lot of ice that came by thousands of years--"

"A moraine? Left by a glacier?"

"A moraine," agreed PeeTee, happily readjusting his approach: "And it got washed away. Just about the time you lost your milk."

"I fell down a hole!"

PeeTee opened his hands in agreement,

"They had to clear it away; the ground is much lower now. The problem is, although you're very near **where** you left your milk, you're not **when** you left your milk."

The boy sat back and placed his spoon carefully on the edge

of his bowl,

"I have read H. G. Wells. How long am I not when I lost my milk?"

"Eighty years."

"And five months," added Petra.

A jet-liner squealed by on its approach to the local airport.

"When can I go back to my milk, your soup is lovely--"

Another lorry made heavy weather of the hill outside. Peter winced,

"But your now is so noisy."

"Finish your soup, and we'll go back upstairs and look at a possible solution. If you simply went back the way you came --"

* * *

"I reckon if you run up the last few stairs and jump upwards into the airing cupboard, like this, aiming to catch hold of the ceiling at the back, you should just about make it. But you have to believe that you're going to jump through the shelves or you might not."

Petra surveyed the obstacles,

"What if we take the shelves out first PeeTee?"

"I'd be happier jumping up through space. I'd grab up through the ceiling quite happily, but I'd prefer space."

"I tell you what. We'll take the shelves out, and then I'll give you the soldiers' hand up. Then you'd be sure of reaching the ceiling."

"Yes. That sounds good."

PeeTee began to strip the cupboard.

"Are we going to do it now?" The boy asked slightly apprehensively.

"PeeTee's parents are coming for lunch. Half an hour, less. A visitor from eighty years ago might be hard to explain."

"Yes!"

They finished their preparations of the cupboard, and PeeTee vanished into his bedroom. When he returned, he placed a chain around Peter's neck. On the chain was a silver half heart.

"Wear that always, to remind you of today."

"I will."

"Erm, Peter love, it might be an idea not to mention today to anyone."

"I might only be a Milk-Roundsman, but that's just because there's no other job available. Stupid I ain't!"

PeeTee crouched down with his back to the hot tank, Petra held the door wide open, and Peter did two slow trial placements of his right foot into the man's cupped hands, while sizing the lift up into the back of the cupboard.

"Remember! You have to **believe** that you're going to do it."

"I know." Peter closed his eyes for a few seconds; when he opened them again, the fire of determination burned brightly. "I'm ready," he said huskily.

"Goodbye and Good Luck," said PeeTee.

"Goodbye and Good Luck," repeated Petra.

"Goodbye and Good Luck. And Thanks!" replied Peter.

He ran forward two steps, stamped his foot firmly into PeeTee's cupped hands and lifted up, reaching high towards the back of the airing cupboard. PeeTee followed through, bench pressing him firmly towards his goal --

* * *

"You might have asked me first, about the heart."

"I knew you wouldn't mind; we'll get it back, you know that."

The doorbell rang, PeeTee went to answer it and admitted his parents, still sprightly despite their Ninety-and-change years of age.

When the guests were settled, Petra made her move,

"You are going to tell me your life story today Peter because we found out an hour ago why you were so unwilling to tell us until now. You knew there was a better one in the offing."

"What are you saying?"

"A boy fell out of our airing cupboard this morning," murmured PeeTee.

Peter sat back in his chair,

"Ah."

"A what fell out of where?" Asked Polly-Jane, leaning

forward, wide-eyed.

"And I told him you were coming for lunch." Added Petra.

PeeTee's father felt for something under his shirt,

"I've had it for eighty years, can I keep it for the few I have left."

"Of course you can," said his daughter in law: "Was your milk still there when you got back?"

**Collected Short Stories And Pomes
{And No It's Not A Typo}
The End**

KAREN, THE GIRL THAT WOULD BE A PLUMBER.

She sat at her computer, finishing her report,

--'I was just about to test it. My warning was ignored. From that height, a cage in free fall hits the ground at crushing speed.'

She paused, phrasing her next sentence, it would be the final sentence of the account proper, then she just needed to write the Conclusion.

The report was just a few short pages, but, bearing in mind the quality of the hovering silks waiting to present it at the inquest, in effect a 'Get away with Murder' card,

Well -- Manslaughter anyway, she thought.

So begins 'Karen', and we have not yet reached Chapter One. Who has been killed, by whom and why is the setting to this unusual erotic novel.

Karen is the most knowledgeable plumber around, except that she isn't a plumber. How and why this oxymoron comes about is the second background theme in this account of the life and loves, testing and success of this feisty Zulu Princess by controversial author, Petra Ceason. The crime fiction whodunit theme running throughout the book may well keep you guessing until the end.

Once again Miss Ceason challenges the hypocrisy of accepted morality, but this time, up front, as well as close and personal in this latest feel-good story.

DELIA, CHEF IN A WHEELCHAIR

Delia Summers is disabled, she needs special ankle supports in a built-up right shoe, which she refers to as a Clump. She is a brilliant intuitive cook with an incisive brain, but she does not tolerate fools gladly.

Delia is bright, ruthlessly ambitious and in love with a married man. If that wasn't dangerous enough she's not yet sixteen, and the object of desire of the wife her amour.

The scene is set for love and tragedy, intrigue and murder and they are all here in generous portions, hopefully, garnished with surprises, chuckles and some laughter on the way.

This is another feel good erotic story from Petra Ceason.

RITA WHO?

Although Rita takes the Title Rôle, this is a Searching for Identity, Voyage of Discovery for all eight of the main characters. I have a certain amount of sympathy for some of those that end up discovering to their cost...

When Rita first appeared in a Creative Writing Homework early in 2004, our Tutor was incensed, mainly because the writing was pretty grotty, but also because,

'The Social would have something to say about an under-age working girl.'

I have endeavoured to sort the grotty writing, **his** area of expertise, but steepled our resolve about the Social, **my** area of expertise.

My ACKNOWLEDGEMENTS and THANKS to an early Twentieth Century edition of Boy's Own Paper, for a vaguely remembered story idea, that I adapted to become that of Mary Richards, {and hence Mary Andrew} fighting for her life on the top of a runaway Stage Coach in America's Old West.

My APOLOGIES to Native Americans who, at that time, were portrayed as anarchic savages, and thus also in the extract. I do know that contrary to the Hollywood Studio image; you had every provocation to wage war on the invaders. Compared to many of them, you were civilised.

My thanks also to my tutor, Mr E. E. Hughes for the imagination stimulus picture of the four men meeting, from which this crime fiction sprang. My first effort you castigated, so did my Canadian dolly, even I wasn't that keen! I like the finished erotic novel a bit better!

Petra.

ROSALIND AND TIMOTHY
{AN ESSAY ON DEFLATED SELF WORTH.}

How do you think you would behave if you thought you were inadequate, substandard, worthless compared to your peers?

One of the eponymous characters takes refuge in daydreams, the other in planning a suicide.

That a 'Feel Good' novel with a crime fiction theme and punctuated by searing love scenes, arises from the ashes of such an unpromising concept is typical of Petra Ceason.

Rosalind and Timothy are two of the central, pivotal characters, in the West Novochester Chronicles Novels.

FRANK, AN ESSAY ON HEALTH
{AND ILL HEALTH AND BULLYING AND EVIL LOCAL GOVERNMENT}

Frank is just your ordinary sort of bloke. You'd chose to sit next to him on a bus, or feel comfortable walking near him in a dark alley, and you wouldn't be wrong. But Frank has a secret and unsuspected talent which grants him success in two very different fields.

This biographical novel about Human Relationships is interesting and thought-provoking, as well as satisfying, and erotically exciting.

The heroine, Amy Whyte, is not your typical 'Nice girl that don't.' She is an engineer 'and a bloody good one,' Amy's own, perfectly accurate, description of herself. By which you can imply that false modesty is not a character trait from which young Miss Whyte suffers. That she is also a top sportswoman makes her the almost complete antithesis of Frank in every way.

Opposites attract in Magnetism and Electricity; the same is sometimes true in Homo Sapiens.

28/12/2018